THE NATURE OF REVOLUTION

The Nature of Revolution

ART AND POLITICS UNDER THE KHMER ROUGE

James A. Tyner

The University of Georgia Press   Athens

Paperback edition, 2023

Athens, Georgia 30602
www.ugapress.org

Designed by Erin Kirk
Set in Chapparal Pro by Graphic Composition, Inc. Bogart, GA.

Most University of Georgia Press titles are
available from popular e-book vendors.

Printed digitally

Library of Congress Cataloging-in-Publication Data
Names: Tyner, James A., 1966– author.
Title: The nature of revolution : art and politics under the Khmer Rouge / James A. Tyner.
Description: Athens : University of Georgia Press, [2019] | Includes bibliographical references and index.
Identifiers: LCCN 2018020211 | ISBN 9780820354392 (hardback : alk. paper)
| ISBN 9780820354385 (ebook)
Subjects: LCSH: Communism and art—Cambodia. | Art—Political aspects—Cambodia.
| Parti communiste du Kampuchea.
Classification: LCC HX521 .T96 2019 | DDC 959.604/2—dc23
LC record available at https://lccn.loc.gov/2018020211

Paperback ISBN 978-0-8203-6491-9

CONTENTS

FIGURES

ACKNOWLEDGMENTS

Leon Trotsky wrote that art must make its own way and by its own means. For Trotsky, art is not something to be imposed or dictated. Rather, art comes from within; it is something felt, something that needs expression. Art cannot be contained; art is emancipatory. And it is this liberating potential that cuts across the grain of politics; and it is for this reason that governments have long sought to harness the freedom offered by artworks and artists.

I did not set out to write this book, but this book materialized nonetheless. My hope has long been to contribute something to our understanding of the political economy of Democratic Kampuchea and how a Marxist critique of the Communist Party of Kampuchea may help clarify the geographies of the Cambodian genocide. But in the process, a stark contradiction haunted my work, a disconnect that resonated with scholarship on the Holocaust and other moments of horror: How could the Khmer Rouge write poetry when so many men, women, and children were dying? A simple answer is that the so-called poems, songs, and so forth were not really art, or perhaps these productions could be dismissed as nothing more than pieces of propaganda. My search for answers resulted in this book.

The research for and publication of this book was a collective effort, an intellectual journey I shared with many others. Primary thanks are extended to Mick Gusinde-Duffy and the entire staff at the University of Georgia Press, who guided the manuscript from initial proposal submission through final production. Special thanks are extended also to the editorial board at the University of Georgia Press and the anonymous reviewers who provided critical feedback. At Kent State University, I express my appreciation to Jim Blank, Todd Diacon, Marcello Fantoni, Mandy Munro-Stasiuk, and Scott Sheridan, for their continued backing of my research. Kent State University has provided an exceptionally supportive environment, and I am deeply grateful for the productive working environment provided by these individuals. In Cambodia I am indebted to the support and assistance of Youk Chhang and the staff at the Documentation Center of Cambodia. The center has been extremely generous in providing documents and photographs for this project and others over the years. More specifically, however, I thank Dara Vanthan and Phirun Suon for their assistance in obtaining permissions for the photographs used in this book. Special thanks are also extended to Sokvisal Kimsroy, Chhunly Chhay, Savina Sirik, and Kok-Chhay Ly for their input and insight and for their translation of documents.

Over the years, I have benefited immeasurably from frank discussions, critical feedback, and pointed comments from my students: Gabriela Brindis Alvarez, Sutapa Chattopadhyay, Chhunly Chhay, Alex Colucci, Gordon Cromley, Christabel Devadoss, Kathryn Hannum, Sam Henkin, Josh Inwood, Sokvisal Kimsroy, Robert Kruse, Kok-Chhay Ly, Mark Rhodes, Stian Rice, Savina Sirik, Dave Stasiuk, Rachel Will, and Chris Willer. I have been truly blessed to work with and learn from them all. I have also drawn inspiration from and have been challenged in my thinking through conversations with some very remarkable scholars over the years, including Stuart Aitken, Derek Alderman, Caroline Bennet, Stéphanie Banzaquen-Gautier, Noel Castree, Kevin Cox, Thom Davies, Michael Dear, Randle DeFalco, Khamboly Dy, Craig Etcheson, Alice Evans, Julie Fleischman, Colin Flint, Jim Glassman, Michelle Hamers, David Hassler, Rachel Hughes, Helen Jarvis, Ben Kiernan, Caroline Laurent, Andrew Mertha, Don Mitchell, Richard Peet, Anne-Laure Porée, Curt Roseman, Vicente Sánchez-Biosca, Ian Shaw, Simon Springer, Sarah Williams, and Melissa Wright.

Portions of this book have appeared in previous publications, and I am thankful for the opportunity to use and expand on this material. Chapter 3 is based on “Nature, Poetry, and Public Pedagogy: The Poetic Geographies of the Khmer Rouge” (*Annals of the Association of American Geographers* 105, no. 6:1285–99), coauthored with Sokvisal Kimsroy and Savina Sirik; portions of chapter 4 appeared as “Music, Nature, Power, and Place: An Ecomusicology of Khmer Rouge Songs” (*GeoHumanities* 2, no. 2:395–412), coauthored with Mark Rhodes and Sokvisal Kimsroy, and chapter 5 is based on “Landscape Photography, Geographic Education, and Nation-Building in Democratic Kampuchea, 1975–1979” (*Geographical Review* 105 no. 4:566–80), coauthored with Sokvisal Kimsroy and Savina Sirik.

As always, I thank my stalwart companion, Bond, my now seventeen-year-old puppy. My daughters, Jessica and Anica, continue to show me what's important in life. And thanks go to Belinda, my partner, for her unwavering support. I thank also my parents, Dr. Gerald Tyner and Dr. Judith Tyner, for their encouragement. Last, I would like to acknowledge my brother, David Tyner. My brother is an accomplished artist and graphic designer; more precisely, though, my brother has often expressed his political commitments and sense of social justice through his artwork. Over the years, dreams have gone unrealized, but his struggles have been a source of inspiration for me. Always, I have appreciated the power of art through him. To my brother, I dedicate this book.

THE NATURE OF REVOLUTION

INTRODUCTION

Between April 1975 and January 1979, the Communist Party of Kampuchea (CPK), also known as the Khmer Rouge, carried out a program of mass violence that led to the deaths of approximately two million people: between one-quarter and one-third of Cambodia's pre-1975 population. Victims succumbed to extreme exhaustion, disease, starvation, torture, murder, and execution as a direct consequence of CPK policies that sought to liberate Cambodia from historical foreign influences, abolish private property and currency, and establish a new society under a Communist-inspired vision of collective ownership.

The broad coordinates of the Cambodian genocide are well documented. Once in power, the CPK mobilized the entire country: cities and towns were evacuated, their inhabitants forcibly relocated to agricultural communes. Work teams were established along military lines as men, women, and children were tasked with growing rice, building irrigation systems, and clearing forests. Education, marriage, religion, and other social institutions were either eliminated or transformed to align with the political philosophy of the Khmer Rouge, namely, strict loyalty to the regime and revolution.

The reintroduction of certain social practices is less acknowledged, but it is through an engagement with these practices that the coordinates of the genocide were established. Upon seizing power, the Khmer Rouge enjoyed neither widespread support nor trust among the citizenry of Cambodia. For the top leadership, this posed only a contradiction to be resolved. Reflecting its Marxist-Leninist roots, the CPK viewed itself as a vanguard of Khmer society and thus understood its immediate role as one of revolutionary mentor. Consequently, the CPK needed to articulate a vision of its newly established country, renamed Democratic Kampuchea. This geopolitical vision was conveyed through numerous artistic means, including poetry, song, dance, and photography.

The Nature of Revolution provides a detailed account of art and politics under the Khmer Rouge. Theoretically informed and empirically grounded, this book serves two purposes. First, it makes a specific contribution to the literature on the Cambodian genocide. To date, little research has examined the social dimensions of the Khmer Rouge. Most existing book-length studies provide general historical (and largely descriptive) accounts of the Khmer Rouge.[1] A subset of literature engages more narrowly with specific economic, security, or military dimensions, focusing especially on the direct and structural violence enacted by the Khmer Rouge.[2] Aside from a handful of articles and book chapters, there has been no sustained study of artistic practices forwarded by the CPK, nor have any previous studies considered how "nature" factors into the aesthetic politics of the Khmer Rouge. And none of these works have applied a Marxist critique to Khmer Rouge policy or practice. This is a crucial omission, for an engagement with nature, art, and politics under the Khmer Rouge provides a much-needed reinterpretation of Khmer Rouge praxis.

Second, *The Nature of Revolution* contributes broadly to the growing literature on the nexus of art and politics, especially as developed within the discipline of geography and related fields that have theorized the spatiality of aesthetic politics.[3] Much of this literature draws heavily on the work of Jacques Rancière, along with the writings of Theodore Adorno, Walter Benjamin, Bertolt Brecht, Georg Lukács, and others.[4] *The Nature of Revolution* likewise draws on this literature but provides also a more extensive engagement with the insights of Leon Trotsky. Here, Trotsky's understanding of the politics of aesthetics specific to socialist revolutions is crucial, for in his writings Trotsky identifies the fundamental tension of individuality and bureaucratic control with respect to artistic creativity and freedom. In so doing, I contribute to our understanding of how artistic productions facilitate the shaping of imaginative geographies and, more precisely, how "art" works as political intervention.

My project is framed broadly within Marxist political philosophy, and I do so for two interrelated reasons. First, the CPK explicitly presented itself as a Marxist-Leninist vanguard. In myriad public pronouncements and official documents, for example, references to Marxist-Leninism abound. By way of illustration, consider Pol Pot's momentous speech of September 29, 1977. On this day Pol Pot identified publically for the first time the Marxist-Leninist foundation of Democratic Kampuchea. He explained: "We have solidly laid the foundations of our collectivist socialism, and we are continually improving them, while consolidating and developing them." He continued: "We promote broad democracy among the people by a correct application of democratic centralism, so that this immense force will mobilize enthusiastically and rapidly for socialist revolution and construction, at great leaps and bounds forward."[5] Accordingly, it is appropriate to question the application of Marxist-Leninist concepts to the actual policies and practices of the CPK. In other words, it is important to document the "actually existing" conditions of the political economy of Democratic Kampuchea in order to better articulate *why* the genocide happened. This points to my second reason, namely, to contribute to the reassessment of twentieth-century Communist movements. As Wilson Au writes, "In the 20th century, communists wrenched great victories out of the horror of each world war: the Bolshevik revolution in the aftermath of World War I, the Chinese revolution through the course of World War II, along with Yugoslavia, Romania, Albania, North Korea, and North Vietnam, followed later by Laos and Cuba."[6] Yet these victories were in many respects short lived and misguided. Indeed, Terry Eagleton acknowledges that "in its brief but bloody career, Marxism has involved a hideous amount of violence."[7] Both Joseph Stalin and Mao Zedong, for example, "were mass murderers on an almost unimaginable scale."[8] However, Eagleton is quick to point out that all is not as it appears, for "to judge socialism by its results in one desperately isolated country would be like drawing conclusions about the human race from a study of psychopaths in Kalamazoo."[9]

Accordingly, *The Nature of Revolution* is situated within a small but vibrant literature that attempts to reinterpret "the setbacks in the struggle for communism that took place during the last half of the 20th century."[10] My purpose, therefore, is straightforward: to reposition Khmer Rouge artworks within their proper political-economic context.[11] We must understand that the Khmer Rouge as a political organization materialized in an era of anticolonial and decolonization movements. Consequently, both its policies and its practices—including its production of poetry, music, and photography—were incontrovertibly shaped by these events. Art does not appear in a vacuum, and we must concede that the creation of Khmer Rouge poems, songs, and photographs is no different. Prior to my substantive engagement with the art and politics of the Khmer Rouge, however, it is necessary to first provide a brief historical overview of the CPK's so-called Communist revolution and, second, a conceptual overview of the "nature" of revolutions as *aesthetic interruptions* more broadly.

The Unlikely Revolution

Cambodia achieved its independence from France in 1953 during the maelstrom of the first Indo-China War, also known as the Franco–Viet Minh War. Since 1946 a Communist-led revolutionary movement in Vietnam, the Viet Minh, waged an armed struggle against the French. Vietnam, along with neighboring Laos and Cambodia, had formed French Indochina. After a brief interlude of Japanese occupation during the Second World War, French authorities sought to regain and retain possession of their former colonies. In turn, throughout Vietnam, numerous nationalist groups formed and reformed in opposition to the French, most notably the Indochina Communist Party (ICP), led by Nguyen Sinh Cung, better known as Ho Chi Minh.

Strategically, the Vietnamese Communists believed that independence from colonial rule could be assured only if the French were defeated throughout the entirety of Indochina. This led to the establishment in 1951 of a Vietnamese-sponsored Cambodian Communist movement, the Khmer People's Revolutionary Party (KPRP). Prior to this watershed event, there was no dominant or united opposition group to challenge French authority. Instead, there existed a disparate assemblage of Khmer Issarak (independence) forces, all exhibiting vastly different outlooks. The short-lived Khmer People's Liberation Committee, for example, was nationalist in orientation, although some members were sympathetic to Communism. Overall, however, Communism was downplayed in Cambodia, both by the Vietnamese and by their Khmer counterparts.

Following independence, the vast majority of Cambodians laid down their arms and returned to village life. Their country was free from foreign rule, and both French and Vietnamese forces were departing. As David Chandler writes, most Khmer "were reluctant to become involved in rebellious politics after Cambodia's independence had been won."[12]

Postindependence politics in Cambodia were dominated by then-king Norodom Sihanouk. Sihanouk was widely popular, but Cambodia's constitution limited his power. Accordingly, in 1955 Sihanouk abdicated the throne in favor of his father in order to take full executive control of the government. Domestically, Sihanouk consolidated a number of contending political parties under the banner of the Sangkum Reastr Niyum (People's Socialist Community) to more fully dictate the future of Cambodia. With respect to foreign affairs, Sihanouk adopted a policy of Cold War neutrality. This approach "was partly a domestic accommodation, an implicit acknowledgment of the local communists' important role in the war for Cambodia's independence and their potential and incentive to disrupt a more pro-Western regime."[13] Most broadly, however, Sihanouk's moves were to safeguard Cambodia's neutrality in the escalating conflict in neighboring Vietnam.

Sihanouk's domestic and foreign policies required a delicate balancing act, a political feat he was able to sustain for over a decade. As Ben Kiernan summarizes, "Sihanouk's foreign policy of independence appealed to moderate nationalists, and his neutrality appeased veteran communists, while his autocracy stifled dissent and co-opted most of Cambodia's political spectrum into a one-party kingdom."[14] In the end, Sihanouk's policies were quixotic and served only to alienate opposition from both sides of the political spectrum. Sihanouk, for example, installed known leftist politicians into the Sangkum, including the Communists Hou Youn, Hu Nim, and Khieu Samphan. Sihanouk also signed a treaty of friendship with the People's Republic of China (PRC), terminated United States assistance programs, nationalized Cambodia's banking and foreign trade, and moved to establish state-owned industries. These decisions failed to placate the political Left and simultaneously angered the right-wing business elite. Furthermore, Sihanouk's decision to turn away from the United States frustrated Cambodia's military and led in part to the rise of his defense chief, General Lon Nol, to the position of prime minister in 1966. Paradoxically, Sihanouk's apparent acquiescence to leftist politics and his favoring of relations with China and the Communist-led Democratic Republic of Vietnam (DRV) were matched by the repression and purge of suspected Khmer Communists.

From the 1950s onward, the Vietnamese Communists proposed dual revolutions. On the one hand, they viewed events in Vietnam as comprising a true people's democratic revolution, one that would withstand American intervention and provide the foundation for socialism. On the other hand, the Vietnamese concluded that conditions in Cambodia were not viable for revolution. This meant, practically, that not only were the Khmer Communists to forestall armed insurrection; they would also be expected to support the ostensibly neutralist Sihanouk. For the Vietnamese, the brewing struggle against the United States was all-important, and it was imperative that Cambodia remain neutral—at least in the short term—to prevent the United States from establishing a base of operations on Vietnam's western border.

The reaction of Cambodian Communists to Vietnam's strategy was mixed, revealing deep fissures both ideological and practical.[15] Some veteran leaders accepted Vietnam's logic and supported, to a degree, an alignment with Sihanouk. Other members were decidedly opposed to Sihanouk and, furthermore, exhibited profound mistrust of their Vietnamese counterparts. This is not to suggest, however, a straightforward opposition between two camps within the Khmer Communist movement. Steve Heder, in particular, has critiqued such a dichotomy, noting that the historiography of the movement is decidedly more complex.[16] What is clear, however, is that a small minority of revolutionaries—including Pol Pot and Nuon Chea—adhered to an approach that closely mirrored Lenin's dictatorship of the proletariat.

The concept of the dictatorship of the proletariat was employed by Marx in reference to the political system adopted by French revolutionaries in 1848. In the nineteenth century, the phrase was normally associated with the politics of ancient Rome, whereby a ruler would be granted—or assume—supreme power for temporary period in order to defend the republic. For Marx, all forms of government rule were dictatorships, and he used the phrase to signal a transitional period of governance. In the early twentieth century, Lenin reformulated both the writings of Marx and the meanings of the dictatorship of the proletariat to align with conditions in Tsarist Russia. For Lenin, the conditions for revolution were not present; Russia was largely a feudal society and lacked an appreciable proletariat. Moreover, the working class had not yet developed an appropriate political consciousness. Consequently, Lenin postulated the formation of a vanguard—a dictatorship of the proletariat—composed of professional men and women who would bring about revolution. Afterward, the vanguard would initiate the task of building socialism among the masses. Pol Pot was drawn to Lenin's argument certainly by the early 1950s. According to Heder, Pol Pot believed strongly in Lenin's proclamation that Communist revolution is possible even if there is no proletariat.[17]

In 1960 Pol Pot and several other cadre leaders met secretively in Phnom Penh. The purpose was to transform the moribund KPRP into a vanguard party, originally called the Workers' Party of Kampuchea, later to be renamed the Communist Party of Kampuchea. Veteran revolutionary Tou Samouth was appointed party secretary, with Nuon Chea and Pol Pot elected as the second and third highest-ranking members, respectively. In two years, following the mysterious disappearance of Tou Samouth, another secret meeting was held. Now Pol Pot was elected secretary-general. Nuon Chea retained the second position and was joined by Ieng Sary, So Phim, and Vorn Vet. Of the twelve central committee members, five positions were held by those who aligned with Pol Pot's strategy. The vanguard, known as Angkar, had formed. Years later Pol Pot would explain that victory had been achieved through "the implementation of the Party's dictatorship of the proletariat in all areas of . . . revolutionary activity."[18]

Meanwhile, Sihanouk's hope that Cambodia would be spared from the escalating conflict in Vietnam was shattered. For years, Communist officials in Hanoi had been engaged in their own balancing act. On the one hand, they adhered to a long-standing objective of a unified, sovereign Vietnam. Since the Geneva Accords of 1954 brought an end to the first Indochina War, Vietnam had been divided into two political entities. To the north there existed the Communist-led DRV; to the south, the U.S.-supported and pro-Western Republic of Vietnam. On the other hand, Vietnamese Communist officials worried about direct military conflict with the United States. Consequently, the leadership in Hanoi restrained insurgents in the south from engaging in armed resistance. This policy changed in 1959, however, with the founding of the National Front for the Liberation of South Vietnam, better known as the National Liberation Front, or NLF.

The DRV's strategy was highly dependent on its ability to provision the southern insurgents. Crucially, this required the establishment of a series of supply lines—the Ho Chi Minh Trail—that wound through eastern Laos, the Central Highlands of Vietnam, and parts of eastern Cambodia. In Cambodia, North Vietnamese access was conditional on Sihanouk's assurance or, at the very least, his acceptance of neutrality. For this reason, Communist leaders in Hanoi continued to press their Khmer counterparts to hold off armed revolution against the Khmer monarch.

As the United States expanded its military operations especially throughout South Vietnam, both the NLF and the North Vietnamese Army (NVA) increased their use of Cambodian territory as places of sanctuary and resupply.

In turn, U.S. officials enlarged their theater of operation to include armed conflict in Cambodia. In 1967 American military advisors initiated Operation Salem House, later renamed Operation Daniel Boone, whereby U.S. combat troops, in combination with the Armed Forces of the Republic of Vietnam (ARVN), entered Cambodia to gather intelligence and conduct limited combat operations. More devastating was the escalation of America's aerial campaign. On March 18, 1969, U.S. president Richard Nixon ordered a series of secret and illegal B-52 bombing raids to be conducted on Cambodian soil. Known as Operation Menu, this campaign would last for fifteen months, during which time more than three thousand B-52 sorties were flown, dropping more than one hundred thousand tons of bombs.

Meanwhile armed rebellion erupted in Cambodia's countryside, leading the CPK to openly declare war against Sihanouk. Officials in the DRV were dismayed by this turn of events but nonetheless were forced to offer support to the Khmer Rouge. Strategically, the top leadership of the CPK retreated to the northeastern quadrant of Cambodia as a base of operations. As Craig Etcheson explains, "There they set about establishing their authority over Ratanakiri, Mondolkiri, and Stung Treng Provinces, using murder to liquidate the existing administration. The nascent revolution moved from village to village, purging local leaders and appointing revolutionary leaders to take their place."[19]

On March 18, 1970, Sihanouk was removed from power in a coup led by Lon Nol and Prince Sisowath Sirik Matak. In response, Sihanouk issued an appeal to the Cambodian people, whereupon Royalist supporters would join the Khmer Rouge in a unified effort to defeat the Lon Nol government. Both Sihanouk and the Khmer Rouge leadership recognized the tenuous basis of their alliance. The Khmer Rouge continued to hold Sihanouk responsible for the war in Cambodia, but it well understood his popularity and was able to exploit this for propaganda and recruitment purposes. Sihanouk likewise understood that his role in the alliance was little more than that of a titular figurehead. He gambled, however, that he might use the arrangement as a means of deposing Lon Nol and eventually returning to power. His gamble failed to pay off.

On March 23, 1970, Sihanouk announced the formation of the National United Front of Kampuchea (Front Uni National du Kampuchea, or FUNK), a political and military coalition of Royalists and the Khmer Rouge, committed to destroying Lon Nol's republican forces. Two months later, the Royal Government of National Union of Kampuchea (Gouvernement Royal d'Union Nationale du Kampuchea, or GRUNK) was announced. Sihanouk assumed the post of GRUNK head of state, while Penn Nouth was designated prime minister. Other high-ranking positions were occupied by members of the Khmer Rouge cadre: Khieu Samphan was designated deputy prime minister, minister of defense, and commander in chief of the GRUNK armed forces; Hu Nim served as minister of information; and Hou Yuon assumed the positions of minister of interior, communal reforms, and cooperatives.[20] It was in part through these structures that members of the CPK solidified their authority. The other approach was more direct: mass murder. For five years, as civil war raged across Cambodia's landscape, the CPK leadership set about purging oppositional members. Indeed, by 1973 the Khmer Rouge began to liquidate Sihanouk's partisans, other allies inside FUNK and GRUNK, hundreds of Khmer Communists who had acquired military and political training in Vietnam, and ethnic Vietnamese who were fighting for the revolution.[21]

War escalated throughout Cambodia, generating the conditions that would ultimately make the Khmer Rouge revolution possible. On April 30, 1970, Nixon ordered U.S. and ARVN combat troops into Cambodia as part of a limited "incursion" designed to eliminate North Vietnamese bases of operation. This operation was followed by Nixon's decision of July 21, 1970, to resume bombing raids over Cambodia.[22] These military actions "gave the Khmer Rouges a propaganda windfall which they exploited to the hilt—taking peasants for political education lessons among the bomb craters and shrapnel, explaining to them that Lon Nol had sold Cambodia to the Americans in order to stay in power and that the U.S., like Vietnam and Thailand, was bent on the country's annihilation so that, when the war was over, Cambodia would cease to exist."[23]

The Nature of Revolution

When the Revolutionary Army of Kampuchea finally captured the capital city of Phnom Penh on April 17, 1975, the CPK enjoyed neither widespread support nor trust among the citizens of Cambodia. Indeed, while people were all too aware of the Khmer Rouge, most had little or no knowledge of the existence of the CPK. Indeed, many if not the majority of recruits to the Khmer Rouge joined not out of ideological commitment to Communism but rather for myriad reasons that centered, on the one hand, on widespread aerial bombing by the United States conducted in the course of the war against Vietnam and, on the other hand, the restoration of Sihanouk. This situation was not wholly unexpected. Secrecy on behalf of the Khmer Rouge during the revolution was deliberate and calculated. Reflecting its Marxist-Leninist foundation, the CPK viewed itself as a vanguard of Khmer society and understood its self-appointed role as one of revolutionary mentor. The lack of support and trust were thus mere contradictions needing to be resolved. Accordingly, in the postwar period, the CPK sought to articulate a vision of its newly established state, Democratic Kampuchea, a vision predicated on the dialectics of nature and society. This geopolitical imaginary, subsequently, was conveyed through numerous artistic means, including poetry, song, and photography.

In *The Nature of Revolution*, I provide a primary-sourced reconstruction of Khmer Rouge artistic practice. More precisely, I consider how "art" was made to work for the Khmer Rouge. I do so from a decidedly *geographic perspective*, in that I critically evaluate the dialectics of art and politics in the production of geographic knowledge. In common usage, geographical knowledge often refers to some understanding about a particular place. Consequently, geographical knowledge may be understood as that information purported to describe, explain, or interpret the distributions and characteristics of people and places. This is a fairly standard approach to geography: the writing of peoples and places. Conversely, geographical knowledge may also encompass a normative dimension in that it prescribes where people are to be located. David Harvey explains that governments, for example, may institute normative programs for the production of new geographical configurations and in so doing become major sites for orchestrating the production of space, the definition of territoriality, and the geographical distribution of populations, economic activities, social services, wealth, and well-being.[24] In either case (the former being descriptive geographies, the latter being normative geographies), geographic knowledges are *representations of reality*.

Edward Said referred to these knowledges as *imaginative geographies*.[25] These "ways of seeing," according to Said, "legitimate a vocabulary, a representative discourse peculiar to the understanding of places that becomes the way in which a place is known."[26] Imaginative geographies are, in effect, geopolitical discourses that provide the foundation for material policies and practices.

Derek Gregory elaborates that imaginative geographies involve a politics of space. He asks: "Who claims the power to represent: to imagine geography like this rather than like that?" In response, Gregory concludes that "the process of articulation is . . . a process of valorization."[27]

Geographical imaginations, especially as articulated in official narratives, are not mimetic representations of reality, however. As Stephen Daniels explains, "In geography . . . the place and status of imagination is shaped by the position and pressure of an array of contrapuntal concepts such as reason, experience, reality, objectivity, morality and materiality; the imagination has conventionally taken up a location somewhere between the domains of the factual and fictional, the subjective and objective, the real and representational."[28] This notion will assume added importance in that artistic productions often work as aesthetic interruptions.

According to Dydia DeLyser, "authenticity is not simply a condition inherent in an object, awaiting discovery, but a term that has different meanings in different contexts, in different places, to different people, and even to the same person at different times."[29] Photographs, for example, perform important framing functions. Not only are the images reproduced framed but a larger geographical imagination is also framed. Only certain elements of the landscape are captured on film, thereby guiding perceptions *and* conceptions toward a particular frame of mind. The mimetic quality of landscape photograph is illusionary, for the scenes depicted (seen) are "scenes" in the filmic sense. As Stuart Aitken and Leo Zonn explain, such images "demand to be read as real *places* with their own sense of geography and history."[30] In other words, the geographies imagined become "real" places that exist virtually but give the appearance of existing materially. Hence, as Jeff Hopkins writes, following Jean Baudrillard, "when the [images] resemble perfectly something that never existed, then the images are not reproductions of the real, but 'simulacra'—copies for which there are no originals."[31]

Throughout his writings, Baudrillard develops the concept of *simulacra*—a reproduction without an original.[32] In other words, social texts, including photographs, songs, and poems, are copies of places or events that never existed or that existed perhaps only in the eye of the composer. Understood thus, artistic practices *may* be considered inauthentic, in that it is not "reality" that is depicted but instead an imaginative geography. Such an understanding, however, negates the politico-aesthetic instrumentality of representations, for it is my contention that such artworks *are* authentic in their depiction of a reality that existed not materially but ideologically.

For Rancière "aesthetics is a historically determined concept which designates a specific regime of visibility and intelligibility of art, which is inscribed in a reconfiguration of the categories of sensible experience and its interpretation."[33] This suggests, on the one hand, that the political is inherently aesthetic, but, on the other hand, this does not imply that formal politics depend solely on mustering emotions and affect via iconic images and spectacle.[34] Instead, as Dixon explains, "art remains an important ensemble of practices, performances and artefacts because it provides an opportunity for reflection upon these very issues. Artistic practices are not autonomous from the political, nor are they political because of the message they send. Rather, they are both a particular form of politics and are capable of commenting on politics in itself."[35] By this I understand that Khmer Rouge artistic practices are illustrative first of particular geographical imaginations, that is, authentic simulacra, but second as indicators of proper revolutionary politics. In other words, we must understand poems, songs, and photographs produced by the Khmer Rouge not simply as works of propaganda but as indices of and contributors to the broader political and spatial transformations envisioned by the CPK.[36]

"Propaganda" in common usage has a pejorative sense; this, however, has not always been the case. As a term, "propaganda" was coined by Pope Gregory XV in 1622 in reference to a form of teaching, preaching, or education. It was only in the twentieth century that propaganda came to be associated with authoritarian or totalitarian regimes, state-controlled media, and broader forms of public brainwashing.[37] Writing during the rise of Nazi Germany, for example, Frederic Bartlett conceived of propaganda as the attempt to influence public opinion and conduct in such a manner that the persons who adopt the opinions and behaviors do so without themselves making any definite search for reasons.[38] In other words, propaganda is regarded as a passive form of politics, whereby audiences uncritically submit to messages forwarded. Accordingly, propagandistic art entails songs, poems, novels, photographs, and other forms of mass communication designed to influence attitudes and behaviors unreflexively.

This is not how the Khmer Rouge approached artistic practices. Indeed, documentary evidence would indicate that the senior leaders of the CPK actually viewed the promotion of songs, poetry, and photographs not as instruments of ideological indoctrination but instead as aesthetic forms of lived experiences. Stated differently, artworks for the Khmer Rouge were intended as means to actively engage in the revolution, for it was through the experiential quality of artworks that political subjects might be transformed. This belief counters the prevalent Maoist interpretation of people as blank sheets of paper to be inscribed with political writings or lumps of clay to be molded by members of the vanguard. Rather, it is suggestive of a dialectic approach to human consciousness and societal transformation. To this end, artistic practices produced and distributed by the Khmer Rouge are best understood as *politico-aesthetic technologies* that animate an alternative future.[39]

In the following chapters, I document how the Khmer Rouge used poems, songs, dance, and photographs as means of translating policy into practice. As a form of public pedagogy, these artistic productions provided instructions to the men, women, and children of Democratic Kampuchea for both proper political consciousness and the right attitudes toward labor. Hence, rather than viewing Khmer Rouge poems, songs, dance, and photography as instruments of political propaganda, I consider how creative expressions were conceived by the Khmer Rouge as aesthetic interventions: socially engaged sites of political action. As Alan Ingram explains, rather than assuming the power of art, it is more useful to attend to the multiple rhetorics and modalities of artistic interventions, to their practices, their reception and effects, in order to investigate how they may corroborate, suggest, or energize other kinds of actions.[40] This being said, it is also necessary to consider the inner contradictions within Khmer Rouge praxis. Notably, throughout Democratic Kampuchea men, women, and children had little opportunity for self-liberation; any semblance of individuality was anathema and potentially fatal. Consequently, while the CPK advanced artistic practices as forms of transformative potential, it decried attitudes and behaviors that deviated from its own prescribed norms. Unlike the emancipatory potential of artworks as understood, say, by Trotsky, artworks under the Khmer Rouge aligned more closely with the rigid, dogmatic promotion of political propaganda as seen throughout Stalinist Russia.

The cultivation of proper political consciousness, from the vantage point of the CPK, could not come about through the rote memorization typical of formal, classroom-based education. Instead, the nurturing of a political consciousness could only be achieved through personal and societal transformation.

Artistic productions were to facilitate this transformation, as aural and visual modes of instruction that, in dialectical fashion, would both reinforce lived experience and project forward a normative vision of what Democratic Kampuchea was to become. Ultimately, therefore, my project is not a simple case study of a bygone revolution that failed but instead a theoretically engaged, empirically grounded discussion of the intersection of art, politics, and nature from a Marxist standpoint. In taking this approach, I contribute to the geographic study of art and politics, the historiography of Cambodia under the Khmer Rouge, and a rereading of artistic practice through the lens of Marxist political philosophy.

The Path Forward

The Nature of Revolution begins with a broad conceptual overview of Marxist political philosophy. This is a strategic effort on my part, one that runs counter to more-conventional accounts of Khmer Rouge artworks. To begin, Marxist political philosophy has long been associated with the study of art, aesthetics, and culture.[41] As Dave Beech elaborates, Marxist aesthetics has made vital contributions to our understanding of literature, film, theatre, radio, painting, sculpture architecture, photography, photomontage, and the media.[42] Yet, just as there is no singular Marxist political philosophy, neither is there a straightforward interpretative framework for the study of art and aesthetics. Thus, following Maurice Merleau-Ponty, Beech distinguishes two broad divisions of Marxist political philosophy, each with its own distinctive approach to art and aesthetics: Classical Marxism and Western Marxism.[43] The former consists primarily of the economic and political writings of Marx and Engels and extends to those of Vladimir Lenin, Leon Trotsky, and Rosa Luxembourg, among others; the latter consists of the more philosophical, aesthetic, and cultural writings of Marxism, including but not limited to Georg Lukács, Theodor Adorno, Walter Benjamin, Ernst Block, and Fredric Jameson.[44]

Broadly, Western Marxism emerged in the 1920s and 1930s as a critique of Soviet-styled Marxism, especially as interpreted by Lenin and Stalin. Western Marxists redirected emphasis from political economy to culture, philosophy, and art; indeed, by rereading Marx with particular attention to the categories of class consciousness and subjectivity, they broke sharply with those who advocated (in their minds) an overly reductionist, materialist Marxism.[45] Accordingly, "in their efforts to rescue Marxism from positivism and crude materialism the Western Marxists argued that Marx did not simply offer an improved theory of political economy" but instead offered a critique of political economy; hence, Western Marxists adopted a position committed to the "abolition of political economy or to emancipation from the rule of the economy."[46] As Russell Jacoby concludes, the "categories of political economy themselves expressed an economic domination that Marxism sought to subvert."[47]

The writings of those aligned with Western Marxism would profoundly shape the study and interpretation of art and artistic practices throughout the remainder of the twentieth century. In effect, "Classical Marxism said a great deal about economics and very little about art; Western Marxism said a lot about art and aesthetics but virtually nothing about economics."[48] Indeed, as Beech elaborates, Classical Marxism "did not regard art as significant enough economically or politically to warrant attention. Western Marxism did not regard economics as providing the best tools for grasping the nuances of art."[49]

To be sure, there is considerably more nuance and complexity to the historiography of Marxist political philosophy than I have provided here.[50] However, my intent in calling attention to the debates and divisions among those who have followed in Marx's wake is to make clear my positioning of Khmer Rouge art and politics within the corpus of Classical Marxism, namely, through a reading of Marx, Lenin, and Trotsky. I do so for two reasons. On the one hand, it is my contention that a Marxist critique of a so-called Marxist social movement—which the CPK clearly was—requires a comparison of apples with apples and oranges with oranges. In other words, it is most appropriate to evaluate CPK policy and practice, including the production of artworks, through their own philosophic grounding. It is necessary to evaluate the CPK, as a self-described Marxist-Leninist vanguard party, from a standpoint of Marxist-Leninism. On the other hand, a critical reading of Khmer Rouge artistic practices provides an opportunity to counter a myopic Western Marxism that has largely stifled any sustained engagement of artistic practice within political economy. To turn once again to Beech, Western Marxism's historic opposition to Classical Marxism too often conflates Stalinism with the writings of Marx and Engels, as the latter is portrayed by the former as a "narrow and direct economic reductionism."[51] Consequently, as David Harvey writes, "Marx and 'traditional' Marxism were systematically criticized and denigrated as insufficiently concerned with more important questions of gender, race, sexuality, human desires, religion, ethnicity, colonial dominations, environment, or whatever."[52] This unfortunate state of affairs is indicative of a pervasive misreading of Marx himself. Christoph Henning finds that "the legacy of more than one hundred and fifty years in the history of the reception of Marx is so powerful that one can never be sure of understanding what he meant to say without being influenced by one of the numerous applications of his ideas."[53]

The study of Khmer Rouge artistic practices must be contextualized within a framework informed by a Marxist political philosophy *as interpreted by the Khmer Rouge*. The Khmer Rouge explicitly attempted to bring about a Marxist-derived socialist revolution. Thus, it is necessary to situate its goals, objectives, and methods within the larger corpus of historical materialism, as this was precisely the approach taken by the Khmer Rouge. To this end, in chapter 1 I build a scaffold on the concepts of historical materialism, dialectics, contradictions, revolutions, and transitional periods. This is followed by a more sustained engagement of the dialectics of nature, labor, consciousness, and freedom. This endeavor has significant ramifications for any subsequent attempt to disentangle nature within the corpus of Khmer Rouge policy documents. On the one hand, references to nature are abundant, as evidenced in meeting minutes, party slogans, and songs. On the other hand, most references are superficial. In the Four-Year Plan, for example, nature appears as a resource, waiting to be seized for productive purposes. My reading of CPK documents suggests a more substantive articulation of nature by the Khmer Rouge, a stance that aligns readily with Marx's nature-society dialectic. Following Marx, the labor process is purposeful activity aimed at the production of use-values, that is, those *things* necessary for life itself. Stated differently, the labor process for Marx was the fulcrum on which transformations in both nature and humanity hinged. In many of Marx's writings, nature *appears* as something external to human activity. A cursory or incomplete reading could lead one to speculate that Marx viewed nature as something to be appropriated by men and women. A Marxist conception of nature, though, is dialectical, for Marx proposed a general unity of "physical" nature with "human" nature. In other words, through labor—the material transformation of trees, soil, and water—humanity itself is transformed. It is for this reason that the production of consciousness is such an integral part of the general production of material life and is dialectically related to the transformative possibilities of labor. Indeed, Marx suggests a unity of nature with society—a unity derived from the concrete activity of natural beings, produced in practice through labor on material nature. This notion has a tremendous bearing on my subsequent understanding of the Khmer Rouge's conception of nature through artistic practice, for it is my argument that forced labor—from the vantage point of the CPK—was foundational to the cultivation of a correct political consciousness. Significantly, this argument runs counter to more-conventional accounts of the Khmer Rouge. That said, I caution that previous explanations have failed to consider more fully the actual Marxist imprint on CPK policy. For example, the Khmer Rouge viewed nature as something to be conquered. This position holds that the CPK sought to defeat nature and in the process create a pure, Communist utopia where rice fields flourish and humanity is free from want. Thus, we hear the Khmer Rouge proclaim, "Let us be master of the water, master of the nature" and "Let us not be defeated by nature." Such superficial readings of slogans, songs, and documents risk losing sight of the fundamental dialectic advanced by the Khmer Rouge. Because the CPK was a political organization influenced by Marxist-Leninist doctrine, it is necessary to follow its line of reasoning. Nature and humanity/society for the CPK were viewed not as binaries but rather as oppositional and contradictory categories. In other words, for the Khmer Rouge, humanity was not something external to a preexisting nature but instead both were mutually co-constitutive. Consequently, the CPK premised a unity of opposites whereby labor, a physical activity that transforms nature, would dialectically transform humanity. Last, I provide an explicit consideration of the "work" of art within Marxist-derived revolutions. Drawing heavily but not exclusively on the writings of Leon Trotsky, this section critically evaluates the different forms and functions of art following socialist revolutions and, significantly, highlights the tensions identified by Trotsky regarding the "bureaucratization" of socialism and the influence of this on the development of art. In the Soviet Union, for example, art came to be dominated by a very restrictive "Socialist Realism"; this was counter to the revolutionary potential of art as identified by Trotsky, namely, the necessity of allowing artists creative freedom.

Theoretically, this section provides an essential foundation for understanding subsequent Khmer Rouge policy and practice with respect to the promotion of arts in Democratic Kampuchea. Crucially, we must not position the Khmer Rouge solely as a dominant or hegemonic form of power or Democratic Kampuchea as always and already a totalitarian state. We must take seriously the fact that the Khmer Rouge was a revolutionary movement and that (from its vantage point) armed conflict was a form of resistance. For prior to military victory, the Khmer Rouge presented itself as waging an emancipatory campaign against imperialism and neocolonialism. Consequently, when one speaks of revolutionary art, for example, as produced by the Khmer Rouge, it is necessary to recognize that these artworks originated during a transitory period and the transformation of one geographic configuration to another.

Chapter 2 provides an empirically documented overview of the Khmer Rouge revolution and the overall political economy of Democratic Kampuchea. Success for the CPK, as described in its Four-Year Plan developed between July 21 and August 2, 1976, was premised on the achievement of two economic goals. The first was to serve the people's livelihood and to raise the people's standard of living quickly, in terms of both supplies and other material goods; second, the CPK would accumulate capital from agriculture with the expressed objective of expanding industry and defense. Agricultural growth would effectively produce the capital that would form the basis for eventual industrial self-sufficiency. But first agricultural surpluses had to be exchanged for foreign capital. And before that, agricultural surpluses had to be created.

Increases in rice production were necessary to produce a surplus to be sold on foreign markets in exchange for basic commodities and inputs (like oil, chemical fertilizers, and pesticides) and manufactured goods (like tractors, medicine, and ammunition). With sufficient growth in agricultural productivity, increasing surpluses would net increasing imports to support industrial development, which would in turn accomplish the goal of raising living standards; a textbook implementation of Walt Whitman Rostow's classic model of economic takeoff. This is not the autarkic, isolationist CPK typified in most accounts of the Khmer Rouge. Instead, documentary evidence reveals a government that used its comparative advantage in rice to secure the means for primary production and, eventually, to establish an economic strategy based on import substitution.

To meet these objectives, CPK leadership determined that not only did the amount of land under rice cultivation need to expand; overall rice *productivity* had to be tripled, to a national average yield of three tons per hectare per year. These increases in productivity were to be accomplished through (1) improvements in efficiency realized through the use of mechanical tools, chemical inputs, and scientifically bred seeds; and (2) the construction of large-scale irrigation works that could supply water to rice fields during the dry months of the year. Regarding the former, tools and chemical inputs were to be either manufactured within Democratic Kampuchea or purchased from abroad using revenues from the sale of surplus rice. Improved varieties of seeds—some developed within the country with foreign assistance, others imported directly—were to be widely disseminated to agricultural collectives. Concerning the latter, the CPK launched massive work projects to construct a network of dikes, canals, and reservoirs. The forced labor employed to complete these irrigation systems endured brutal working conditions, and many workers succumbed to exhaustion, malnutrition, and exposure to disease.

There was an important social dimension to the establishment of the Khmer Rouge political economy. Upon assuming power in 1975, the CPK well understood that its hold on power was tenuous. Consequently, the CPK turned to education as a means of establishing both legitimacy and political control. However, the CPK explicitly refused to appropriate former, more "traditional" forms of education. Thus, the Khmer Rouge dismantled preexisting educational institutions (e.g., public schools and universities) and replaced them with more "public" and "experiential" forms of education, including poetry, music, dance, and photography. Chapters 3 through 5 consider these in turn.

In chapter 3, I argue that the CPK used poetry as a form of public pedagogy. Thus, while geographers and other scholars laud the revolutionary and liberating possibilities of, for example, public art and dance, not all revolutions are liberating. As Ingram explains, "attempts to assess the significance and implications of art for geopolitics should begin with a more critical and evaluative approach towards the supposed emancipatory possibilities that have preoccupied the literature to date."[54] In addition, violence can, and often does, surround the displacement of the status quo in society. More specifically, I advance the argument that Khmer Rouge–era poetry presented nature as the fulcrum on which society was to be transformed. The cultivation of a proper political consciousness required the nurturing of a collective identity of what

Democratic Kampuchea was to become. In so doing, this chapter draws on, and contributes to, two themes in geography, namely fictive geographies and public pedagogy. As Jo Sharp explains, "Geographers undoubtedly have a contribution to make to the analysis of fiction. The 'imagined geographies' created through all sorts of media are central to the geographies used by people when going about their daily lives, so that it is important that such imaginings are understood by those of us trying to get to grips with . . . geographical relationships and identities."[55] Poetry, as recent scholarship demonstrates, is especially informative with respect to everyday geographies, in part because poems "can engage reader's humanity and allow for a visceral resonance."[56] Indeed, it is because of the potential transformative powers of poetry that we turn to public pedagogy as our second theme. Public pedagogy, broadly conceived, explores the possibilities for pedagogic interventions outside the formal learning environment. To this end, a growing body of literature has examined the possibilities—and limitations—of myriad artistic and creative public practices, including graffiti, music, dance, theater, and photography as political activism.[57] As Henry Giroux explains, these forms of public pedagogy are radical, in the sense that there "is a moral and political practice premised on the assumption that learning is not about processing received knowledge but about actually transforming it as part of a more expansive struggle for individual rights and social justice."[58] Public displays of art, for example, "can not only challenge, question, displace, destabilize, and overturn the *status quo* in a society, but also open up a space for radical alternatives and different futures."[59] Indeed, it is this transformative potential that Nick Schuermans and his colleagues announce in their "call and ambition . . . to promote a 'public pedagogy turn' in geographical studies of art, as well as in social and cultural geography at large."[60] I am in general agreement with this—but with a caveat. For in the promotion of radical alternatives and alternative futures, we must remain cognizant that education is always and already a political practice, that revolutions may be simultaneously progressive and repressive.

Music forms the subject of chapter 4. Khmer Rouge–era songs reflect a remarkable diversity of subject matter. Often the standard narrative renders Khmer Rouge songs as mere instruments of propaganda and thus emphasizes revolutionary fervor and collective heroism. And certainly, many songs do reveal a hypernationalism. Yet Khmer Rouge songs also speak to day-to-day activities, mostly but not exclusively related to agriculture. This should not be construed as a mindless and clichéd romanticism of the peasantry, for as John Marston finds, many songs prior to the Khmer Rouge likewise extolled the virtues of the peasantry and centered on agricultural activities.[61] Songs of the Khmer Rouge do, however, privilege communal or collective activities as opposed to earlier Khmer songs, which accentuated the family or village. Likewise, Khmer Rouge songs are noticeably silent on tales of romantic love or individual exploits. In this chapter, I understand Khmer Rouge–era songs, quite literally, as political performances, as narratives of revolution and nation building, but also as a normative exegesis to build socialism. Consequently, I approach Khmer Rouge–era songs as narratives that purport—in their totality—to present a story of Democratic Kampuchea. Songs, in other words, form the basis of constructing an imaginative geography of Democratic Kampuchea as a real place—but a place that is in the process of "becoming." Consequently, the repeated transmission of songs over the radio or the material performance of song in agricultural collectives or at worksites reiterate the history and geography of revolutionary and postrevolutionary society. However, apart from narrating the past as a sequence of interconnected events (e.g., revolutionary victory and postvictory practice), these songs provide a normative lesson, specifically, how the transformation of nature (through the development of irrigation schemes and other forms of hydropower) contributes to the transformation of society and the promotion of a shared sense of purpose.

Chapter 5 considers the promotion of photography, and specifically landscape photography, as a form of public pedagogy in Democratic Kampuchea. Since its inception, photography has emerged as a widely employed medium of landscape representation and, by extension, a politically important instrument of nation building. Tim Hall, for example, notes that "the idea of the photograph as a true record is almost universally accepted."[62] Steven Hoelscher likewise writes of the "thoroughly convincing illusion of factuality" of photographs.[63] Simply put, the power of photography is derived from its apparent mimetic quality—its ability to ostensibly represent the "real" world in an authentic, truthful, objective manner—thereby obfuscating its artificial basis. From this vantage point—a point that judicial systems are often quick to uphold—photographs become key documentary and evidential sources. Herein lies the power and paradox of photographic representation. Photographs are powerful devices that purport to represent authentically, yet paradoxically the images produced and reproduced are anything but authentic.

This paradox has tremendous political and judicial implications. Just as recovered photographs from the Khmer Rouge era are used to "substantiate" crimes against humanity, it must be acknowledged that these same images are not as they seem. Throughout the Extraordinary Chambers of the Courts of Cambodia (ECCC; better known as the "Cambodian genocide tribunal"), for example, photographs have been used to establish the guilt of high-ranking Khmer Rouge officials. However, to use Khmer Rouge–era photographs as evidence is to afford a "truthfulness" to these images that may not be warranted. This is akin to robbing Peter to pay Paul: on the one hand, we uphold the veracity of images as evidence of crimes against humanity; on the other hand, we simultaneously dispute the "authenticity" of the photographs as instruments of political propaganda. How then is it possible to call into question the truth function of photographs while not denying their evidential quality? A way forward is to consider Khmer Rouge–era landscape photographs as *authentic simulacra*.

As authentic simulacra, the landscape photographs of the Khmer Rouge are "faithful" copies of a landscape that existed virtually in the rhetoric of the Communist Party of Kampuchea. They are representations of a landscape envisioned but not realized, scenes of everyday life that never materialized but served as pedagogic devices informing citizens of how life was to be lived. That the landscape photographs of the Khmer Rouge appeared in "public" magazines and, especially, elementary school textbooks is therefore not inconsequential. As Guntram Herb observes, "All texts with a wide audience, including popular magazines, schoolbooks, novels, films, or news reports, are important in the 'common-sensical construction' of the nation."[64] This observation highlights an uncomfortable irony: Geographers have long recognized the importance of using landscape photographs as teaching tools. However, geographers have also critiqued the supposed neutrality of photographs. It is my contention that the CPK well understood the political power of photographic representation and that the effectiveness of photographs is found in the supposed truthfulness of photography's apparent mimetic quality.

By way of conclusion, in chapter 6 I move beyond Khmer Rouge artistic practice to consider the political aesthetics from a Classical Marxist perspective. More precisely, I provide an exegesis of freedom, labor, and artistic production with the purpose of advancing a progressive politics for the twenty-first century. David Harvey argues that it is necessary to engage critically with

Marxism.[65] Neil Smith agrees, noting that "the major challenge for Marxist work today is to take the wealth of insights generated from Marxist explorations in and around geography during the last three decades and to apply these to the task of understanding and criticizing a highly dynamic geographical world, and formulating alternatives."[66] To this I would add that it is more important than ever to critically engage in geographically informed studies of "actually existing" conditions in so-called socialist or Communist states, for the alternative is to cede the legacy of Marxist political philosophy to its detractors.

1 The Materiality of Art and Politics

In January 1976, party statutes were adopted by members of the Communist Party of Kampuchea. According to the preamble, the Communist Party of Kampuchea "is the party of the worker class," and the members of the CPK constitute "the most enlightened workers and peasants, walking at the very forefront, the most audacious and determined, and the very best of models." In effect, senior leaders of the CPK codified themselves as the true vanguard of the socialist revolution and thus were responsible for the transition of Cambodian society from an era of feudalism and capitalism to one of Communism. Crucially, the statutes affirmed that "the Party holds Marxism-Leninism as the foundation of its views and as the compass for all its activities by lively implementing Marxism-Leninism in accordance with the concrete situation of Kampuchea, . . . absolutely, along the principles and stances of dialectical materialism and historical materialism."[1]

In the pages that follow, I provide a theoretical framework for my subsequent evaluation of Khmer Rouge art and politics. Such an approach is necessary, for it is my argument that the CPK was both inchoate and inconsistent in its deployment of historical materialism and dialectics. In making this argument, however, it is necessary to first establish a foundation for understanding Marxist political philosophy. The past century has witnessed substantial confusion over many key terms and concepts, including, for example, *contradictions*, *vanguard*, *mode of production*, and *dialectics*. Even a cursory review of documents produced by the CPK illustrates considerable ambiguity and incoherence in the use of these and other terms.

In the pages that follow, I do not provide or advocate a "true" reading of Marx, although I do believe some readings are more appropriate and coherent than others. Nor do I make the claim that Marx was necessarily correct in his interpretation of history or society; this debate has raged for over a century and shows no sign of abatement. I do maintain the importance of reading CPK policies and programs against the grain of Marx to highlight different interpretations and to challenge the dominant narrative that Democratic Kampuchea represents a "pure" or "extreme" form of Marxism, Communism, or, for that matter, any other "ism." To cite but one example, Leo Cherne argues that the establishment of Democratic Kampuchea constitutes "the creation of the first pure Communist society anywhere in the world."[2] We must interpret and evaluate the CPK on its own terms, but this requires a robust engagement with the complexities of these terms. This chapter accordingly provides a scaffold for subsequent chapters. More precisely, in building my argument, this chapter proceeds block by block, as key concepts are added in support. I begin with the concept of historical materialism.

Historical Materialism

A materialist conception of history begins "with real individuals, their activity and the material conditions of their life."[3] Such a beginning is not arbitrary but instead predicated on what Karl Marx and Friedrich Engels termed the first premise of all human history, that is, "the existence of living human individuals."[4] At a bare minimum, obtaining food, water, shelter, and clothing are the conditions for a living existence, for both individual and collective survivability.[5] A first step in approaching history, therefore, is to consider how humans satisfy these needs, in short, to ascertain how societies are organized to provide the material conditions necessary for survival and reproduction.

Any given society will exhibit particular forms of acquiring and sustaining its material needs; these will be manifested in certain social relations, both internal and external to that society. For example, is the society self-sufficient in terms of growing its own foodstuffs? Conversely, does the society engage in trade with its neighbors? If so, how is trade conducted? At a more micro-level, how are various tasks performed, that is, how are laboring tasks divided among the society? By beliefs surrounding perceived age or sex differences? Marx's basic premise, in other words, was that the way people organize with one another to produce their subsistence is dependent on the type of productive technology they use, and that the type of productive methods in turn determine the kind of social organization they can have.[6]

For Marx, the production of material life was paramount, with the term "production" used in an expansive way to indicate how the basic necessities of existence are satisfied. To this end, Marx forwarded the abstraction *Produktionsweise*, translated as "mode of production." As a fundamental concept of Marxist political philosophy, this term has generated much debate and controversy and has resulted in considerable misunderstanding among supporters and critics alike. To begin, Marx used the term in different ways, depending on the task at hand. In some sections of *Capital* or the *Grundrisse*, for example, *Produktionsweise* is used narrowly in reference to labor processes; elsewhere, the term is deployed more generally in reference to various "stages" or "forms" of social development. Adding to the confusion are myriad other, related terms, including "forms of production," "epochs of production," "periods of production," or "historical organizations of production."[7]

Marx's clearest exposition of the concept—and the one most often cited by his followers—appears in his *Contribution to the Critique of Political Economy*, wherein he writes:

> In the social relations of their existence, men inevitably enter into definite relations, which are independent of their will, namely *relations of production* appropriate to a given stage in the development of their material *forces of production*. The totality of these relations of production constitutes the *economic structure* of society, the real foundation, on which arises a legal and political *superstructure* and to which correspond definite forms of social consciousness. The mode of production of material life conditions the general process of social, political, and intellectual life.[8]

Conceptually, this is a heavily laden passage and requires some explanation. We begin, as does Marx, with the proposition that any society will exhibit a certain form of social organization necessary for its survival and reproduction. From this, we may surmise that any specific mode of production—for example, foraging, horticulture, slavery, feudalism, capitalism, Communism—will have its own set of social relations, that is, the social arrangements by which people interact in the production and reproduction of their lives and those of the society in question.[9] Furthermore, each mode of production will exhibit certain levels of technology and make use of precise raw materials; these constitute the forces of production. Both the relations of production and the forces of production form the "base" of society, or its "economic structure." Emanating from the base is the superstructure, that is, those institutions, relations, and practices that encompass politics, law, education, and religion. These are not mere reflections of the economic structure of society but are interrelated. More precisely, the base and the superstructure are dialectically related; the mode of production, therefore, must be understood as a totality—a nuanced reading often missed by Marxists and non-Marxists alike, who simply reduce modes of production to static forms of social organization. Before expanding on this point, I must first work through the Marxist notion of dialectics.

Dialectics

Key documents produced by the CPK proclaim an adherence to dialectical materialism. Regrettably, nowhere did members of the CPK articulate with any degree of clarity what they meant when using this phrase. Perhaps such discussions took place, perhaps in the various political training sessions held by high-ranking officials, as they tried to disseminate their ideology to their subordinates. Before we pursue this avenue, however, it is necessary to establish a baseline for subsequent discussion, for *dialectics* remains a much-used and much-abused idiom.

According to Bertell Ollman, "dialectics is a way of thinking that brings into focus the full range of changes and interactions that occur in the world."[10] Let's pause for a moment on this statement. Ollman suggests that dialectics is a method—a way of thinking. The object of inquiry, though, is not a static object but instead one of transformations and connections; in a word, history, but history understood as unfolding not as linear progression but as the result of adaptations and contingencies. Thus if historical materialism constitutes the ontology of Marxist political philosophy, dialectics is its epistemology.

Such an approach is counter to more conventional and pervasive epistemologies—of which empiricism is exemplary—that disaggregate the world into discrete and unrelated entities. So conceived, a disaggregated epistemology limits analysis to the surface appearances of objects, of things understood having been sensed, that is, having the qualities of being measurable. By way of example, we may envision a table laden with foodstuffs: meats, fresh fruits, vegetables, and bread. Sensually, we experience these as discrete objects, individually placed on the table. Objectively, we may see, taste, touch, and smell the food. Dialectics, conversely, opens space for a deeper and more profound analysis. Reality, from a dialectic vantage point, consists not simply of disparate "things" but instead of processes and relations. Consequently, our awareness of the food should be informed by the underlying factors that made possible the bounty before us: for instance, the labor that went into the planting and harvesting of crops; and the labor that made possible the transportation of crops from field to market to our table. Reality is therefore more than the epiphenomena that can be counted, classified, and mapped; it is more than the observation that strikes us immediately and directly, which masks the underlying structures and social relations.

For Hegel, the presumption of discrete objects contributed to another faulty logic, namely, the *principle of noncontradiction*. Aristotle, for example, premised that an object cannot be both "A" and "Not-A." This binary form of thinking continues to permeate much of Western society, including that of the law. In the legal system, one is considered guilty or not guilty; it is generally not possible to be "just a little guilty." Hegel also drew on two concepts explored by the Greek philosopher Heraclitus. Heraclitus famously forwarded the idea that one can never step in the same river twice. This simply means that everything is in a state of flux and that while surface appearances suggest that the river is the *same* river, in actuality it is in constant motion, constantly changing. Heraclitus also called attention to the idea that "unity" exists in apparent opposites. Day is separate from night, and night separate from day, and just as day follows night, so too does night follow day. But neither can be understood—or even be said to exist—without the other, complementary element. These two concepts, of constant, permanent change and the unity of opposites, would greatly inform Hegel and, in turn, Marx.

Hegel argued that the principle of noncontradiction distorted the complexity of how the human mind and the objective world operate. For Hegel, the only permanent reality was the reality of change, and the key to understanding reality *as process* was to understand that everything in existence in some sense contained within itself its opposite, or its negation.[11] Thus any given society, Hegel maintained, would contain within it the seeds of its own negation. These are to be found in the myriad social relations and practices evidenced in society.

For Hegel, societies are composed of various institutions, laws, morals, and beliefs. These concepts embody certain ideals and are related to particular developmental stages of reason, or what Hegel termed the spirit of the age. It was the spirit of the age that informed one's preconception of reality, comparable to contemporary notions of localized knowledge. Following Hegel, these ideals inform how one understands reality. By extension, representations of reality are internally related to consciousness, which is both historically and geographically grounded. Societies change, Hegel argues, because of systemic contradictions that emerge within the collective consciousness of society. I will return to the very important concept of contradictions later; for now, suffice it to say that Hegelian contradictions lead to societal transformation and that these contradictions are dialectical in that the conditions for potential transformations are found within society itself.

Marx was in general agreement with Hegel that societies are in constant flux and that change is predicated on contradictions internal to society. Marx also shared Hegel's understanding that ideas or concepts did not have an independent existence, that laws, regulations, and institutions are not transhistorical but rather particular to any given society. He departed from Hegel, however, on the latter's assertion that change is found in some mystical consciousness that seemed to float above or beyond society. The fundamental problem for Marx was that Hegel began with an abstraction: the spirit of the age. Marx, writing with Engels, professed that

> in direct contrast to German philosophy which descends from heaven to earth, here it is a matter of ascending from earth to heaven. That is to say, not of setting out from what men say, imagine, conceive, nor from men as narrated, thought of, imagined, conceived, in order to arrive at men in the flesh; but setting out from real, active men, and on the basis of their real life-process demonstrating the development of the ideological reflexes and echoes of this life-process. *The phantoms formed in the brains of men are also, necessarily, sublimates of their material life-processes, which is empirically verifiable and bound to material premises. Morality, religion, metaphysics, and all the rest of ideology as well as the forms of consciousness corresponding to these, thus no longer retain the semblance of independence*. They have no history, no development; but men, developing their material production and their material intercourse, alter, along with this their actual world, also their thinking and the products of their thinking.[12]

Elsewhere, Marx inverts Hegel or, as he puts it, stands Hegel on his head: "My dialectical method is, in its foundations, not only different from the Hegelian, but exactly opposite it. For Hegel, the process of thinking . . . is the creator of the real world, and the real world is only the external appearance of the idea. With me the reverse is true: the ideal is nothing but the material world reflected in the mind of man, and translated into forms of thought." What does Marx mean in this passage and, more to the point, why is this important for our subsequent interpretation of Khmer Rouge art and politics? Simply this: Marx is saying that those elements that constitute the superstructure, such as law, education, and religion, do not magically appear in society but are dialectically related to the dominant mode of production. Legal systems within capitalism, for example, are interrelated with practices of landownership and property rights. Accordingly, within a communal subsistence-based economy there would be no laws protecting private ownership, for such a relation would not exist and no protection would be required. The imposition of such a law would emerge ex post facto, or at minimum contemporaneously, with a corresponding change in the economic sphere, such as the separation of workers from the means of production. In Democratic Kampuchea, we might presume that artistic practices—and the political use of art—would emanate dialectically from the dominant mode of production introduced by the CPK and that high-ranking officials, as self-proclaimed dialecticians, would understand art in this manner. In other words, art cannot be imposed "from above" on society but must germinate from within. This thesis will be a recurrent theme in subsequent chapters.

Returning to the topic more broadly, Marx argued that "the mystification which the dialectic suffers in Hegel's hands by no means prevents him from being the first to present its general forms of motion in a comprehensive and conscious manner. Within him it is standing on its head. It must be inverted, in order to discover the rational kernel within the mystical shell."[13] From this vantage point Marx and Engels are able to assert, "It is not consciousness that determines life, but life that determines consciousness."[14] In other words, instead of succumbing to something akin to the nebulously abstract spirit of the age, Marx and Engels posit that ideologies are materially grounded. Rather than descending from above as angels or demons, ideologies ascend, workmanlike, from the activities surrounding the production, circulation, and consumption of life's necessities. As Marx explains, "Neither legal relations nor political forms could be comprehended whether by themselves or on the basis of a so-called general development of the human mind." Instead, "they originate in the material conditions of life."[15] This is not to suggest that production *determines* all facets of social realty; this is a misunderstanding propagated primarily by postmodernists and other critics who fail to appreciate Marx's precise usage of the word "determinant."

For Marx, determinism refers neither to teleological inevitability nor to fatalism.[16] Rather, a *Marxist* determinism is based on the identification of key factors derived from *reading history backward*. Stated differently, Marx approached history inductively through an examination of concrete relations and processes. By way of illustration, consider your ability to read this present monograph. If we read history backward, we realize that numerous things had to happen: You obviously had to acquire this book, but equally, I had to write this book. Without a publisher, though, this monograph would not have appeared in its present form—if it appeared at all. And before writing the manuscript, I had to be in a position to gather and interpret vast amounts of documentation.

By reading history backward, Marx sought to identity those key *determinants* that contributed to the present condition. Capitalism, as it manifested itself in the late nineteenth century, exhibited a certain social form: private property, currency, production for exchange, and so forth. By reading history backward, Marx identified certain points in history whereby social relations were transformed and technological innovations were advanced in particular ways that contributed to the emergence of capitalism as a dominant mode of production. These transformations were dialectically related to changing forms of social consciousness, legal orders, and educational systems. These included the legal basis of private ownership, for example, or the rise of labor unions. Going forward, Marx suggested that if certain relations hold, we would expect the future to take on a particular form. In essence, Marx's method was a form of projection, more akin to meteorological or demographic analyses. Demographers, for example, routinely *project* future population sizes based on reading history backward. Assumptions are made based on determinant factors, such as fertility and mortality rates; given present levels (or deviations from these levels), a range of future forecasts is made.

Marx's approach to history but also to anticipatory revolutions is based on a similar logic. Crucial in this regard was the concept of contradictions and how the resolution of contradictions systemic to any mode of production would "impel" society forward. It is at this point we turn to Marx's deployment of contradictions.

Contradictions

For Marx, the idea of contradictions presupposes the existence of opposing tendencies or properties within phenomena. In formal logic, a contradiction exists when something is said to have two oppositional characteristics, or identities, in the Aristotelian form of A and not-A. These contradictions are logically inconsistent, as in the dominant belief in many Western societies that an individual cannot be both male and female. Indeed, much of Western philosophy is predicated on the privileging of singularity and dichotomous logic. Marx's understanding of dialectics differed. By way of illustration, think of a laborer. On the one hand, in capitalism, workers produce; they are responsible for the transformation of materials into commodities. Indeed, the labor theory of value presupposes that laborers are the ultimate source of value and that profit is the direct result of exploitation. On the other hand, laborers are also consumers. In capitalism, surplus value can be realized only if the commodities produced (by workers) are consumed, that is, purchased. Yet those "consumers" are also the "producers." Any given laborer thus embodies a particular "unity of opposites," in that he or she is simultaneously producer and consumer. This marks an inherent contradiction within capitalism. Owners of the means of production—the capitalist class—seek to minimize wages in an attempt to garner greater profits; yet if workers are paid too little, they are ineffective consumers.

Contradictions, for Marx, are at the center of class struggle and societal transformation. Indeed, Marx identified a number of systemic flaws in capitalism, and these, he argued, would greatly determine the transition from capitalism to socialism. Consider, for example, the assembly line, arguably the archetypical social formation of capitalism. As economic processes are reorganized away from artisanal to industrial production, workers increasingly find themselves as mere cogs of the assembly line. No longer in control of their own labor, they experience an isolated and alienated existence; they become, in effect, individuated as nothing more than replaceable parts of a larger machine. However, for any assembly line to function, these individuated cogs must work together; in other words, the assembly line itself constitutes a "collective." Unlike artisanal production, on the assembly line no one person is responsible for the entirety of production. Paradoxically, through this process capital's seeds of destruction are sown. The unity of individual workers into a collective whole facilitated the growth of labor unions; workers were able to unite against their own alienated existence. Thus, for Marx, contradictions between the forces of production and the relations of production would grow to a point where there would be an epoch of social revolution whereupon contradictions, manifested in antagonism between contending classes, would burst forth.[17]

Marx elaborates that "at a certain stage of development, the material productive forces of society come into conflict with the existing relations of production or—this merely expresses the same thing in legal terms—with the property relations within the framework of which they have operated hitherto. From forms of development of the productive forces these relations turn into their fetters. Then begins an era of social revolution."[18] We have, therefore, an incipient theory or framework of social revolution, an understanding grounded not for, example, in abstract ideals of, say, national identity but instead in the concrete structures and relations of society. Marx continues that the "changes in the economic foundation lead sooner or later to the transformation of the whole immense superstructure," but in "studying such transformations it is always necessary to distinguish between the material transformation of the economic conditions of production . . . and the legal, political, religious, artistic or philosophic—in short, ideological forms in which men become conscious of this conflict and fight it out." He concludes that "one cannot judge such a period of transformation by its consciousness, but, on the contrary, this consciousness must be explained from the contradictions of material life."[19]

We can readily see the implications of dialectics and contradictions for our understanding of societal transformations, including that following the Khmer Rouge revolution. History for Marx consists of changes brought about by human beings in the process of producing their existence.[20] Far from being a determinist in a crude usage of that term, Marx's historical approach was premised on the dialectics of human agency and structural conditions. Unfortunately, as Paul D'Amato explains, the socialists who followed Marx and Engels—including, as well, the Khmer Rouge—tended to read into Marx and Engels's historical materialism a kind of schematic list of stages that every society must pass through according to its level of economic development.[21]

Properly speaking, modes of production should be conceived as *processes* and *relations*. For many theorists who followed Marx, however, modes of production became reified as discrete, discernable *things*. This decidedly undialectical understanding of history has misdirected theorists and revolutionaries ever since. For Marx, Jairus Banaji writes, the task of scientific history consisted in the determination of the laws regulating the movement of different epochs of history, their "laws of motion," as they were called following the example of the natural sciences.[22] It bears repeating, though, that these laws did not operate as those in the natural sciences, such as the law of gravity. Rather, for Marx, human history involves people acting together or in conflict to achieve more or less conscious goals. Human agency, however, is contingent on material conditions that shape the consciousness of historical actors and also shape and limit the scope and character of their actions.[23] Indeed, Marx was emphatic that abstract laws do not exist in history, that the laws of motion operating in history are historically determinate laws; and that the scientific conception of history could be concretized only through the process of establishing these laws, specific to each epoch, and their corresponding categories.[24]

Subsequent revisions of Marx's historical approach both perverted the concrete grounding of Marx's conceptualization of modes of production and largely vacated the dialectic foundation of social transformations. Most notable in this regard was the maladaptation of Marxist political philosophy to align with the political machinations of Joseph Stalin and the Soviet Union. Under Stalin, Soviet Marxists uprooted the scientific foundations of both historical materialism and dialect materialism. Thus "for the dialectic as the principle of rigorous scientific investigation of historical processes . . . Stalinism substituted the 'dialectic' as a cosmological principle prior to, and independent of, science."[25] The end result was a presentation of self-contained "modes of production" that were premised to follow a predetermined and general sequence. As Banaji concludes, this "lifeless bureaucratic conception, steeped in the methods of formalism, produced a history emptied of any specifically historical content, reduced by the forced march of simple formal abstractions to the meagre ration of a few volatile categories."[26] Inexorably, capitalism followed feudalism; socialism followed capitalism; and Communism followed socialism. All that was required was an explication of conditions that were conducive to social revolution.

The so-called stages of economic development became ossified even during Marx's lifetime. In fact, Marx was compelled to respond to those who rendered his "historical sketch of the genesis of capitalism in Western Europe into a historico-philosophical theory of general development, imposed by fate on all peoples, whatever the historical circumstances in which they are placed."[27] Engels, likewise, spilled considerable ink in an attempt to correct the growing misinterpretations of Marx's historical materialism, noting that

> according to the materialist conception of history, the ultimately determining element in history is the production and reproduction of real life. Other than this neither Marx nor I have ever asserted. Hence if somebody twists this into saying that the economic element is the only determining one, he transforms that proposition into a meaningless, abstract, senseless phrase. The economic situation is the basis, but the various elements of the superstructure . . . also exercise their influence upon the course of the historical struggles and in many cases preponderate in determining their form.[28]

Neither Marx's nor Engels's admonitions were sufficient to prevent a reductionist and vulgar form of historical materialism and dialectic materialism from gaining ascendency. Indeed, by the second decade of the twentieth century most so-called Marxists—and their detractors—interpreted societal revolutions from such a misreading. It was this misreading that greatly informed the Communist revolutions in Russia and China. This misreading would also manifest itself in the Khmer Rouge's attempt to make a "super great leap forward."

Revolutions

In *The Communist Manifesto* Marx and Engels famously declare that "the history of all hitherto existing society is the history of class struggles." They continue, "Freeman and slave, patrician and plebian, lord and serf, guild-master and journeyman, in a word, oppressor and oppressed, stood in constant opposition to one another, carried on an uninterrupted, now hidden, now open fight, a fight that each time ended, either in a revolutionary constitution of society at large, or in the common ruin of the contending classes."[29] But how is this revolution to be accomplished?

Marx did not establish a coherent theory of revolution. Nor did he specify how a capitalist society, for example, would transform into a socialist society. And neither did Marx provide a blueprint of what a socialist or Communist society would look like. These lacunae would provide considerable difficulties—and opportunities—for those revolutionaries who followed in Marx's wake.

The thought of revolution for many people is anathema. As D'Amato explains, sudden, abrupt changes are seen as disruptions of a normal functioning society. However, a Marxist perspective holds that a revolution is not an aberration in an otherwise smoothly functioning society but instead is "a period when the gradual accumulation of mass bitterness and anger of the exploited and oppressed coalesces and bursts forth into a mass movement to overturn existing social relations and replace them with new ones."[30] Indeed, one reading of Marx holds that revolutions arise spontaneously, that when the exploited classes develop an appropriate political consciousness, when the fundamental contradictions within society become too pronounced, the downtrodden will replace the dominant ruling class. And for much of his life, Marx held out hope that such a revolution would materialize in Europe, whereby the proletarian class would rise up in unison to overthrow the bourgeois. Throughout the 1840s and 1850s, for example, Marx anticipated that as capitalism matured, the proletariat would come to understand their exploited condition, a crucial spur for revolution.

Marx's promotion of spontaneous revolution requires further clarification, if not for the fact that subsequent theorists have misunderstood this idea. As a dialectician, Marx did not promote a position of inevitability, nor did he subscribe to an ontology whereby ideas—including that of revolution—simply appear. Rather, a revolutionary consciousness is materially grounded in laboring activities, but it also requires social organization. As D'Amato writes, "all struggles throughout history have involved at least a rudimentary form of organization. In that sense, there is no such thing as pure spontaneity."[31] To this end, spontaneity and organization, Duncan Hallas explains, "are not alternatives; they are different aspects of the process by which increasing numbers of workers can become conscious of the reality of their situation and of their power to change it. The growth of that process depends on a dialogue, on organized militants who listen as well as argue, who understand the limitations of a Party as well as its strengths and who are able to find connections between the actual consciousness of their fellows and the politics necessary to realize the aspirations buried in that consciousness."[32]

For Marx (and Engels), social organization was a necessary requirement, not least because "the ideas of the ruling class are in every epoch the ruling ideas: i.e., the class which is the ruling material force of society, is at the same time its ruling intellectual force."[33] In other words, according to Marx, those who control the means of production, that is, the capitalist class, also control the ideological foundations of society, including education and the law. In capitalism, for example, private ownership *appears* natural and enduring because it forms the basis of power for the ruling class. Thus the "ruling ideas are nothing more than the ideal expression of the dominant material relations, the dominant material relations grasped as ideas; hence of the relations which make the one class the ruling one, therefore, the ideas of its dominance."[34] This assertion will have profound implications for our subsequent engagement with Khmer Rouge artistic practice for it calls into question the ideological struggles over political consciousness.

A key question that occupied the attention not only of Marx but also of his followers was why exploitative societies are even possible. In other words, why do workers persist and even support a society where they are oppressed, either socially, economically, or politically? Even today, pundits grapple with the fact that voters often appear to vote against their own interests. In part, the explanation centers on the production, distribution, and consumption of knowledge. The basic Marxian view "sees information as limited and incomplete. There are some circumstances in which people can have a better grasp of possibilities than in others. In most circumstances, people are obstructed by limited knowledge due to their inhibited access to others, inhibited access to communication, and inhibited access to education."[35] People appear to willingly support their own exploitation and oppressive life conditions because they do not necessarily realize they are exploited or oppressed; they embody a form of *false consciousness*. Subsequent writers working in the tradition of Marx have elaborated in considerable detail the concept of false consciousness and, more precisely, how this interacts with ideology. In the writings of Antonio Gramsci and Georg Lukács, for example, a distinction was forwarded whereby "false consciousness came to mean a distorted and limited form of experience in society," while "ideology was applied to those explanations offered by intellectuals to legitimate such experience."[36] For our present purposes, the fundamental takeaway is that social organization is a vital aspect of revolutionary movements.

Social organization *in response to* and in challenge of the hegemonic ideas of the ruling class was absolutely central to the overthrow of capitalism. If an appropriate proletarian consciousness had not fully developed, it would become necessary to "build socialism," that is, to cultivate an appropriate level of consciousness among the people. In *The Communist Manifesto*, Marx and Engels emphasized the importance of class solidarity and organization among the proletarians.[37] The working class, in other words, needed to build an organization of socialist militants.[38] This organization would ultimately take the form of Communist parties.

Marx's understanding of revolutionary transformations was fundamentally a process of *grassroots democracy*. More precisely, social organizations were to be inclusive and democratic, composed of all peoples who stood against the ruling class. This concept of organization, D'Amato writes, "sees socialists neither as mere participants in the struggle, nor as an elite that dictates to the masses, but as comrades in struggle."[39] In time, Marx's conception was radically altered by subsequent revolutionaries, notably those advocating for revolution in Russia.

Throughout the late nineteenth and early twentieth century, countless Russian writers, theorists, and revolutionaries increasingly turned their attention to the promotion of a vanguard party. Lenin, for example, favored the establishment of a subset of professional revolutionaries whose task was "to train working class revolutionaries who [would] be on the same level in regard to Party activity as intellectual revolutionaries."[40] Lenin elaborates that "attention must be devoted principally to the task of raising the workers to the level of revolutionaries, and not to degrading ourselves to the level of the 'labor masses' . . . or necessarily to the level of the average worker."[41]

Neither Marx nor Engels favored the idea of a vanguard or any nondemocratic form of rule. Indeed, both Marx and Engels were revolted by the idea of a "program which divided the movement into those who monopolized the revolutionary idea and those who served as cannon fodder."[42] To this end, according to Richard Hunt, both men "struck at the essence of the vanguard idea, which implicitly or explicitly denies the capacity of the masses to emancipate themselves and therefore assigns the responsibility for thinking and leading to a self-appointed general staff drawn—inevitably—from the educated classes."[43] Ominously, Engels would write: "People who boasted that they had made a revolution have always seen the next day that they had no idea what they were doing, that the revolution made did not in the least resemble the one they would have liked to make. That is what Hegel calls the irony of history."[44]

In Russia and later China, the idea of a vanguard party was extremely seductive. Simply put, in these countries, conditions were not favorable for Communist revolution—as understood conventionally by Marx. Russia at the turn of the twentieth century exhibited only a nascent proletariat; society was effectively feudal in composition. China was predominantly agrarian, with a large peasantry, and only at the beginning of the process of industrialization.[45] It is at this point that the caricature of Marx's modes of production assumes tremendous importance.

Transitions

Much debate has centered on the Marxist concept of transitions and transitional periods.[46] To begin, the crux of the debate is relatively straightforward. If we agree that societies reflect different modes of production, for example, feudalism and capitalism, how does the transformation from one social formation to another occur? For Marx, we have seen, systemic contradictions within any given mode of production will necessarily lead to revolutionary transformations. This follows, however, from the development of an appropriate political consciousness and an awareness of one's own oppression. Accordingly, the overthrow of capitalism and the subsequent foundation of a Communist society require certain preconditions to be manifested in society. Capitalist relations of production, the assembly line, for example, need to be developed sufficiently to the point that a proletarian consciousness can emerge.

But what if conditions are not yet appropriate? Is it possible to foment a Communist revolution in, say, a predominantly feudal or peasant-based society? This question would haunt revolutionaries in a number of countries, including Russia and China. In time, so too would revolutionaries in Cambodia confront this dilemma. Ironically, these questions reveal a decidedly undialectical historiography, one based on a vulgar caricature of discrete epochs through which all societies must pass. It was within this context that so-called Marxists countenanced the idea of skipping stages, that is, bypassing capitalism altogether in their promotion of a Communist society. Early Chinese

Marxists, for example, read into Marx and Engels justification for leaping over capitalism. For these theorists, Adrian Chan explains, the main criterion for revolution was the presence of exploitation, rather than the existence of a fully fledged capitalist economy. Therefore, in agrarian societies, the dispossession of the peasants' landholdings during the commercialization of agriculture was sufficient to transform them into a rural proletariat.[47]

Having determined that it was possible to skip or leap over stages, theorists in both Russia and China were still confronted with several interrelated problems. For example, was socialism a distinct mode of production or merely a transitional period leading to Communism? If it was a distinct mode, how would the transition from socialism to Communism occur? Conversely, if socialism was a transitional period, how long would it last? And again, how would socialism transition to Communism? Coupled with these seemingly objective concerns were other issues of a decidedly more subjective nature. Certain material transformations were possible through revolutionary action: private lands could be appropriated; and communal forms of economic production could be introduced. How, though, could an appropriate level of political consciousness be cultivated?

This is not the place to engage directly with the complex histories of Russian or Chinese Communism. Rather, my purpose in raising these questions is twofold: first, to highlight the intricacies surrounding the many Communist revolutions that transpired during the twentieth century; and second, to call attention to the salience of purportedly appropriate forms of political consciousness to these movements. Even so, such an academic deliberation may seem fairly unrelated to the overarching task at hand, namely, a critical interpretation of art and politics forwarded by the Khmer Rouge. Yet in many respects, this seemingly academic debate is perhaps the most crucial question to ask when studying the Cambodian genocide. Simply put, for senior leaders of the CPK, the matter of transitional periods was anything but a philosophical nut to be cracked. Instead, it was very real, very concrete, and ultimately determined the course of action adopted by the CPK. It is necessary, therefore, to provide something of the broad coordinates of the transitional debate, not to resolve this dispute to the satisfaction of Marxist political philosophers but as a means of teasing out how the CPK approached the problem. Required, therefore, is a more direct assessment of the dialectics of labor, nature, and consciousness. This, in turn, necessitates an engagement with a Marxist conception of freedom.

Nature, Labor, Consciousness, and Freedom

Within Marxist political philosophy, nature appears as an abstraction. This is not to deny a material reality, that trees, rocks, and rivers do exist. Rather, it is a proposition that *ideas* about nature are constituted by (and simultaneously constitute) a particular historical and geographical moment. As Ollman explains, "Our knowledge of the real world is mediated through the construction of concepts in which to think about it; our contact with reality, in so far as we become aware of it, is contact with a conceptualized nature."[48] To view nature as an abstraction, therefore, is to contemplate *which* concrete realities constitute nature. For example, are humans part of or apart from nature? In contemporary capitalist society, nature is often premised as something separate from humanity, as if people were external to nature. As Noel Castree writes, "Once we distinguish ideas of nature from the things they refer to we can make an apparently startling claim: namely, that there is no such thing as nature! Nature is simply a name that is 'attached' to all sorts of different real-world phenomena. Those phenomena are not nature as such but, rather, what we collectively choose to call 'nature.'"[49]

We recall that for Marx and Engels the first premise of human history is the existence of living human beings. Therefore, any conception of nature would necessarily begin with the ability of humans to individually or collectively satisfy—produce—the material conditions of survivability: food, water, shelter, and clothing. By extension, the dialectic relationship between humans and nature must proceed from the conception of *production in general*. As explained by Marx:

> Labor is, first of all, a process between man and nature, a process by which man, through his own actions, mediates, regulates and controls the metabolism between himself and nature. He confronts the materials of nature as a force of nature. He sets in motion the natural forces which belong to his own body, his arms, legs, head and hands, in order to appropriate the materials of nature in a form adapted to his own needs. Through this movement he acts upon external nature and changes it, and in this way he simultaneously changes his own nature.[50]

In this quote, nature *appears* as something external to human activity. As Neil Smith explains, humans are born with certain natural needs, such as food, water, and shelter, and they are born into a world where nature provides, either directly or indirectly, the means for fulfilling these needs.[51] But a Marxist conception of nature, as Smith points out, is dialectical and thus would pivot on a general unity of physical nature and human nature.[52] Thus Marx writes: "Nature is man's inorganic body—nature, that is, insofar as it is not itself the human body. Man lives on nature—means that nature is his body, with which he must remain in continuous intercourse if he is not to die. That man's physical and spiritual life is linked to nature means simply that nature is linked to itself, for man is a part of nature."[53] As such, to countenance that humanity (or, more properly, human consciousness) is external to nature is to promote a Hegelian vision of mystical origin, for if humans are external to nature, whence did humanity arise?

The production of consciousness is an integral part of the general production of material life and is dialectically related to the transformative possibilities of labor. This, according to Marx, is what separates so-called humans from so-called animals.[54] In a widely cited passage, Marx elaborates on this process:

> We presuppose labor in a form in which it is an exclusively human characteristic. A spider conducts operations which resemble those of the weaver, and a bee would put many a human architect to shame by the construction of its honeycomb cells. But what distinguishes the worst architect from the best of bees is that the architect builds the cell in his mind before he constructs it in wax. At the end of every labor process, a result emerges which had already been preconceived by the worker at the beginning, hence already existed ideally. Man not only effects a change of form in the materials of nature; he also realizes his own purpose in those materials. And this is a purpose he is conscious of, it determines the mode of his activity with the rigidity of a law, and he must subordinate his will to it. This subordination is no momentary act. Apart from the exertion of the working organs, a purposeful will is required for the duration of the work.[55]

Here, Marx forwards a general unity of nature with society—a unity derived from the concrete activity of natural beings, produced in practice through labor on material nature.[56] To this end, following Marx and Engels, "consciousness is . . . from the very beginning a social product."[57] But it is a social product that has not descended from the heavens but rather arises from the ground up, the product of human material activity. Consequently, the specific form of human activity both constitutes and is constituted by consciousness itself. Consciousness, therefore, is material, relational, and processional. It is material from the standpoint that consciousness is derived from the physical act of labor—the transformation of physical nature through human activity. It is relational, both from the standpoint of how humans relate to nature but also from that of how humans relate to one another. And finally, it is processional, in that consciousness is not something we are born with and is unchanging throughout our lives. Rather, consciousness is always in a process of becoming.

Marx posited also a fundamental transformation between *production in general* and *production for exchange*. Within those societies characterized by production in general, humans produce objects based on particular use-values. If a shovel or a bucket is needed to facilitate agriculture, members of the community will make a shovel or a bucket. Under systems of production for exchange, however, the relation with nature is no longer exclusively a use-value relation, in that objects are produced no longer for direct use but for exchange. This is crucial, for as Smith concludes, "with production for exchange rather than direct use, there arises first the possibility and then the necessity for alienation of the individual."[58] A particular form of nature transformed, in other words, works to estrange humans from their human nature.

Marx's theory of alienation is most fully developed in the posthumously published *Economic and Philosophic Manuscripts of 1844*, where he presents alienation as comprising four broad relations that cover the totality of human existence: workers' relationships to (1) their productive activity, (2) their products, (3) other people, and (4) the species-being, that is, humanity.[59] First, alienation is experienced when laboring activities become external to the worker. Those workers assigned to assembly lines, for example, exist as mere appendages to the factory; they do not control their own productive activities but instead function at the beck and call of those who own the means of production. Second, under such conditions workers become alienated from the object of their labor: the commodities produced are owned not by the worker but rather by those who own the means of production. Workers derive no satisfaction from their labor activities. Third, workers become alienated from other people; all become mere cogs in the machinery. Last, workers become alienated from humanity itself. This final form, species alienation, is of a qualitatively different type and requires some elaboration. To begin, this form of alienation does not mean that there is some essential human nature that is not produced by human activity but is instead given a priori. Species alienation should be understood not as alienation from an ideal human nature but as alienation from historically created human possibilities and especially from the human capacity for creativity.[60]

According to Marx, under an exploitative system of production for exchange, men and women—but humanity as a whole—are precluded from developing an unalienated, unestranged consciousness. As Ollman concludes, "The human species is deprived of its reality, of what it requires to manifest itself as the human species."[61] Indeed, the exploitative practices of an economic system built on a system of production for exchange reduces humanity "to performing undifferentiated work on humanly indistinguishable objects among people deprived of their human variety and compassion."[62] For this reason, Marx believed Communism, as a collective, nonindividuated form of production, was necessary to overcome the alienated life that typified capitalism. A Communist revolution, accordingly, was premised not solely to affect political and economic change; it would also occasion a *moral* transformation. With the abolition of those structures and relations that bring about alienation, work would be experienced as a free and fulfilling expression of life.[63]

Throughout his writings, Marx is somewhat circumspect on the topic of unalienated life. In part, this results from his dialectical epistemology. For Marx it was improper to specify with any degree of certainty or finality how a future Communist society might appear or function. Nevertheless, scattered among his writings are various clues that shed insight into his thinking. To this end, much attention has focused on Marx's forwarding of the "realms of freedom" and the "realms of necessity."[64] Together, these concepts have generated substantial debate among historians and philosophers; they are also of considerable interest vis-à-vis the aesthetic politics promoted by the Khmer Rouge.

Briefly stated, the "realm of necessity" refers to work, while the "realm of freedom" refers to time outside the working day.[65] Beyond this simple explanation, however, lies a more nuanced journey into the ideas and ideals of freedom, democracy, and labor. At issue is not merely how humans spend their time, whether at "work or at play," but instead how the temporal allocations of productive and reproductive tasks impinge on political participation, yes, but more importantly on how individuals (and society) may promote and lead an unalienated life.

Depending on the context, Marx uses the terms "work" and "labor" in precise ways. Regarding the realm of necessity, Marx refers to labor as that directed toward satisfying the basic needs of society.[66] This aligns with historical materialism and Marx's first premise: the production of food, water, shelter, and clothing are necessary requirements for the biological, material reproduction of society. The realm of freedom would thus *appear* to be in opposition to the realm of necessity. Indeed, one reading would suggest that the realm of freedom equates with leisure, or time away from the drudgery of work. As Jan Kandiyali explains, the "natural temptation is to see the 'realm of freedom' and the 'realm of necessity' as being opposed to one another, so that the contrast is between a 'realm of freedom,' that comprises all that is free, and a 'realm of necessity,' comprising its opposite, namely, alienation, unfreedom and such like."[67] This is not Marx's intention. Kandiyali suggests that Marx is actually positing two "realms" of freedom: freedom as *self-determination*, understood as collectively determining one's activity instead of being ruled by external forces; and freedom as *self-realization*, understood as the development of one's distinctly human capacities and potentialities.[68]

A materialist understanding of history holds that societies at a basic level are concerned first and foremost with satisfying the conditions necessary for life itself. In so-called primitive societies, notably those characterized as hunter-gatherer, labor is performed by humans, but it is labor marked by necessity. Ollman explains: "Such labor is mere energy expended to satisfy immediate physical needs and has little in common with human productivity activity."[69] In this context, human labor is largely indistinguishable from that of animals; all species by necessity need to acquire food and water and to seek shelter. In such a society, the human condition is one of unfreedom, for everyday life is characterized by the perennial struggle to satisfy the most basic physical needs.[70] Humans, however, have the capability of *something else*, namely, genuinely creative work.[71]

Throughout human history, the productive means of satisfying these needs are transformed. Technological innovations, reconfigured divisions of labor, and complex systems of barter and trade all steadily distance humans from the realm of necessity. In other words, humans are gradually, almost inexorably becoming free from the physical constraints of nature. Indeed, the dialectic relationship between humans and nature is transformed. Eventually, under capitalism, the industrialization and automation of the labor process initiated unprecedented levels of productive power. Paradoxically, these transformations brought about a fundamental societal contradiction. Production under capitalism should have provided the means to humanize labor, reduce the working day, and lead to greater leisure time.[72] More wealth, likewise, should contribute to a better quality of life, one where children no longer go to bed hungry or paupers die in the streets for lack of housing. Yet, Marx observed, under capitalism, societal inequalities became more pronounced, and humans became alienated. Children were starving, and the homeless did die from exposure.

Communism, for Marx, would transcend the stultifying conditions of alienation, exploitation, and oppression and, in turn, would provide the necessary freedom for the development of human creativity and personal fulfillment. This is not to suggest that humanity no longer dwells in the realm of necessity, for material production remains necessary to maintain life. However, under Communism men and women cooperate with one another in a nonexploitative fashion, and the absence of exploitative and oppressive relations provides the opportunity to fully cultivate one's life activities and aesthetic endeavors.[73] As Kandiyali concludes, while the realm of necessity may be understood as a realm of self-determination, where men and women exercise control over their economic activity, the realm of freedom is the realm of self-realization, the sphere of life where individuals develop their distinctly human powers and capacities.[74]

In Communism, for Marx, both self-determination and self-realization become possible. Men and women, while engaging in labor necessary for the production and reproduction of society, exhibit self-determination; they are no longer subject to structures of domination imposed by a ruling class. Work is voluntary, communal, unalienated, and personally fulfilling. Moreover, men and women are able to develop and express their creative capabilities and potentialities—something that appears most prominently in the cultivation of artistic practices.

The "Work" of Art

Aesthetic production for Marx was intimately associated with his conceptualization of work.[75] As evidenced in his presentation on the realms of necessity and the realms of freedom, Marx premised that only in a communal society could men and women achieve self-determination and self-realization. Perhaps nowhere is this more evident than in the production of art. Thus Marx premised that work is not only a means to satisfy material needs (e.g., a necessity); it is also an expression of a fundamental human drive for personal fulfillment. Hence, under conditions of freedom, beauty could be found even in the most seemingly banal task or chore. Nevertheless, the products of laboring activities are always destined to be consumed; these objects have a pragmatic use-value and therefore forever remain within the realm of necessity.[76]

Artistic activity is different. Artistic productions are not instrumental; these activities are not undertaken to satisfy an immediate (or delayed) material need, such as the gathering of water or the provision of food. Indeed, artistic productions are *not* to be consumed but instead are meant to be appreciated for their intrinsic appeal.[77] Thus, in the *Economic and Philosophic Manuscripts*, Marx writes: "Animals also produce. They build themselves nests, dwellings, like the bees, beavers, ants, etc. But an animal only produces what it immediately needs for itself or its young. . . . It produces only under the dominion of immediate physical need, while man produces in freedom therefrom." In elaboration, Marx continues: "An animal forms things in accordance with the standard and the need of the species to which it belongs, while man knows how to produce in accordance with the standard of every species, and knows how to apply everywhere the inherent standard to the object." Crucially, Marx concludes that "man . . . also forms things in accordance with the laws of beauty."[78]

Marx premised Communism as a necessary corrective to an alienated existence systemic to capitalism. Consequently, emphasis was placed primarily but not exclusively on economic transformations. "The changes in the economic foundation," Marx writes, "lead sooner or later to the transformations of the whole immense superstructure. In studying such transformations it is always necessary to distinguish between the material transformation of the economic conditions of production . . . and the legal, political, religious, artistic or philosophic—in short, ideological forms in which men become conscious of this conflict and fight it out."[79]

Artistic productions and creative expression figure prominently in Leon Trotsky's materialist understanding of postrevolutionary society. He notes, for example, that a failure on behalf of society to provide the basic conditions of life would lead to obvious failure of the society. However, he also declares that "even a successful solution of the elementary problems of food, clothing, shelter . . . would in no way signify a complete victory of the new historical principle, that is, of socialism."[80] He elaborates that "only a movement of scientific thought on a national scale *and the development of a new art* would signify that the historic seed has not only grown into a plant, but has even flowered."[81]

Trotsky's understanding of art is profoundly dialectic. For Trotsky, the blossoming of future art, that is, of postrevolutionary artistic creations, is germinated in the fields of past art. Thus, while Trotsky quips, "It is silly, absurd, stupid to the highest degree, to pretend that art will remain indifferent to the convulsions of our epoch," he also contends that "it is fundamentally incorrect to contrast bourgeois culture and bourgeois art with proletarian culture and proletarian art."[82] The explanation is twofold. First, as indicated, culture and art for Trotsky are *transformed* by revolution; this is decidedly different than premising that the culture and art of the bourgeois will be replaced by the culture and art of the proletarian. Second, and more pointedly, any replacement by proletarian art is impossible, for—according to Trotsky—there is no such thing as a proletarian culture.

An orthodox reading of dialectic materialism holds that the proletariat—as a social class—must be transitory, for the simple reason that under Communism classes will cease to exist. It holds, therefore, that there cannot be any such thing as a proletarian culture or proletarian form of art in a Communist society. Trotsky writes, "The historic significance and the moral grandeur of the proletarian revolution consist in the fact that it is laying the foundations of a culture which is above classes and which will be the first culture that is truly human."[83] This readily aligns with Marx's belief that Communism will provide the opportunity for humanity's creative expression to be developed to its greatest potential.

Trotsky advocated that artistic creations be enlisted in support of the revolution but decried the possible appropriation of art and artists by revolutionary bureaucrats. "Our policy in art," Trotsky writes, "during a transition period, can and must be to help the various groups and schools of art which have come over to the Revolution to grasp correctly the historic meaning of the Revolution." That being said, Trotsky clarifies that people should be afforded "complete freedom of self-determination in the field of art."[84]

In his support of artistic freedom, Trotsky did provide a rather substantial qualification: It must be put before the artist "the categorical standard of being for or against the Revolution."[85] Does this not negate his entreaty that artists are to enjoy complete freedom of self-determination? A possible response is found in his criticism of artistic "fellow travelers." Today, the phrase "fellow traveler" has been misappropriated by Marxists and non-Marxists alike; contemporary usage tends to equate a fellow traveler with someone who is supportive of or sympathetic to Marxist ideals but is not a party member. For Trotsky, the term was laden with pejorative connotations: fellow travelers "do not grasp the Revolution as a whole and the communist ideal is foreign to them."[86] With this in mind, Trotsky's qualification of artistic freedom reads differently. Thus, in reference to the early years of the Soviet Union, Trotsky laments, "Between bourgeois art, which is wasting away either in repetitions or in silences, and the new art, which is as yet unborn, there is being created a transitional art, which is more or less organically connected with the Revolution, but that is not at the same time the art of the Revolution."[87] In this statement, Trotsky concludes that the free and creative expression of women and men has yet to materialize; artistic works, most assuredly, are being produced; and these are produced under the mantra of revolution. Ultimately, though, these so-called artists are nothing more than fellow travelers. For Trotsky, therefore, the artists of the early Soviet Union were "not the artists of the proletarian Revolution, but her artist 'fellow travelers'" and, as such, the "work of the 'fellow travelers' [was], in its way, a new Soviet populism."[88] Artistic works produced as such were not *for* the revolution, in the sense that the artists themselves creatively expressed personal self-determination.

Trotsky's condemnation of fellow travelers mirrors his disdain for party influence on artistic production and creative expression. Trotsky writes: "The actual development of art, and its struggle for new forms are not part of the Party's tasks, nor is it its concern. The Party does not delegate anyone for such work."[89] Elsewhere, he writes: "The new forms must find for themselves, and independently, an access into the consciousness of the advanced elements of the working class as the latter develop culturally. Art cannot live and cannot develop without a flexible atmosphere of sympathy around it."[90] In these passages, Trotsky acknowledges that art is not produced in a vacuum but rather that art, politics, technique, and economics are intertwined.[91] He allows that artistic endeavors are produced and must be understood within the totality of society. His contempt was directed at the ham-fisted appropriation of art to serve party propaganda as opposed to a material activity that reflects a revolutionary consciousness, where art is understood as being expressive of an unalienated freedom. Trotsky explains, "Our Marxist conception of the objective social dependence and social utility of art, when translated into the language of politics, does not at all mean a desire to dominate art by means of decrees and orders. It is not true that we regard only that art as new and revolutionary that speaks of the worker, and it is nonsense to say that we demand that the poets should describe inevitably a factory chimney, or the uprising against capital!"[92]

Communism, for both Marx and Trotsky, held the potential for humanity's creative possibilities to be fully realized. Artistic productions could, of course, provide support for the revolution. However, art was not to be held captive by the revolutionary party. Revolutionary art was not, according to Trotsky especially, a predetermined form dictated by party apparatchiks. Truly revolutionary art expressed self-determination and self-realization; it was the concrete manifestation of the transformed consciousness of men and women in communal society. All of which begs the fundamental question: How was art and politics forwarded by the Khmer Rouge?

Trotsky's assertion is important for my present work *not* because I believe that senior leaders of the CPK were Trotskyites. To my knowledge, no documentation has been put forward indicating that Pol Pot, Nuon Chea, Ieng Sary, or any other leading party member was either conversant with or influenced by the writings of Trotsky. Trotsky's writings are important insofar as his ideas provide a framework from which to interpret art as promoted and practiced by the CPK. Both Trotsky and the CPK were materialists; both subscribed to a dialectical historiography; and both recognized that creative expression was crucial to the socialist revolution. Yet art and politics under the Khmer Rouge were pursued in ways quite distinct from the ideal proposed by Trotsky.

Conclusions and Prologs

Having achieved victory on April 17, 1975, the Communist Party of Kampuchea set itself the herculean task of transforming society in its entirety. Key leaders within the CPK endeavored to fashion a society free from class rule, exploitation, and oppression. They were guided in their efforts by the utopian goal of creating a free and unalienated society, whereby men and women would experience both self-realization and self-determination. This was their dream; reality was starkly different.

High-ranking members of the CPK understood that they did not enjoy popular support. In part, this was a condition of their own making. Because the CPK was a self-professed Marxist-Leninist party, secrecy was paramount. Throughout the long years of revolution, both the party and its platform remained shrouded in mystery. Neither the CPK nor its leaders were formally acknowledged, and Communist doctrine was downplayed if not downright neglected. Political training sessions were cursory at best; complex concepts such as "contradictions" or "self-determination" were presented in simple terms, and the populace learned by rote memorization. Most men and women who joined the Khmer Rouge did so in response to armed conflict and a sustained United States–led bombing campaign that had a devastating effect on Cambodia. Others joined in support of the ousted former monarch, Norodom Sihanouk, who was removed five years earlier in a coup. Very few soldiers of the Khmer Rouge were ideologically motivated.

Consequently, having liberated Cambodia and, in so doing, having apparently leaped over any transitional stages, the leadership of the CPK recognized that it would be necessary to cultivate a proper political consciousness. Indeed, countless documents testify to the imminent need to both recruit new party members and to reeducate and refashion non–party members. I posit that the CPK internalized Marx and Engel's proposition that "it is not consciousness that determines life, but life that determines consciousness." I argue that the CPK recognized that political consciousness—the "building of socialism"—was dialectically associated with a particular production of nature; and that the transformation of nature through necessary labor would affect a transformation of self and society. Indeed, both self-determination and self-realization would emerge as stalwart fixtures within CPK slogans, speeches, and publications. The incorporation of these terms signify a particular Marxist interpretation by the CPK—a reading not fully appreciated by previous scholarship on the Khmer Rouge.

More precisely, key officials of the CPK acknowledged that creative expression and artistic production were foundational to the building of socialism. Song, poetry, and photography were also developed as forms of public pedagogy in an attempt to forward CPK ideology. In so doing, however, CPK officials deviated from Marx's understanding of creative expression. Consequently, they succumbed to the same failings of artistic production present under Stalin in the former Soviet Union. Art was transformed from an activity of personal fulfillment and self-realization into a bureaucratized, staid form of propaganda. And in a final, tragic irony, the perversion of aesthetic expression to party needs would ultimately constitute a fundamental contradiction that became the basis of mass violence.

2 Transformations

Marxist-Leninist political philosophy holds that it is neither possible nor desirable to reform or remold the state. According to Marx and Engels, previous revolutions largely failed precisely because the revolutionaries attempted to co-opt or reform the existing state apparatus. In *The Eighteenth Brumaire*, for example, Marx concluded that previously "all revolutions perfected this machine instead of smashing it."[1] Heretofore, Marx reasoned, revolutions failed because the prevailing state—a concrete manifestation of class rule—was appropriated by revolutionaries as opposed to being dismantled. This is a theme picked up and expanded by Lenin, who would write: "All the revolutions which have occurred up to now have helped to perfect the state machine, whereas it must be smashed, broken."[2] For Lenin, revolutionary violence was administered, coordinated violence; it was not sporadic or chaotic. He explained that "the proletariat needs . . . the centralized organization of force, the organization of violence, for the purpose of crushing the resistance of the exploiters and for the purpose of leading the great mass of the population . . . in the work of organizing socialist economy."[3]

It is not surprising, therefore, that the specter of failed revolutions should assume such a prominent place in a speech delivered by Pol Pot, an admirer of Lenin, in September 1977.[4] Throughout the course of its two-thousand-year history, according to Pol Pot, Cambodia was witness to a series of class-based revolutions. In previous slave societies, for example, Pol Pot explained that the "exploited class struggled against the exploiting class," but, he cautioned, "this struggle was not guided by a correct line."[5] Likewise, he identified a revolutionary struggle against feudalism. Victory, again, "was temporary, because those who were the victors did not possess a correct line to really liberate the country and really liberate the people, the exploited masses who comprise the peasant class."[6] Failings, according to Pol Pot, stemmed from the fact that those who overthrew the previous class "made themselves warlords and ruled like kings and viceroys, and they became the new exploiters of the peasant class."[7] Pol Pot's interpretation falls squarely in line with that of Lenin vis-à-vis the state following a socialist revolution. The dialectic transformation from a feudalist-capitalist society to a Communist society entails, on the one hand, the complete annihilation of the previous state and, on the other hand, the establishment of a transitory form of government—a dictatorship of the proletariat—that, at a certain point in the future, would simply wither away, thereby leaving in place a classless, Communist society free of exploitation, oppression, and alienation. The immediate concrete objective of the socialist revolution, from a Marxist-Leninist standpoint, is thus the material obliteration of the capitalist state and, by extension, those social relations that constitute the state.

It is imperative, following Lenin, for revolutionaries to concentrate their forces on the destruction of the previous state and "to regard the problem, not as one of perfecting the state machine, but one of smashing and destroying it."[8] Only with the complete annihilation of the former regime is a transition to Communism possible, for the elimination of capitalist relations of production—including those of governance—marks the beginning of a new phase of the revolution. It is also no surprise, therefore, that a captured Khmer Rouge document dated 1975 reads, "The immediate goal of the party is to lead the people to succeed in the national democratic revolution, to exterminate the imperialists, feudalists, and capitalists, and to form a national revolutionary state in Cambodia." The document continues: "The long range goal of the party is to lead the people in creating a socialist revolution and a communist society in Cambodia."[9] Leading members of the CPK accordingly viewed themselves as forming a dictatorship of the proletariat. Having waged a successful military revolution, after April 1975 they needed to begin the crucial task of building socialism.

Building socialism would be a recurrent theme throughout Democratic Kampuchea. In the CPK's Four-Year Plan, developed between July 21 and August 2, 1976, for example, party leaders deemed it necessary to "build the country quickly, and build socialism quickly."[10] To this end, a guiding question that informs this and subsequent chapters is deceptively simple: *How did the Communist Party of Kampuchea attempt to build socialism?* My response is similarly straightforward, although it will require considerable explication and documentary evidence. To begin: forced labor—from the vantage point of the CPK—was foundational to the cultivation of a correct political consciousness. It was through the material transformation of nature by a laboring population that the Khmer Rouge sought to build socialism. However, this experiential form of consciousness building required guidance and organization. For the CPK as self-proclaimed vanguard, it was necessary to provide an alternative form of education whereby the citizenry would understand its labors as forming a crucial component of nation building. Far from simply a means of indoctrination, the public promotion of art was to provide a framework within which a proper political consciousness would emerge. Thus, rather than dismissing songs, poems, photographs, and other creative expressions as blatant forms of propaganda, these materials are most properly understood as *aesthetic interventions* or *imaginative geographies* of the CPK.[11] Following Edward Said, imaginative geographies are ways of seeing that legitimate a vocabulary, a representative discourse peculiar to the understanding of places that becomes the way in which a place is known.[12] Consequently, the music, songs, poems, and other artistic productions of the Khmer Rouge are authentic simulacra in their truthful representation of how the CPK leadership envisioned both the revolution and Democratic Kampuchea. They also become crucial building blocks in the production of a correct political consciousness.

In this chapter, I provide a political-economic context for interpreting the specific contours of artistic production under the Khmer Rouge. As both Marx and Trotsky understood, art and education are dialectically related to any given mode of production. Accordingly, it is essential that creative expressions, whether pursued in more formalized productions such as revolutionary magazines or informally through song and dance, will reflect those practices required for the satisfactory production and reproduction of society.

Building Socialism through Agricultural Work

When the Khmer Rouge achieved military victory on April 17, 1975, its political future was far from certain. This posed two immediate obstacles to subsequent forms of governance initiated by the CPK, the resolution of which would have considerable repercussions throughout the country. On the one hand, leaders of the Khmer Rouge were impelled to further disseminate, albeit guardedly, their overall political-economic objectives. Drawing in part on Leninist doctrine, Pol Pot and other senior leaders determined that a strong central authority remained necessary, for until the masses had elevated themselves to the appropriate level of political consciousness, a dictatorship of the proletariat remained indispensable. So cautious was the CPK in its openness that it was not until 1977 that the CPK's existence and Pol Pot's leadership were publically acknowledged.[13]

On the other hand, a politically derived social structure was established, in part to isolate trustworthy cadres from potential internal enemies. As specified in the Party Statutes of 1976, all party members must "be good and clean and be pure politically, ideologically, and organizationally."[14] Consequently, whereas in theory all citizens over the age of eighteen were eligible to become party members, strict qualifications had to be met. For example, party members "must have had good and constantly combative activities, tested in successive revolution work in the unions, in the cooperatives, and in the Revolutionary Army" and "must have good and clean life morals and be good and clean politically."[15] To this end, new recruits were required to complete an eleven-page biographical form. Most of the thirty-two questions sought information about the applicant's family members; questions about political activities and social networks were paramount.[16]

Beneath these cadres were two main groups: "base" people and "new" people. The former class included men, women, and children who lived in rural areas that were liberated by the Khmer Rouge prior to April 1975. New people, also known as "April 17" people, included all those who were not Khmer Rouge cadre, party members, or base people. New people were almost exclusively urban in origin. Base people were classified as full-rights people, meaning that they were allowed to vote and serve in positions of authority; they also received relatively better rations and were treated less harshly. New people, conversely, were largely excluded from any political position, had fewer rights, and were subject to more brutal treatment.

To govern the country, CPK leaders initiated a hierarchical form of government known as democratic centralism. Not found in the writings of Marx or Engels, the term "democratic centralism" was first specifically formatted as the organizing principle by both Bolshevik and Menshevik factions of the Russian Social Democratic Labor Party in the early twentieth century.[17] It was Lenin, however, who most effectively formulated the dialectic combination of "democracy" and "centralism" into a principle of political organization in which workers, not state administrators, would be responsible for production decisions. In principle, all members are to express freely their ideas and concerns; a decision is then made collectively and enforced by the upper echelon. Over time, democratic centralism acquired different meanings, as the concept was adopted and adapted by Communist parties in other countries, including China and Vietnam. In 1921, for example, the Chinese Communist Party accepted Marxism-Leninism as its political canon and modified democratic centralism as a core feature of its policies and programs.[18]

In his speech of September 1977, Pol Pot explained, "We have solidly laid the foundations of our collectivist socialism, and we are continually improving them, while consolidating and developing them."[19] He continued: "We promote broad democracy among the people by a correct application of democratic centralism, so that this immense force will mobilize enthusiastically and rapidly for socialist revolution and construction, at great leaps and bounds forward."[20] In practice, democratic centralism was not applied correctly, in that the party leadership never relinquished ultimate authority over political, economic, or social programs.[21]

The principles of democratic centralism did inform the administrative infrastructure of Democratic Kampuchea. As stated in its constitution, drafted in December 1975 and promulgated the following month, democratic centralism was to provide the bedrock on which legislative, executive, and judicial power was to be built. Article 5, for example, states that "the legislative power lies with the Assembly of workers, peasants and other laborers' representatives," while Article 7 proclaims that "justice is exercised by the people."[22] Democratic centralism is also codified in the 1976 Statutes: "The Communist Party of Kampuchea takes the principle of democratic centralism as its organizational foundation." Consequently, Democratic Kampuchea was governed (in theory) according to a territorially based hierarchy. At the apex of the hierarchy was an administrative unit known as *phumipeak*, or zone. Zones were referred to by cardinal directions (e.g., Southwest or East Zone), although each was given a numeric code. Each zone was composed of *damban*, or regions (also translated as "sectors"). These were largely based on former provinces, but there was no one-to-one correspondence; indeed, many regions crossed old administrative boundaries. Regions were designated by number, often but not always indicating a level of systemization. The Northwest Zone, for example, was composed of seven regions, numbered one through seven. The East Zone consisted of five regions numbered twenty through twenty-four. Other regions, however, were less straightforward, reflecting in part the ongoing shuffling of regions between zones.[23] Administrative divisions below the zone and regional level conformed to prerevolutionary terminology. Each region was composed of several districts (*srok*), each district was composed of several communes (*khum*), and each commune was composed of numerous villages (*phum*).

As of April 1975, the CPK had divided Cambodia's nineteen provinces into five zones: The Northeast, North, Northwest, Southwest, and East. A "special zone" was also created, to include the area around Phnom Penh. In the ensuing months and years, administrative divisions changed often, usually as the result of internal purges or power plays among CPK leaders. Toward the end of 1975, for example, the Southwest Zone was split into two, forming a new West Zone and a smaller Southwest Zone. The Phnom Penh "special zone" was also dissolved and thereafter categorized as a distinct territory not within the formal administrative structures. Later, two autonomous regions were formed: Region 106, consisting mostly of the former Siem Reap and Oddar Meanchey Provinces, and Region 103, composed of the former Preah Vihear Province. The port facility at Kampong Som was also organized as a separate entity. And still later, toward late 1976 and early 1977, a seventh zone was created when Regions 103 and 106 were merged to form a new North Zone; the old North Zone was renamed the Central Zone.[24]

Each political division was administered by a three-person committee consisting of a secretary, deputy secretary, and member, responsible for politics, security, and economics, respectively. At the commune and village level, the two senior-ranking committee members were usually identified as "chief" and "deputy chief." The zone committee was responsible for overseeing the implementation of CPK plans and policies throughout its respective zone and for delegating plans and policies to all other levels (e.g., regions, districts) in its zone. Likewise, the committees at the region, district, and commune levels fulfilled similar functions of implementing tasks designated by the higher levels. Each political division, from the zone level down, included a variety of three-person committees responsible for specific tasks, including economics, transportation, finance, medical, mobile, military, social affairs, fishing, textile production, and security.[25]

Despite the references to democratic centralism and the imposition of a hierarchical infrastructure that, in theory, should afford citizen participation, governance was effectively centralized among a few key individuals who constituted the true locus of power, this being the Standing Committee of the CPK. As of April 1975, the Standing Committee included Pol Pot (secretary general), Nuon Chea (deputy secretary general and vice-chair of the Military Commission), Ieng Sary (deputy prime minister of foreign affairs), So Phim, (secretary, Eastern Zone), Vorn Vet (deputy prime minister for the economy), Ros Nhim (secretary, Northwest Zone), Ta Mok (secretary, Southwest Zone), and Son Sen (deputy prime minister for defense). The Standing Committee was itself a smaller component of the Central Committee.[26] By statute, the Central Committee was the highest decision-making body in Democratic Kampuchea. Likewise, as a more broadly representative body, the Central Committee was given responsibility to "implement the Party political line and Statute throughout the Party" as well as to "govern and arrange cadres and Party members throughout the entire Party."[27] In practice, though, the Central Committee remained subservient to the dictates of the Standing Committee.

On March 20, 1976, a suite of ministries to replace the previous government was also introduced.[28] These included the Ministry of Foreign Affairs (headed by Ieng Sary), the Ministry of the Economy (Vorn Vet), the Ministry of Defense (Son Sen), the Ministry of Information and Propaganda (Hu Nim), the Ministry of Health (Thioun Thioeun), the Ministry of Social Affairs (Ieng Thirith), the Ministry of Public Works (Touch Phoeun), the Ministry of Culture, Education, and National Studies (Yun Yat), and the Ministry of Interior, Cooperatives, and Communes (Hou Youn).[29] Pol Pot was appointed prime minister. In addition, six committees were established under the direction of the Ministry of Economy: agriculture, industry, commerce, rubber plantations, transportation, and energy.[30] Boraden Nhem describes the administrative structure of Democratic Kampuchea as an "empty government," noting that many of the ministries were "nominal only and had no notable activities."[31] For a Marxist-Leninist organization, however, this is readily understandable and explains also the indifference exhibited by CPK officials in their smashing of civilian and military officials of the previous regime.

For our present purposes, Hu Nim's Ministry of Information and Propaganda is most salient. Regrettably, however, very little is known of this ministry.[32] According to Andrew Mertha, the ministry appears to have combined party and government functions and was subdivided into several units, each known by a particular code number. Located at the printing house of the former *National Liberation* newspaper in front of the Olympic Stadium in Phnom Penh, K-25 was the office in which the political magazines *Revolutionary Flag* (*Tung Padevat*) and *Revolutionary Youth* (*Youveak Chon Youveak Neary Padevat*) were published. *Revolutionary Flag* was a magazine published monthly by the CPK between January 1975 and September 1978, whereas *Revolutionary Youth* ran from January 1974 to November 1978.[33] Initially developed as a recruitment instrument during the civil war, *Revolutionary Youth* in particular was promoted as a means of fostering appropriate behavior among Khmer youth. Published articles, replete with photographs, focused on the everyday life of the Khmer Rouge, that is, the imagined everyday life of a prosperous communal society. These articles, coupled with poems and other written materials, also served as social forms of instruction.

Here, the experiences of Kim Vun are particularly helpful.[34] Between 1975 and 1979, Kim Vun worked in various subunits affiliated with the Ministry of Propaganda, including those sections responsible for writing, printing, and broadcasting; he also was trained and performed duties as a photographer for the CPK. In 1971, at the age of twelve, Kim joined the Khmer Rouge. He was motivated not out of any ideological commitment; indeed, he was only dimly aware of Khmer Rouge politics. Rather, his impetus was material, driven by sustained aerial bombings and the overthrow of Prince Sihanouk. He recalls, "If we looked into the sky, there would be airplanes. . . . In my village, some families perished because of the aerial bombardments. So we had suffered a great deal from this, and we supported the former King. My villagers and I and my family never wanted the war; we wanted peace."[35] As the war intensified, Kim listened intently to the radio broadcasts disseminated by both China and the Khmer Rouge. He learned of the many demonstrations held throughout the country in support of Sihanouk; he heard of the violence that ensued, as civilians were gunned down while protesting; and he was moved by Sihanouk's appeal to join the revolution.

Kim was not sent to the front lines as a soldier but instead was tasked with transcribing documents. He recalls that his penmanship was very good. Working in a makeshift printing house located on a rubber plantation, Kim dutifully copied onto carbon paper handwritten materials: political documents, reports from the battlefield, statements made by the leadership. These materials would then be forwarded to another location and reproduced for wider circulation. When not transcribing, Kim was required to attend political training sessions and to continually practice his handwriting.

After the fall of Phnom Penh, Kim was reassigned to work at K-25. His primary responsibilities included the transcription and editing of articles for the revolutionary magazines. Kim also contributed to the composition of articles. These writings, he explains, were broad in scope and mostly conveyed the importance of agricultural production and the national reconstruction of the country. He was frequently called on to prepare for publication articles of a more political nature; these would often explain in simple terms the meaning of "contradictions" or "historical materialism." According to Kim, these articles were principally, if not exclusively, written by members of the Central Party, in that only these men and women were knowledgeable enough to compose such commentaries.[36]

When contributing to the content of *Revolutionary Flag* and *Revolutionary Youth*, Kim explains, "we tried to write in order to encourage people to build irrigation, try to grow crops, and do agricultural works." He notes, "We could not write freely; we had to follow the policy line of the Party."[37] This stricture extended also to the composition of poems and the use of photographs, both of which were not viewed as creative expression of individuality but instead were approached as pragmatic forms of learning. Members of K-25 were required to attend regular political training sessions and also staff meetings, where the upper echelon would indicate the type of stories to be covered. If the party sought to promote the objective of producing three metric tons of rice per hectare, Kim recalls, "we had to expand to that, for example, in order to ensure that people had surplus of production for export."[38]

The procedures of photographing the revolution were similar. Kim explains that in pursuit of a particular story or event, he would travel throughout the countryside, staying anywhere from two to seven days depending on the assignment. He could not travel freely but was instead required to obtain proper authorization and travel permits. While working as a photojournalist, he was responsible for providing photographs of inaugural events, such as the completion of an irrigation project, or to document the arrival of foreign dignitaries. Other times he was called on to photograph the everyday lives of workers; these images assumed the form predominantly of men and women planting or digging canals. Kim was under strict orders to photograph only those scenes that depicted a harmonious and productive existence. If he encountered anything that could be construed as negative, such as hunger, he was to report directly to the supervisor but—under no circumstances—was he to capture these scenes through photography or text. Kim explains: "We had to be vigilant, and there was restriction [on] taking photographs because we had to cover the same confined topics. As a photographer, we had been trained to the technicality of taking photographs and also the political aspects of taking the photographs. For example, for each photograph, what kind of elements could a photographer take into account before taking the shots, whether the photo had contributed to the reconstruction of the country or not after it being taken."[39]

Beyond Kim's work at K-25, countless other Khmer Rouge cadres served the Ministry of Propaganda in various guises. Other key offices, all located in Phnom Penh, included K-30, which occupied a former school along Monivong Boulevard, and K-32, located near Monivong Bridge. K-30 assumed important educational functions, including the publication of textbooks.[40] K-32 was referred to as "the office of art" (*montie silapak*) and was divided into two sections: a division tasked with writing stories and composing poems—which would appear in various magazines and other outlets—and a second division composed of performance actors who would travel throughout the country. K-33 was Radio Kampuchea, located by Wat Phnom. Initially, broadcasts were aired only in Khmer, but later programs were transmitted also in English and Vietnamese; preparations were also apparently under way to be broadcast in Thai. Last, Office K-34, located east of the former Phnom Penh University, was responsible for producing documentary and propaganda films, mostly dealing with dam and canal constructions but also films about the ongoing military campaigns against Vietnam.[41]

The propagation of informational materials appears to have been mostly confined to the Ministry of Information and Propaganda and thus reflects party policy. According to Mertha, there were no counterpart propaganda committees at the zone level or below. However, each zone did apparently have its own newspaper, independent from those published in Phnom Penh and directly overseen by the CPK. The Eastern Zone, for example, reportedly had a newspaper called *Light of the East* (*Ponleu Bophea*). Zone-level newspapers reported on agricultural and defense issues within their respective zones and thus served a crucial dissemination function for political and economic matters.[42]

Having sketched with broad strokes the CPK bureaucratic apparatuses, I now consider broadly the dialectics of nature and labor within the context of agricultural production, for it is on this pivot, I maintain, that the CPK attempted to build socialism. Subsequently, the processional transformation of self through a transformation of nature was disseminated throughout Democratic Kampuchea in the form of artistic productions.

Nature, Labor, Consciousness

In the CPK's Four-Year Plan, two primary objectives were identified: "to aim to serve the people's livelihood, and raise the people's standard of living quickly, both in terms of supplies and in terms of other material goods" and "to seek, gather, save, and increase capital from agriculture, aiming to rapidly expand our agriculture, our industry, and our defenses rapidly."[43] These objectives are not mutually exclusive but instead point to a materialist approach to Democratic Kampuchea's political economy in its totality. Agricultural growth would produce the capital that would form the basis for eventual industrial self-sufficiency; these economic strategies, in turn, would facilitate the provision of the necessary conditions for production and reproduction. The crucial component was that agricultural surpluses had to be exchanged for foreign capital, but before rice for currency could be exchanged, agricultural surpluses had to be achieved.

Elsewhere I have argued that CPK policy during this period was far from unique; indeed, the programs enunciated within the Four-Year Plan readily align with those forwarded by other members of the Non-Aligned Movement.[44] During the 1950s and 1960s, many former colonies embarked on a particular economic strategy known as import-substitution industrialization (ISI).[45] Proponents of ISI argued that lesser-developed countries should first substitute domestically produced simple consumer goods for those previously imported and then substitute domestically produced goods for a wider range of more sophisticated manufactured items.[46] In other words, advocates of ISI promoted an economic strategy predicated on self-sufficiency. Variously understood within broader theories of dependency or underdevelopment, the argument was this: For decades, if not centuries, the economies of colonies were held in check by unfair trade arrangements and production processes that consigned the colonies to positions of subservience within the global economy. Colonies and former colonies were forced to import most of their manufactured goods in return for the export of primary products, such as sugar, bananas, coffee, tea, and cotton. Under ISI, governments of former colonies would be able to protect their domestic industries and by extension encourage the production of domestic consumer goods. Revenue saved from not having to import these goods could then be used to purchase other manufactured commodities that could not be produced given the country's overall level of industrial development. Such an approach is readily apparent in CPK documents. For example, minutes from a meeting held on May 8, 1976, state: "We will decrease importing items next year, including cotton and jute, because we are working hard to produce ours. We will import only some important items such as chemical fertilizer, plastic, acid, iron factory, and other raw materials."[47] This strategy was deemed most appropriate, in that solutions were not to be found "by taking loans from the West or Eastern Europe," for in so doing the CPK would lose its "self-reliant stance."[48]

Operating within an overall policy of ISI, the CPK needed to identify those items that could be effectively produced, both for domestic consumption and for foreign trade. On the home front, plans called for the promotion of items necessary to facilitate the people's livelihood: plates, pots, spoons, mosquito nets, shovels, hoes, and so on. In practice, most of these industries never materialized, although textile factories and some machine shops were in operation within a few months. Surviving documents indicate that the CPK was receptive to any number of imported goods but that economic efficiencies would be the determining factor in deciding the conditions of foreign trade.

Within a system of production for exchange, which the CPK clearly pursued, it matters little if linen or coats are produced; whichever offers the best opportunity for capital accumulation will, in principle, be produced. Marx refers to this tendency as "indifference to use-value," and the CPK was in many respects indifferent to use-value. A report prepared in 1976 notes, "We can export and sell many products such as kapok, shrimp, squid, elephant fish, and turtles. All of these products can earn foreign exchange. There are great possibilities for exporting peanuts, wheat, corn, sesame, and beans. The objective would be to save up these products for export. Almost anything can be exported, so long as we don't consume it ourselves, but set it aside."[49] The report offers further details: "We have the potential to achieve full quotas in rubber, cement, railroads and salt. We have progressed nicely, almost with empty hands. We have achieved good results. But the possibilities are even greater. We must expand the Plan. Our line is to stress industry and the working class as the basis."[50]

The CPK determined that agriculture was to be the country's comparative advantage. This point is developed in the Four-Year Plan: Democratic Kampuchea is full of "such things as land, livestock, natural resources, water sources such as lakes, rivers and ponds," and these "natural characteristics have given [the country] great advantages compared with China, Vietnam, or Africa. Compared to Korea, [the country] also ha[s] positive qualities."[51] Paramount among these, of course, was agriculture. The Four-Year Plan asserted, "We stand on agriculture as the basis, so as to collect agricultural capital with which to strengthen and expand industry." And among the possible agricultural crops that could be pursued, rice was preeminent. To this end, Pol Pot declared in August 1976: "We have greater resources than other countries in terms of rice fields. Furthermore, the strength of our rice fields is that we have more of them than others do. The strength of our agriculture is greater than that of other countries in this respect. . . . It is the Party's wish to transform agriculture from a backward type to a modern type in ten to fifteen years. A long-term strategy must be worked out. We are working [here] on a Four-Year Plan in order to set off in the direction of achieving this 10–15 year target."[52]

Contrary to conventional scholarship on Democratic Kampuchea, the CPK leadership did not intend to construct an agrarian utopia. Rather, it initiated a pragmatic course of action based on capitalist principles. From a competitive standpoint, rice was the clear choice. And while other agricultural products were identified, including rubber, corn, beans, fish, and forest products, these were largely gratis. The CPK argument was profit based: "For 100,000 tons of milled rice, we would get [U.S.] $20 million; if we had 500,000 tons we'd get $100 million. . . . We must increase rice production in order to obtain capital. Other products, which are only complementary[,] will be increased in the future."[53]

High-ranking members of the CPK—not the workers—determined initially that the country would need to *triple* rice production to a national average yield of three tons per hectare per year. Only by attaining such a surplus would it be possible to raise sufficient revenues to obtain necessary goods and commodities from abroad. Consequently, it was necessary to introduce rational and efficient agricultural techniques. Throughout Democratic Kampuchea, rice fields were classified into two categories: those harvested once a year and those harvested twice. Calculations provided by the CPK indicate that in 1977 there were 2.4 million hectares of land suitable for rice production; of these, 1.4 million hectares were determined capable of sustaining a single harvest per year; the remaining would be conducive to two harvests. Over the next four years, according to Pol Pot, the land devoted to single harvests would remain constant, while the amount of double-cropped lands would progressively increase from 200,000 hectares in 1977 to 500,000 in 1980. It was further determined that new agricultural lands would generate two harvests per year.[54]

For the CPK, an overriding difficulty associated with increased rice production was the problem of water. According to the Four-Year Plan, it was necessary to "increase the degree of mastery over the water problem from one year to another until it reache[d] 100 percent by 1980 for first-class rice land and reache[d] 40–50% for ordinary rice land."[55] Following a table of calculations indicating the annual percentage increase projected between 1977 and 1980, the text continues: "In order to gain mastery over water there must be a network of dikes and canals as the basis. There must also be canals, reservoirs, and irrigation pumps stationed in accordance with our strategy."[56] The rapid and massive development of irrigation was crucial, necessitating the completion of thousands of kilometers of dikes, dams, and canals, and the construction of hundreds of reservoirs.[57]

The preliminary remarks of Pol Pot given in a speech delivered during the third week of August 1976 are crucial in understanding the underlying geographical imagination systemic to CPK policy. In his statements, Pol Pot stressed the salience of "building socialism in economic terms" and stated, "It is the Party's wish to transform agriculture from a backward type to a modern type in ten to fifteen years."[58] He noted that in earlier plans, it was incorrect to set a target of three tons per hectare; accordingly, he explained, the CPK "rearranged and improved our line, classifying some places as ones which could be harvested once a year and other places as ones which could be harvested twice a year."[59] He then indicated that "the Party ha[d] a grasp of geographical factors—what earth to cultivate, what earth to set aside."[60] It is not clear how these factors were determined, nor is the salience or validity of these factors apparent. However, while there is to my knowledge no documented understanding that members of the CPK were aware of local drainage patterns, soil types, rainfall patterns, diurnal and seasonal temperature differences, crop diversification, microclimate humidity levels, or leaching potential, interviews with former Khmer Rouge cadre and other survivors do indicate that (1) local knowledge was used in the planning and implementation of various hydro projects; and (2) Chinese engineering and technical assistance was widely employed.[61]

In his remarks of August 1976, Pol Pot does discuss in broad outline the geographies of Democratic Kampuchea's administrative zones. Recall that the CPK's governmental structure positions the zone level as preeminent, followed in rank by regions, districts, cooperatives, and villages. With respect to the Northwest Zone, for example, Pol Pot stated, "We must grasp the nature of the available soil and the nature of water resources. Having grasped the geography, we can assign first-grade land to two harvests and second-grade land to one. In addition, we must estimate the water-power available. We must know where to construct dams and where to dig canals."[62] Similarly, he explained that in the Southwestern Zone, the "soil in Region 25, if harvested twice, [would] yield sizable crops, compared with Region [33] which produce[d] only 1.5 tons per hectare; Region 25 produce[d] four to five tons per hectare, a very significant difference."[63]

Throughout his remarks, Pol Pot called for the production of "charts, lists and figures for certain zones and regions so that those attending this meeting [could] observe whether these [were] in accordance with reality or not."[64] This in fact is a long-standing demand of Pol Pot—and perhaps indicative of the lack of detailed knowledge vis-à-vis local environmental conditions. At an assembly meeting of officials from the Western Zone held between June 3 and June 7, 1976, a speaker—most likely Pol Pot—stated: "I ask the Zone to make maps and give the figures for the area of land in each Region and the figures for each sector of the economy: statistics sector by sector, period by period."[65] He continued: "As for the Regions, I ask them all to have their own maps and statistical tables." These are necessary, he explained, so that "the Zone Committee [could] grasp things and so [could] other people." He concluded by reiterating an earlier point: "Now I ask the Zone, Region and district (administrations) to have maps. By mid-1977 there will be statistics right down to the co-operative level. Each co-operative must have its own map."[66]

In this speech, Pol Pot also discussed the necessity of forest clearance but also noted the potential consequences. He explained:

> The problem of clearing the forest: In fact this forest must be cleared, but we must set a limit. Because if we clear all the forest around the Tonle Sap, in ten years' time the Tonle Sap will have dried up; we will have no water source and no fish. Moreover, when the water coming down the Mekong stops going into the Tonle Sap, the Tonle Sap will dry up. Water from the Mekong enters the belly of the Tonle Sap. If the Mekong water does not enter the Tonle Sap, the area around Phnom Penh and the river banks downstream will be all submerged by the flooding Mekong.[67]

Phnom Penh sits at the confluence of the Tonle Sap and Mekong Rivers. During the rainy seasons, the waters of the Mekong rise precipitously. This increased flow, in turn, causes the Tonle Sap to reverse course. This seasonal change of the Tonle Sap subsequently leads to the annual flooding of Tonle Sap Lake. By November and December, the lake expands fourfold in size. The enormous volume of water and nutrients in the flooded lake provide the vital conditions for fish and other aquatic life that, in turn, provide life for the people of Cambodia. It is noteworthy—and counter to prevailing accounts—that the CPK was aware of the significance of the seasonality of the Tonle Sap. Indeed, the Tonle Sap's hydrological process is so important for Cambodia that it was common knowledge—even for the Khmer Rouge. In the above quote, Pol Pot demonstrates a particular apt understanding of the "reflexive relation" between human society and the environment.[68] Deforestation practices are coupled with increased siltation and flooding, and the consequences of both siltation and flooding on agriculture, fishing, and urban life are acknowledged. In their attempt to construct an autonomous, self-reliant society, the CPK *at this level* sought to ensure that environmental constraints were taken into consideration in its management approach; being minimally aware of potential environmental degradation, the CPK attempted to manage resources in a sustainable fashion.

The rapid expansion of agriculture and irrigation systems was complemented by a system of food rations imposed on the population that appears to be related to Marx's much-maligned phrase "from each according to his ability, to each according to his needs!"[69] Thus, workers were classified as either *kemlang ping* (full strength) or *kemlang ksaoy* (weak strength), with the former consisting mostly of adults and the latter consisting of small children and the elderly. Those designated as full-strength were further classified into two subgroups: *kemlang* 1, which consisted of young, able-bodied, single men and women who composed mobile work brigades (*kong chhlat*); and *kemlang* 2, composed of married, able-bodied men and women who were divided by sex but generally worked closer to the village. The heaviest tasks were generally reserved for *kemlang* 1 persons. These work teams were segregated by sex; males belonged to *kong boroh* and females to *kong neary*. These brigades were set to work primarily clearing land, digging canals and reservoirs, and constructing dams and dikes. *Kemlang* 2 workers generally worked closer to their villages, performing such tasks as local wood cutting (for building materials or fuel), preparation and cultivation of agricultural fields, and maintenance of irrigation schemes. Last, the "weak strength" laborers (*kemlang* 3) performed lighter tasks. Elderly workers were grouped into work teams known generically as *senah chun*; male groups were termed *senah chun boroh* and female groups *senah chun neary*. Duties for members of *senah chun* groups included sewing, gardening, collecting small pieces of wood, and caring for children. Depending on the conditions and the attitudes of the cooperative chief, some elderly workers might be required to labor in the rice fields or engage in other, more strenuous work. Children under fourteen years of age were assigned to work groups known as *kong komar*, with boys and girls separated into *kong komara* and *kong khomarei*, respectively. Children were responsible for looking after cows and water buffalo, light digging in gardens and fields, collecting firewood, and gathering cow dung for fertilizer.[70] Under the Khmer Rouge, consequently, food rations were in theory to be allocated based on the scale and scope of work performed. Workers who performed the heaviest manual labor were to receive the largest rations; those who engaged in the lightest tasks, as well as the elderly and the sick, received the smallest rations. Pregnant women, or women who had just given birth, were supposedly to be given higher rations.

These social structures, systemic to the concrete production of agricultural commodities and irrigation projects, are foundational to the production of political consciousness as forwarded by the CPK. The Four-Year Plan specifies that Cambodian society had leaped over the "neo-colonial, semi-feudalist society of the American imperialists, the feudalists and capitalists of every nation, and . . . achieved a socialist society straight away."[71] In effect, the CPK simply declared that it had "leaped from a people's democratic revolution into socialism."[72]

Paradoxically, though, the Four-Year Plan makes clear and repeated reference to the necessity of building socialism. Even more perplexing is the statement,

"We leap from a people's democratic revolution to a socialist revolution, and quickly build socialism. We don't need a long period of time for the transformation."[73] How are we to interpret these oppositional claims whereby, on the one hand, the CPK leadership asserts that no transitional period is necessary, yet, on the other hand, an indeterminate period of transformation was required? The resolution pivots on the transformation of nature through labor, embodied in the production of agriculture.

During an assembly of party officials and lower-ranking cadres held between June 3 and June 7, 1976, a speaker, presumably Pol Pot, identified the presence of "contradictions," noting that there are always contradictions associated with socialist revolutions. Pointedly, the speaker acknowledged that the CPK "cannot escape them [contradictions]" but that it was possible to take appropriate measures. How? "We do so by grasping politics tightly," he continued, "to make people understand the very important political line of the party." To this end, the speaker explained, it was necessary to "grasp hold their consciousness, make things clear to them. The Party's every task and plan must be explained to them until they understand and things become clear."[74] This is an obvious reference to the need for ongoing political training sessions. Yet there appears to be a more nuanced argument within the speech.

On the subject of the socialist revolution, the speaker asserted, "We must pursue the socialist revolution by pursuing the fight against any remnants that are not proletarian, and not collective or are still private."[75] He continued, "The socialist revolution demands further strength and expansion so that our national society becomes a true revolutionary society."[76] However, he warned, "There are still inadequacies in the field of politics and consciousness. Socialist consciousness and the collective relationship . . . are still inadequate. This shows that socialist consciousness and socialist relationships are still not very strong."[77] Therefore, it was necessary to "further strengthen socialist consciousness so that it becomes the rippling sinews of the collectivity."[78] Of significance, the strengthening of socialist consciousness was to be found in the promotion of agriculture. The speaker explained: "We stand on agriculture in order to expand other fields; industries, factories, metals, oil, etc. The basic key is agriculture."[79]

From 1976 onward, party officials exhorted the populace to meet rice production quotas of three tons per hectare. However, in support of my overriding argument, I suggest that the CPK's promotion of agriculture extended far beyond the building of the country economically; it was also essential for the building of socialism and the making of a proper political consciousness. As explained in the assembly speech in June 1976: "To make socialist revolution is to move towards collectivism, to strengthen collectivism. The real key is three tons."[80] Consequently, we begin to see how the experiential lessons derived from agricultural labor would translate into a proper political consciousness and how this knowledge was disseminated throughout the country in the form of speeches, slogans, magazine and newspaper articles, and, significantly, artistic productions.

Consider, for example, an article that appeared in the July 1975 issue of *Revolutionary Youth*. Titled "Revolutionary Youth Are Determined to Go Down into the Fray of Productive Labor in Order to Forge and Strengthen Their Revolutionary Stance and Actively to Defend and Build Up the Nation," the article notes that during the period of revolutionary war the youth had "forged, tested, built up and strengthened their revolutionary stance" through concrete actions, namely, fighting the enemy, obtaining water in liberated areas, and engaging in the "struggle" to refashion members within the ranks.[81] In short, a revolutionary consciousness emanated from, and youth were transformed through, physical activities. Once peace had been achieved, the article continues, the "most seething and biggest movement" is the "movement to increase production" to enable "the country to escape agricultural backwardness and ensure its rapid advance toward the status of being a modern agricultural and industrialized country."[82] Thus the article serves to disseminate in broad outline the goals and objectives of the party. However, it accomplishes something else. Specifically, the article explains that enthusiasm was lacking among some members and, ominously, states that "erroneous views of the old society" must be "utterly cleansed" and replaced with "a solidly correct revolutionary stance vis-à-vis productive labor."[83]

This point warrants closer attention. Revolutionary youth were being instructed that a correct revolutionary stance, namely, a proper political consciousness, would come about through productive labor. Hence, when it was demanded that a "one-hundred-fold increase" in rice production be achieved, this was not simply to achieve agricultural self-sufficiency—although this would be a positive outcome. No, the article stresses that in proceeding with agriculture, it was imperative to have an outlook and stance that independence, mastery, and self-reliance are important, which would result from manual labor and *not* a reliance on mechanization. It is telling that conventional scholarship on Democratic Kampuchea notes that tractors and other machinery were not always employed by the Khmer Rouge; and that this supposedly provides evidence that the party was either anti-technology in outlook or intent on creating an agrarian utopia modeled after the ancient Angkor kingdom that flourished between the ninth and fourteenth centuries. The article makes clear, however, that manual labor was understood as having transformative effects. In the immediate future, "the most important thing [was] relying on [their] own labor power, and not on machinery." In part, this was because the country lacked sufficient knowledge regarding machinery, and tractors consumed substantial amounts of gasoline. Mechanization would be forthcoming, the article explains, once the country was in a position to be more self-reliant. However, the article also makes clear that failure to engage in productive labor would result in a people "incapable of forging and refashioning themselves or strengthening their revolutionary stance."[84] In essence, it was not that the Khmer Rouge eschewed modern production techniques because of an antipathy toward technology but rather that it premised manual labor as a form of experiential consciousness building.

Similar pronouncements are made in an article appearing in the October 1975 issue of *Revolutionary Youth*. In the lead article, readers are informed of the crucial role that agricultural cooperatives would assume, namely, that these would function as "the greatest of universities . . . for the study of revolutionary knowledge."[85] More precisely, the article counsels that those who "fight to forge, train and refashion themselves on the seething battlefield of the co-operative movement" will be "truly endowed with a firm revolutionary stance" and thus be able to build the "socialist revolution" and proceed to the "communist revolution."[86] To be sure, readers are not informed of key conceptual knowledge; there is, for example, no discussion of the differences between a socialist or a Communist revolution. What is stressed, however, is the necessity to engage in productive labor, specifically the production of agriculture within cooperatives. This article continues: "There have hitherto been a number of erroneous phenomena in the ranks . . . in terms both of outlook and stance." These errors would include "fearing work involving hardship, exhaustion and heavy labor." People with such failings, the article concludes, are "incapable of studying from the movement" and cannot "develop or flourish along with the co-operative movement."[87]

Conclusions

In *The German Ideology*, Marx and Engels famously write: "It is not consciousness that determines life, but life that determines consciousness."[88] This proclamation provides the basis on which senior leaders of the CPK attempted to build socialism. Personal sacrifice was required of the citizenry of Democratic Kampuchea but also something else: the CPK demanded that its people actively contribute to their own internal transformation via physical labor. A correct political consciousness was forthcoming not through formal education but through hard work, through laboring activities that would concurrently contribute to the satisfaction of society's basic material conditions. Accordingly, the strategies adopted by the CPK leadership conform to another aphorism of Marx. In his *Theses on Feuerbach*, Marx declares that philosophers had only interpreted the world, while the point was to change it.[89] Marx's statement is in part a critique of Hegelian idealism: concrete action is required as opposed to idealist thinking. Thus we find the CPK declaring, "We have not relied on theory. We have acted clearly."[90] The CPK was being disingenuous, of course. Countless documents testify to the incorporation of especially Marxist and Leninist "theory" in policy and planning. The point rather is that senior officials of the CPK understood direct action—productive labor—as the determinative element moving forward. This is readily apparent in writings published in various newspapers and magazines, speeches delivered at political rallies, and messages broadcast over the radio. In the chapters that follow, I consider in-depth the "lessons" of the CPK in the context of poetry, music, and photography.

3 Poetic Geographies

Rice scattered to all places
Flourishing in all seasons
On mountain sides, in valleys, or road sides
Mints, garlic, bitter gourd, and sesame.

"Determine to Turn Our Great Cambodian Homeland to Bright Green Rice and Crop Fields," author unknown

"One of the most significant shared qualities of a landscape and a poem," Owen Sheers writes, "is their ability to 'situate' us by translating the abstract world of thought and feeling into a physical language."[1] Hayden Lorimer continues this idea, noting that "once shared, poems generate a common sense of place."[2] The coming together of poems and place is illustrated in the epigraph to this chapter. Nature appears bountiful; the landscape is plentiful. The *imaginative geography* of the poem expresses vitality and fertility, unlimited possibilities. And while the precise location is not mentioned, the emotional tug of the stanza resonates with anyone familiar with agrarian life.

Pointedly, the poem was published anonymously, in *Revolutionary Youth* in August 1976. Its appearance coincided with a meeting of senior members of the CPK, held in Phnom Penh. At the assembly held over a three-day period, Pol Pot told his audience, "We have greater resources than other countries in terms of rice fields," and "In order to gain capital the important thing is rice."[3] Quickly, though, he noted, "In order to make our socialism ever stronger we must seek capital from other crops as well. However small they may be, we must work on them so as to save capital."[4] The occasion of Pol Pot's remarks and his audience are vital in understanding the broader context of the publication of a poem in a journal aimed at Khmer Rouge youth. Pol Pot was lecturing key officials of the CPK about party policy. In turn, these men and women would disseminate these policy lessons down the chain of command, to zone-level officials who, in turn, would inform sector-level officials, and so on, down to the village level. Thus as the youth of Democratic Kampuchea received lectures from their superiors, they would simultaneously be reading poems about the provision of material abundance. We witness, therefore, a form of education whereby state-level policies are indirectly conveyed and legitimated throughout the country.

Missing, of course, are the details of specific plans and the resulting disconnect between the imaginative geographies of the poem and the stark economic realities of CPK policy. For example, while on the one hand, Pol Pot explained: "While taking rice as the basis . . . we must also consider planting other crops. We should consider red corn, legumes, and sesame," he also added. "Growing red corn . . . is part of our strategy. Red corn can feed animals and it can be exported. Foreigners today are asking to purchase corn and beans as well."[5] The mountainsides and valleys, for Pol Pot, would brim with sesame and rice and red corn; these crops, however, were destined not for the citizens of Democratic Kampuchea but instead as fodder for livestock or as commodities for export to foreign markets.

The juxtaposition of an anonymous poem published in a revolutionary magazine and Pol Pot's speech delivered to the upper echelon introduces two main themes that are developed in this and subsequent chapters. First, poetry and other artistic expressions constituted a form of public pedagogy used by the CPK. In a society with markedly high levels of illiteracy, such an alternative, experiential-based educational practice was ideal. Second, artistic productions, with vivid imagery of natural abundance, imposed a contradiction that stood in opposition to the lived experiences of most people throughout Democratic Kampuchea. This incongruity between appearance and reality generated substantial discontent among men, women, and children. Consequently, as the CPK attempted to build socialism through the imposition of forced labor, a deep-seated alienation emerged. Ongoing complaints by senior officials within the CPK of treason and betrayal, of a lack of correct political consciousness, was understood by the leadership not as a failure of policy but as a refusal among bad elements to support the revolution. The mass violence perpetuated throughout Democratic Kampuchea was thus complementary, a synthesis of structural conditions (e.g., the imposition of harsh labor and starvation-level rations) and direct actions (e.g., the murder of suspected traitors who complained about or challenged these conditions).

In this chapter, I argue that the CPK used poetry as a form of public pedagogy. More precisely I advance the argument that Khmer Rouge–era poetry presented nature as the fulcrum on which society was to be transformed through the material practice of building socialism. Methodologically, this chapter is based on a reading of approximately two dozen poems published in various issues of the Khmer Rouge publication *Revolutionary Youth*. These poems are archived at the Documentation Center of Cambodia, located in Phnom Penh, and were translated by Cambodian researchers at this institution.

The overall argument of this chapter is situated, conceptually, within the field of literary geographies. The geographic engagement with literature has a long history, dating to at least the first decades of the twentieth century. John K. Wright, for example, notes that "some men of letters are endowed with a highly developed instinct. As writers, they have trained themselves to visualize even more clearly than the professional geographer those regional elements of the earth's surface most significant to the general run of humanity."[6] For Wright, literature constitutes an alternative way of (re)presenting the landscape—a theme he develops more fully in his article on *terra incognita*. Here, Wright introduces the neologism "geosophy," defined as "the study of geographical knowledge from any or all points of view."[7] Although the term did not widely permeate the discipline, the underlying sentiment, that literature can inform geography, remains highly influential.

Beginning in the 1970s, a small but vibrant community of geographers explored the nexus of literature and geography.[8] Most prominent were studies addressing the dialectics of landscape and literature, especially as presented in novels. In part, geographers were motivated by the premise that an "artists' imagination and sensitivity towards human attitudes, values, and perceptions, as well as his ability to filter the essence of our relations with nature help us understand our interactions with the landscape, its cultural value, and our deep roots in the environment."[9] Christopher Salter and William J. Lloyd concur, noting that literary geographies "encourage the mind to explore more willing and freely, to respond, and, in essence, to see the landscapes of the world."[10] Accordingly, they conclude that "by reading literature with a more pensive appreciation and consideration of the signatures of the cultural landscape, we advance our comprehension of the world of fiction. At the same time, we gain in our ability to apply acute observation to real world landscapes."[11]

Well into the twenty-first century, the fields of literary geography specifically and aesthetic geographies more broadly have expanded rapidly. One key trend has been the move toward textual geographies as opposed to literary, or fictive, geographies.[12] Anghard Saunders, for example, found that it was no longer "the fictional which impels geographical interest, but increasingly the richness of the non-fictional and the broader issues of textuality within which the written word operates."[13] A second trend has been that of geographers expressing their research, or the research process, in nontraditional forms, such as poems.[14] Here, as Hayden Lorimer writes, greater attention "is being placed on the creative performance, presentation and writing of geographical studies of place."[15] Accordingly, more and more geographers have turned toward "enacting or creating geographically-oriented aesthetic works themselves."[16] And to this end, Miranda Ward has introduced the concept of "creative-critical place writing" as "a valuable mode of engaging with geographical thought and expanding debates, a research method, a tool for dissemination of ideas, and a way of solidifying geography's place as both a field of study and an art."[17]

Geography's creative (re)turn has raised innumerable epistemological questions and stimulated a renewed interest in the artistic practice of geography. These debates are equally applicable to the historical study of art and politics. Khmer Rouge poetry, I suggest, constitutes a mode of place writing, a medium in which the CPK's imaginative geography—of what Democratic Kampuchea *could become*—was disseminated throughout society. In other words, it is possible to reevaluate Khmer Rouge poems as a poetics of place: as a pedagogic intervention into politics. However, unlike the spontaneous and unbridled creative expression advanced by Trotsky, Khmer Rouge–era poetry (and other fictive geographies) mirrored more a Stalin-like bureaucratic form of place writing.

The Transformative Potential of Public Pedagogy

Schools are crucial sites in the socialization process. At school, students develop a sense of self, take stock of their feelings, and come to understand their ability to relate to their peers and to adults.[18] Socialization also takes place outside the formal classroom setting. To this end, scholarship needs to "acknowledge the primacy of culture's role as an educational site where identities are being continually transformed, power is enacted, and learning assumes a political dynamic as it becomes not only the condition for the acquisition of agency but also the sphere for imagining oppositional social change."[19] Henry Giroux's comments are situated within a broader discussion of public pedagogy, a multidisciplinary approach that considers the praxis of learning not in the school but rather in public space. I find in Giroux's exposition a means by which it is possible to reconfigure CPK educational practice to better capture the transformative potential of alternative teaching methods. This is especially salient, given the professed aim of the CPK—as a vanguard organization—to smash preexisting institutional forms and replace them with nonconventional methods.

There is no singular theory or method of public pedagogy. Rather, the term refers to "various forms, processes, and sites of education and learning occurring beyond formal schooling."[20] Gert Biesta distinguishes three forms of public pedagogic interventions: pedagogy for the public, pedagogy of the public, and pedagogy that enacts a concern for publicness.[21] The first, pedagogy for the public, constitutes a form of instruction whereby various media serve to instruct the citizenry. As illustrated, for example, in consumer marketing and advertising, this form of public pedagogy entails a normative function. This form is enacted whenever a government instructs its citizens, either explicitly or implicitly, in proper behavior and decision making. A second form, pedagogy of the public, attempts to empower marginalized groups by altering their self-conception as political subjects.[22] This is accomplished by facilitating the incorporation of these groups into the political process via public participation. A final form is one in which "public pedagogy appears as an enactment of a concern for 'publicness' or 'publicity,' that is, a concern for the public quality of human togetherness and thus for the possibility of actors and events to become public."[23] This form encompasses a transformative potential, in that interruptions and interventions in public space facilitate counternarratives. Enacting a concern for publicness is not about teaching individuals what they should be nor about demanding from them that they learn; rather it is about forms of interruption that keep the opportunities for becoming public open.[24]

Public pedagogy has, in recent years, garnered the attention of geographers and other cultural theorists interested in the place-making possibilities of these alternative forms of learning. Indeed, it is the place-making potential of public pedagogy that resonates with the promotion of art education, for art and other cultural practices are understood to initiate learning processes that differ fundamentally from those generated in the context of formal schooling.[25]

Popular forms of writing, for example, have long been recognized as important conduits in the promotion, the enactment, of imaginative geographies.[26]

Do artistic expressions, such as poetry, music, and photography, practiced by the Khmer Rouge constitute a form of public pedagogy? This is a crucial question and highlights the haziness of public space. At one level, public space can be considered any space that is not private—that is, privately owned, privately used, and privately determined.[27] Ironically, as a purported socialist state, all of Democratic Kampuchea could, in theory, be considered *public space*. Indeed, this is part of the imaginative geography promoted rhetorically by the CPK. Those in a position of authority, however, such as the CPK leadership, may have quite different visions of public space. Here, a particular understanding of public space is created and maintained by those who seek order and control. On this level, therefore, public space assumes a normative function, and public pedagogy adopts a programmatic interpretation. As detailed in this chapter, Khmer Rouge poetry was presented as a transformative public and political intervention whereby society, collectively, was encouraged to participate in the crafting of an alternative imaginative geography. In actuality, poetry assumed the role of a pedagogy for the public whereby anonymous poets instructed the citizenry in proper forms of work activity and, in so doing, actively facilitated the cultivation of a "correct" political consciousness.

Throughout the early months of CPK rule, the necessity of developing a proper political consciousness was an ongoing refrain. On January 9, 1976, members of the Standing Committee of the CPK lamented, "Speech, explanations, arts performances . . . do not reflect the heroism of the people and our Revolutionary Army, and do not yet demonstrate for all to see that great force of solidarity between the workers and the peasants, between the people and the Army, and do not yet reflect in a lively way their daily lives."[28] Likewise, at a meeting of the Ministry of Social Affairs held on June 10, 1976, ranking CPK officials acknowledged that a proper political consciousness remained lacking in that "the party's path ha[d] not yet been well-soaked into the heart and in the soul. Consequently, the stance of [the] proletariat of the party is still poor."[29]

In chapter 1, I introduced the concept of authentic simulacra to capture the extent to which artistic practices and artworks can serve as authentic copies or depictions of imagined geographies that have not yet been, nor may never be, materially realized. Khmer Rouge–era poetry often focused on idealized scenes of everyday interactions with nature. Stanzas evoke vivid images of familiar activities: transplanting rice, plowing fields, and harvesting crops. Interspersed are more-emotive pleas that connect seemingly banal tasks with a greater good, namely, lessons on citizenship. Poetry for the Khmer Rouge was intended to create a sense of belonging. This belonging, in turn, assumed an environmental dimension, in that the CPK's imaginative geography was grounded, literally, in the fields of Cambodia. In the end, poetry as public pedagogy was anything but transformative, for state apparatuses of repressive control precluded the democratic and participatory potential seemingly offered by aesthetic interventions.

Education under the Khmer Rouge

In conformance with the Leninist doctrine that bourgeois institutions must in the context of revolution be smashed, the CPK brutally dismantled most facets of the pre-1975 education apparatus. Traditional forms of education were brutally suppressed if not eradicated: Schools were destroyed or converted to other uses; libraries were ransacked and books burned; and upward of 90 percent of all teachers at all levels of education were killed during the Khmer Rouge era.[30] To concentrate solely on the destructive aspects, however, deflects attention from other practices initiated by the CPK—components that must figure prominently in any discussion of Khmer Rouge art and politics. This is not to minimize the violence of the Khmer Rouge. Rather it is an effort to more properly contextualize CPK policy and practice and thereby provide a more accurate understanding of the intersection of violence and education.

Thus, while preexisting structures were demolished, a qualitatively different educational system was introduced.[31] Classrooms were abandoned in favor of communal learning that took place outdoors, and teachers were drawn from the masses, in an effort to ostensibly promote a more participatory form of learning. In addition, a remarkable volume of learning materials was produced: textbooks, magazines, songs, and poetry. This is not to paint a too-rosy picture of life under the Khmer Rouge. Communal learning was at best sporadic and at worst part of routine political training sessions that were more apt to identify traitors for elimination than to disseminate knowledge. Nevertheless, the educational system forwarded by members of the CPK, in its ideal form, provides insight into the mind-set of Khmer Rouge governance.

After seizing power, the CPK did not enjoy widespread support among the citizenry of Cambodia. Furthermore, among those who were loyal to the party and the revolution, knowledge about Marxism-Leninism was woefully incomplete. For the upper echelon, this posed only a contradiction to be resolved. As a self-professed vanguard, the CPK understood its immediate role as one of ideological mentor. Consequently, the CPK required its imaginative geography to be conveyed throughout the entire society. As Jo Sharp writes, the "'imagined geographies' created through all sorts of media are central to the geographies used by people when going about their daily lives, so that it is important that such imaginings are understood by those of us trying to get to grips with . . . geographical relationships and identities."[32]

Following Henri Lefebvre, "a revolution that does not produce a new space has not realized its full potential," otherwise, such a revolution "has failed in that it has not changed life itself, but has merely changed ideological superstructures, institutions or political apparatuses." Consequently, a "social transformation, to be truly revolutionary in character, must manifest a creative capacity in its effects on daily life, on language and on space."[33] Lefebvre's forwarding of the creative coordinates of revolution conforms to Khmer Rouge practice—although not necessarily as Lefebvre may have wanted. This is seen most clearly in CPK Marxist-Leninist policy as it relates to education. As Marx and Engels maintained:

> The ideas of the ruling class are in every epoch the ruling ideas: i.e., the class which is the ruling material force of society is at the same time its ruling intellectual force. . . . The class which has the means of material production at its disposal, consequently also controls the means of mental production, so that the ideas of those who lack the means of mental production are on the whole subject to it. The ruling ideas are nothing more than the ideal expression of the dominant material relations.[34]

Moreover, as Lenin argued, revolutionary struggle required the organization of professional revolutionaries—the so-called vanguard. Practically, it was the task of the vanguard to educate the peasantry and the proletariat to the ideals of socialist revolution and the imposition of a Communist society. Within months of assuming power, the CPK turned to education as a means of establishing both legitimacy and political control. Consequently, having smashed the preexisting educational system, the CPK set in motion its own supposedly nonexploitative and nonoppressive form of public pedagogy.

Significantly, the destruction of Cambodia's pre-1975 educational system does not, contra other interpretations, indicate an overriding anti-intellectual stance.[35] Challenging the assertion that the Khmer Rouge was anti-intellectual is not synonymous with portraying the Khmer Rouge as pro-intellectual. Such a stance perpetuates a false dichotomy and risks masking the complex practices surrounding the so-called intellectual class. For example, the Khmer Rouge did often target individuals with education for arrest, detention, and execution.[36] Likewise, the CPK encouraged Cambodians living abroad to return, ostensibly to help in rebuilding the country, only to execute these men and women when their services were no longer required. As recent scholarship documents, however, the CPK also solicited educated individuals to assist in engineering projects and to facilitate financial transactions between Democratic Kampuchea and other governments, including China, Sweden, and Hong Kong.[37] My point is not to promote the CPK as pro-intellectual but to caution against overly reductive portrayals of the Khmer Rouge as wholly anti-intellectual and therefore antagonistic toward education.[38] Moreover, when analyzing Khmer Rouge educational policies, it is necessary to understand that the destruction of schools and the elimination of teachers violates conventional Marxist doctrine; education is of primary importance within Marxist writings, as the political and economic revolutions are part and parcel of cultural and educational revolutions.[39] The Khmer Rouge did not necessarily fear the ability of people to read and write; rather, it was what certain people read and wrote that made them suspect.[40]

For this reason the CPK proposed a qualitatively different educational system, one that was dedicated to the transformation of a revolutionary political consciousness. As detailed in its Four-Year Plan, the CPK proposed a relatively traditional educational curriculum that, on the one hand, would provide a "system of learning through the collective and in the concrete movement of the socialist revolution and the building of socialism."[41] Education was to be provided at primary, secondary, and tertiary levels, for a total of nine years. General subjects were to include reading and writing, arithmetic, geography, natural science, politics, and the history of the revolutionary struggle. It is true that most of these elements were not put into practice; this should not, however, be taken as prima facie evidence that the CPK was opposed to education and wanted to cultivate an illiterate and uneducated population. For beyond the formal education system proposed—but never fully pursued—were other, alternative forms of education that were implemented to a greater extent. The CPK, for example, made significant use of radio broadcasting as a form of public pedagogy. As explained in a CPK document dated March 8, 1976, radio broadcasting was an "opportunity for political reeducation."[42] The broadcast of songs, therefore, afforded the Khmer Rouge an opportunity to "open up a space for radical alternatives and different futures."[43] In other words, these forms of public pedagogy—as a technique of instruction beyond the formal classroom setting—were in principle used to transform what the CPK viewed as a society beset with the trappings of an oppressive, imperialistic educational system that had been initiated and developed by its former colonial overseer. It was in this context that poetry was also identified by the CPK as a means to build a revolutionary culture and to cultivate an appropriate political consciousness.

Khmer culture has a strong poetic tradition, and the CPK sought to exploit this lineage.[44] Historically, Khmer society made use of normative poems (*chbap*) that are "concerned with the activity of the entire society, and not merely the ceremonial behavior of the elite."[45] In precolonial Cambodia, normative poems centered on various social relations and the inherent contrasts that existed between different segments of society. Effectively, these poems provided an important guiding force in proper behavior and morality. Indeed, as David Chandler's analysis of precolonial Khmer poetry reveals, "discovering one's place in society and acting in accordance with it is one of the messages of the *chbap*."[46] Similarly, as specified in the Four-Year Plan, poems for the Khmer Rouge were to "reflect good models in the period of political/armed struggle and in the revolutionary war for national and people's liberation."[47] These models were based on the CPK's understanding of labor and the dialectics of nature-societal transformations. Crucially, however, this understanding deviated significantly from the ideals set forward by Trotsky, for under the Khmer Rouge poetry emerged not from the people as an expression of self-realization but instead conformed more with the bureaucratic approach that typified the Soviet Union.

The Poetics of Building Socialism

I contend that the CPK, as a Marxist-Leninist vanguard party, understood nature and humanity not as binaries but instead as oppositional contradictions. Humanity, consequently, was not external to nature, but rather nature and humanity were dialectic. The CPK, therefore, premised a unity of opposites whereby labor, a physical activity that transforms nature, would dialectically transform humanity and thereby build socialism. This is illustrated in the CPK Four-Year Plan: "In our educational system there are no examinations and no certificates; it is a system of learning through the collective and in the concrete movement of the socialist revolution and the building of socialism in the specific bases especially the cooperatives, factories, and military units."[48] It was this transformative quality on which Khmer Rouge citizenship was founded.

Thus, beyond the aforementioned rudimentary curricula designed to provide a minimum level of school-based learning (e.g., reading, writing, arithmetic, and geography), the CPK promoted a collective and public form of education based on hard work and sacrifice. An equivalency was established whereby the cultivation of rice fields would equate with a cultivation of political consciousness; dialectically, a proper political consciousness would contribute to increased agricultural productivity. In this way, socialism was to be built rapidly—and properly. The Four-Year Plan explains, "We must choose [people with] backgrounds that adhere to the revolutionary movement and have the quality to grasp the Party's educational line and are able to expand their own capacity in the concrete movement."[49] Likewise, a classified report dated May 28, 1977, noted that "enemies" were inciting citizenry to oppose the construction of dams and the planting of rice, claiming that the harvests would not be shared by the workers. Khmer Rouge cadres, in turn, were to properly "educate" the people. Ominously, this was to "isolate enemies and further investigate them."[50] In other words, it was necessary that people understand the significance of their work, that labor—and not the individual gain of foodstuffs—was paramount. Dialectically, this education would draw out those internal enemies who lacked proper political consciousness and hence would resolve the so-called contradictions between appropriate work efforts and those deemed inappropriate.

This was the purported vanguard role of the CPK. For this reason, men, women, and children were deployed to wage war on nature, not simply (or even primarily) to defeat nature but rather to nurture a proper revolutionary attitude. By extension, it was for this reason that the CPK used a form of public pedagogy. Through poetry, youth, in particular, were to imagine a world different from that of their elders—a world ostensibly free of monarchies, feudalism, and imperialism. This provided a balance, therefore, to the widespread use of fiery language deployed during the civil war.

Military metaphors were still used by the CPK after the revolution, and numerous slogans, songs, speeches, articles, and even poems reflected this usage. However, once in power, the CPK subtly altered its procedures for publicizing its policies. At a meeting held March 8, 1976, the Standing Committee of the CPK cautioned, "We must explain, not be wild and disorderly, do not let it be seen that we want to suppress."[51] In other words, it was still necessary to rally the troops, so to speak, but this was to be approached more circuitously; people were not to know that these actions included an ulterior motive. Perhaps drawing inspiration from Frantz Fanon, the CPK in this statement revealed its understanding that hatred and anger are valuable emotions for active revolution but insufficient to the task of building a society.[52] The aesthetics of poetry, in this way, could in principle nurture more positive emotions while attempting to both mask the continued coerciveness of Khmer Rouge practices, including arrest, detention, and execution, and legitimate the imposition of forced labor and starvation-level food rations.

The CPK viewed poetry specifically but the arts more generally as forms of public pedagogy. A series of staged and creative interventions, published through various outlets including *Revolutionary Youth*, were to provide a collective form of learning, one calculated to foster a proper and correct political consciousness through labor. Conforming to the CPK's overall dialectics of destruction-construction, it was necessary to first eliminate previous forms of public art.[53] As specified in the Four-Year Plan, the CPK commanded cadres to "continue the struggle to abolish, uproot, and disperse the cultural, literary, and artistic remnants of the imperialists, colonialists, and all of the other oppressor classes. This [would] be implemented strongly, deeply and continuously one after the other from 1977 onwards."[54] This accounts, in part, for the burning of books; the destruction of musical instruments, masks for dance, and Buddhist sculptures; and the murder of dancers, musicians, and other cultural artists.[55] The CPK was not so much anti-culture as it was intent on quickly and violently eliminating any form of art that did not conform to its ideal. Consequently, between 1975 and 1979, "no writer in Cambodia was able to express his reflections, ideas, or feelings, and no real literary work was created."[56]

The CPK routinely published, as a form of public pedagogy, poems in the magazine *Revolutionary Youth*.[57] Unfortunately, the authorship of these poems is not known with any certainty, for they appear anonymously in the magazine. There is some suggestion that high-ranking CPK leaders, most notably Pol Pot and Nuon Chea, authored poems. No doubt these leaders would have given approval to any poem prior to its publication. The anonymity of publication, though, is important because it speaks to the attitudes of CPK leaders toward the negation of individualism. People's actions were no longer to be based on individual profit; rather, a selfless dedication to the collective well-being of Democratic Kampuchea was promoted. This is seen, for example, in a poem titled "Cambodian Natural Resources."[58] Here, the penultimate stanza reads: "Join us as a force. Do not boast, be patient. It is only an illusion that farmers are living from hand to mouth." The poem calls on the youth to work in unison, as a collective force, and to not be boastful, that is, call attention to one's self. It also warns against surface appearances; rather poverty and the possibility of famine are illusory. Youth are encouraged to look beyond any visible signs of neglect. Instead they should focus on the bounties provided throughout their country, as illustrated in the first four stanzas:

> Oh, beautiful nation Cambodia, where many kinds of plants flourish,
> And birds and animals thrive in the jungle and under water.
>
> Our country is full of natural resources, including diamonds and rice.
> They are invaluable and have existed everywhere since ancient times.
>
> Rivers, lakes, and seas are numerous.
> Our fish are everywhere. This season's transplanted rice is healthy.
>
> Forest products and tree fruits are available in all seasons.
> The songs of birds, big and small, imply that their numbers are great.

Although Cambodia is presented as being a land of plenty, not all Khmer were able to enjoy these abundances. As explained in the last stanza, "Some of the rich have gone, and the rest, which amount to 90 percent, are poor as a result of exploitation. They have no clothes to wear, rice to eat, or money to spend. This has nothing to do with sin, but with exploitation." In a surprising reference to spirituality, the Khmer Rouge poem concludes that it is not fate that causes suffering and hardship but rather exploitation at the hands of the wealth. Poverty existed in the past—the result of unfair landowners and corrupt merchants—but under Angkar a hand-to-mouth existence is no more. Through the benevolent leadership of the party, men and women would once again be able to flourish in a natural environment endowed with fish, fowl, rice, and other resources. Ominously, the poem alludes to the disappearance of "some of the wealthy", a not-so-veiled reference to the murder of former landlords, merchants, and other prosperous members of society.

In a poem titled "We Are Grateful to the Revolutionary Angkar," the theme of exploitation is further developed.[59] The poem emphasizes the neglect of or indifference to nature displayed by the wealthy:

> We children lived in the darkness of a canopy of dense forests,
> Where the sunlight could never reach, where we lived in a world without light.
> We lived in the wealth of a society with corruption,
> Where earth was no object of thought and concern to any man no matter how fertile it was.
> But now we live happy lives since our Kampuchean Revolutionary Angkar made us understand
> That the old regime was the cause of all worries.
> . . . .
> Therefore, we children have to spare no effort in our struggle until the end of our lives.

In this poem, a particular geography is imagined, based on a careful construction of how the CPK justified and legitimized its rise to power. Prior to the revolution, Khmer society was shrouded in darkness; it was a world dominated by a corrupt society in which the powerful classes of society ignored and neglected nature. For this reason, misery existed, and revolution was necessary. And now, following the revolution, the poem suggests, greater care will be taken to preserve the natural beauty and bounty of Cambodia, and all will be well. This is not the fire-and-brimstone view of nature as something to be defeated; instead, nature appears as being in need of protection and conservation.

Cryptic lessons in Marxian political philosophy are also developed. In a theme common to many Khmer Rouge poems, prerevolutionary Cambodia is presented as a society rife with contradictions, of rich and poor, abundance and scarcity. To be sure, the concept of contradictions is only minimally developed, used mainly as a form of conflicting binaries. Nevertheless, poetically, contradictions are portrayed in sensual and oppositional metaphors, most prominently that between light and dark. But with effort, sacrifice, and loyalty to Angkar, contradictions may be negated: both the rich and the poor disappear, replaced by equal prosperity. This negation, according to the poem, requires sacrifice, both in the form of hard work and in the elimination of those who corrupted society. Crucially, the promotion of difference—between those members of society worthy of participation and those who threatened society—did not always nor necessarily take the form of blatant dehumanizing language. Thus, while many policy documents and even some speeches refer to traitors, for example, as "parasites," in these poems the enemy is identified in a more nuanced manner.

Other poems call more directly for the sacrifice and education of Khmer citizens. An excerpt from a poem published in December 1976 reads: "Young farmers are strong / cultivating the fields giving their best / They take no rest from dusk till dawn / adjusting the water level in the field."[60] Through the collective transformation of agriculture, "Male and female revolutionary youths / accomplish their great duties / determined to reeducate themselves / to protect the revolution." Work in cooperatives, rice fields, and factories are forms of education, practices that are geared toward the continuation—and protection—of the revolution. Consequently, youth are called on to "fight strenuously" and to "work quickly with a pure heart"; they are to "stand strong and read" while keeping "their eyes . . . vigilant." Thus it is only through these efforts that a "grieving landscape" can be turned into a "cheerful one." Notably, this poem makes subtle reference to surveillance practices as a means to resolve fundamental contradictions within society.[61]

As a final example, consider once more the poem that appeared as this chapter's epigraph. The first two stanzas of the poem read:

> Oh! Mighty Kampuchea
> Feudalism capitalism and traitors
> Made our nation and people
> Become poverty-stricken servants.
>
> Our prosperous Kampuchean Party
> Leads Kampuchean Society
> This new society is perfect
> There is no rich or poor or loss of reputation.

The contradictions of prerevolutionary society are clear. The poem nevertheless illustrates how the resolution of contradictions is made possible not only through self-sacrifice but also through the combined efforts of building and defending society through the transformation of nature:

We are youths, peasants, workers
For we are free from sorrow
We swear to change our homeland
Plenty of rice, corn, bananas, potatoes, hemp.
Turn fields with new dikes and irrigation systems
Late rice, early rice, and October rice
Change village lands, and hill lands
To grow fields of chili, eggplant, taro.
Arum, pumpkin, cucumber, melons
Which burst in green everywhere
While we are soldiers
And at times cultivate the land.

As an artistic expression, the poem presents a cornucopian vision, but read in connection with party policy, the poem accentuates the various crops to be cultivated. The necessity of building irrigation schemes is likewise stressed, for through this labor village lands and hill lands may also burst forth with abundance. As for the workers, they remain soldiers, ever vigil in the defense of the party, the revolution, and Democratic Kampuchea, but they are also farmers, needed to literally bring to fruition the sage policies put forth by Angkar.

Effectively, Khmer Rouge–era poetry illustrates the literary production of an imagined geography. For the CPK, Cambodia was a land blessed with a surfeit of natural resources. Centuries of exploitation and corruption by feudalists, capitalists, and imperialists had resulted in widespread poverty and misery, matched only by a callous and irresponsible use of nature. The fundamental contradiction, explained through poetry and only through guarded references to Marxist political philosophy, was the juxtaposition of poverty amid plenty. The subtext of many poems is that the private ownership of nature, and the attendant disregard for the unity of nature and humanity, is the underlying cause. These poems were published, however, to achieve yet another objective, namely, the cultivation of a correct political consciousness.

That such a political consciousness did not materialize is readily observed in the ongoing arrest, detainment, and execution of thousands of men, women, and children throughout Democratic Kampuchea. For the Khmer Rouge, sickness was symptomatic not of any medical condition but rather of a political ailment; to be unable to perform labor was tantamount to treason. So too was the acknowledgment of depression or deprivation.[62] For this reason, CPK cadres initiated and supported a series of purges of those deemed unable to conform to the new society; not educated people per se but rather those who embodied an incorrect education were targeted, as citizenship and survival were articulated around a selfless dedication to the party and the revolution.

Conclusions

The dialectic between physical nature and human nature guided CPK policy and practice. When the Khmer Rouge forced men, women, and children to fight in the agricultural fields, they were to labor with a purposive will and not simply to work as spiders or bees do. Labor became a unity of the cultivation of rice and the cultivation of a correct political consciousness. In advancing this policy, the CPK envisioned a means to build both socialism and a nation. This vanguard role, in turn, required different forms of education. On the one hand, plans were developed—but never fully implemented—to provide a more formal curriculum, designed principally to satisfy the rudimentary tasks of reading, writing, arithmetic, and learning geography. On the other hand, a more experiential form of learning was proposed and to a certain extent more widely promoted. The publication of poems, notably in *Revolutionary Youth*, constituted a form of public pedagogy, a deliberate political intervention designed to rapidly bring about individual and societal transformation. Poetry was thus used by the Khmer Rouge as a creative intervention to serve political ends. This in and of itself is not especially noteworthy. Few scholars of Democratic Kampuchea would be surprised to learn that poems, along with other artistic productions, were used to affect change. What is salient is how the *poetic expression of nature* as expressed in Khmer Rouge–era poetry provides insight into the Marxist-Leninist ideology of the CPK. This is crucial in that it contributes, on the one hand, to a more theoretically grounded understanding of CPK doctrine and, more generally, to the synergy of public pedagogy and the politics of aesthetic interventions.

"How we write about the world," Simon Springer postulates, "constitutes a deeply political choice."[63] That the Khmer Rouge sought to disseminate party policy through poetry and other expressive forms of writing is not inconsequential. Indeed, it appears as if the Khmer Rouge understood that "a poetic-political project is imperative to breaking with colonial knowledges," in that creative geographical expression constitutes alternative epistemological ways of knowing.[64] Thus, while the CPK was resolute in its attempt to provide a scientific understanding of agricultural and water problems, it was equally forthright in its use of poetry as a form of public pedagogy. In this way, the CPK's *writing* of its imaginative geographies was dialectic, a unity of opposing epistemologies required for the ultimate objective of building socialism.

4 The Lyrics of Revolution

Much scholarly attention has focused on the widespread prevalence of torture, famine, and murder under the Khmer Rouge—and rightfully so.[1] Apart from the systematic arrest, detainment, and execution of innumerable men, women, and children at any one of the approximately two hundred security centers located throughout Democratic Kampuchea, countless other people were murdered through random acts of violence. In addition, hundreds of thousands of people succumbed to malnutrition, disease, exhaustion, and other forms of structural violence.

Decidedly less attention has been directed toward the aesthetics of Khmer Rouge practice—an observation that on the surface appears incongruous. Given the sheer scale of human atrocities committed during the Khmer Rouge era, to speak of aesthetics would seem to be the zenith of insensitivity. Yet such an omission holds tremendous importance for our understanding of both direct and structural violence. As recent scholarship surrounding the Holocaust has detailed, "it is one thing to recognize that a given political movement may make greater or lesser use of art and another thing to conclude that aesthetics is identical to ideology."[2]

The scholarly disregard of Khmer Rouge cultural practices limits our understanding of the broader political-economic objectives that underscored the mass violence in Democratic Kampuchea. Consider, for example, Stephen Mamula's abbreviated and inaccurate portrayal of music and performing arts under the Khmer Rouge: "During its regime, the Khmer Rouge was systematic and brutal in dismantling institutions perceived as opposition to revolutionary practice and ideology, including radio and television transmissions, cinema houses, theatres, record stores, as well as nightclubs and discotheques."[3] Although it is true that the Khmer Rouge did dismantle (selectively) various

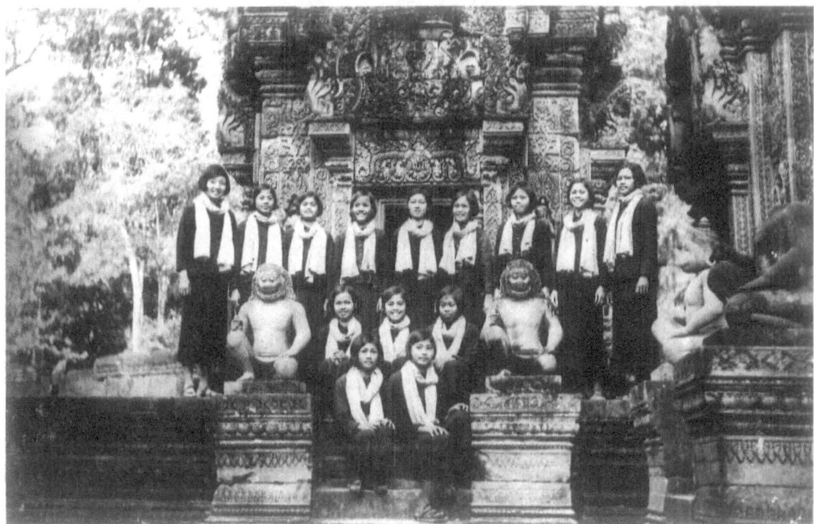

Figure 4.1. Female Khmer Rouge dance troop at the Banteay Srey Temple. Courtesy of the Documentation Center of Cambodia Archives.

institutions, it is also true that many others were transformed to conform to CPK policy. Indeed, cultural institutions, including cinemas and theaters, were explicitly promoted as a means of furthering revolutionary practice. Music was transmitted via radio, and specialized dance troupes were formed to promote revolutionary ideology through cultural performances (figure 4.1). It is imperative that a more complete picture be presented to understand both the day-to-day conditions of life under the Khmer Rouge and the legacy of CPK policy and practices on contemporary life—including that of music and the arts after the Khmer Rouge. It is necessary to reconsider that the performativity of Khmer Rouge songs should not be reduced to a form of political indoctrination but instead be understood as a crucial form of public pedagogy, that is, a material practice associated with building socialism.

In this chapter, I consider the lyrics of eleven Khmer Rouge–era songs that address nature in general but irrigation projects specifically. The analysis is framed, broadly, within the study of the geographies of music.[4] Geographers and other social scientists have long considered music a key component of nation building. Indeed, as Andrew Leyson and his colleagues identify, "music has always been implicated in the social and political world. Its power to affect, disturb, rouse and subdue has been used to great effect by monarchies, armies and governments throughout history."[5] As such, it is possible to demonstrate how geographies of music and literary geographies may come together as part of wider aesthetic interventions into the politics of place making.

To date, approximately one hundred Khmer Rouge–era songs have been cataloged, transcribed, and archived at the Documentation Center of Cambodia.[6] The precise number of songs, however, remains unknown. Many of the archived songs are variations of other songs; likewise, identical songs might have different titles or lyrics that have been only slightly altered. This is not surprising, given that many Khmer Rouge–era songs are based on oral testimony or derived from written records, such as diaries or Khmer Rouge cadre notebooks.

Khmer Rouge–era songs reflect a diversity of subject matter. Often, the standard narrative renders Khmer Rouge songs as mere instruments of propaganda; scholarship, accordingly, focuses most explicitly on the revolutionary fervor and collective heroism of the lyrics. Certainly, many songs do reveal a hypernationalism, but Khmer Rouge songs, similar to poems, speak also of day-to-day activities, mostly but not exclusively related to agriculture. To a degree, agrarian life is idolized, and thus songs often represent farmers and fisherfolk as part of a heroic rural proletarian in the making. However, such a conclusion must be tempered. Indeed, Khmer Rouge songs should not be construed as mindless and clichéd romanticism of the peasantry.[7]

It is important to remember, following Nichola Wood, that music is more than something that is seen (through a focus on musical lyrics); it is something that is also heard and felt.[8] According to Marston, the Khmer Rouge used popular and traditional melodies rather than writing their own scores.[9] New lyrics, written in conformance with basic CPK policy, were set to these melodies, thereby establishing a crucial relationship between past, present, and future. In this manner, Khmer Rouge songs provided a tangible connection to the past, while the lyrics themselves spoke of a radical departure from the past. Likewise, the familiar narratives' daily life centered on agriculture also signified both a temporal and a spatial connection between prerevolutionary Cambodia and Democratic Kampuchea.

In effect, this chapter presents Khmer Rouge–era songs as political performances: as narratives of revolution and nation building, but also as a normative exegesis to build socialism. Consequently, these songs are understood as lyrical narratives that purport—in their totality—to present a story of Democratic Kampuchea. Songs, in other words, form the basis of constructing an imaginative geography of Democratic Kampuchea as a *real place*—but a place that is in the process of becoming. Thus the repeated transmission of songs over the radio or the material performance of songs in agricultural collectives or at work sites reiterate the history and geography of revolutionary and postrevolutionary society.[10] Apart from narrating the past as a sequence of interconnected events (e.g., revolutionary victory and postvictory practice), these songs provide a normative pedagogic lesson, specifically, how the transformation of nature contributes to the transformation of society and the promotion of a shared sense of purpose.

Transforming Nature through Song

Within Democratic Kampuchea, music emerged as a dominant mode of artistic expression by which a correct political consciousness could be fashioned. As noted earlier, CPK officials determined early in their regime that radio broadcasting, and particularly the transmission of songs, offered an opportunity for political reeducation. To this end, Marston speculates that it was probably through broadcasts that songs had the greatest impact on people living in the agricultural cooperatives.[11] Other venues were used, however, including public performances held at reeducation sessions, festivals, and celebrations, often marking the completion and inauguration of irrigation projects.

These forms of public pedagogy—as a means of instruction beyond the formal classroom setting—were in principle used to transform what the CPK viewed as a society beset with the trappings of an oppressive, imperialistic educational system that had been initiated and developed by its former colonial overseer. By way of illustration, a song titled "Best Wishes for the Great Cambodian People" explains, "We have accomplished the Leap Forward victory in our history because we transformed our society to move forward in a manner which has never existed before / Our society has become pure, and there is no oppression. There are no rich nor poor people. It is a democratic society [in] which men and women live prosperously."[12]

The transformation of political consciousness among Democratic Kampuchea's subjects was crucial to the transition to Communism, and for this reason, it is necessary that Khmer Rouge–era songs be understood within the context of CPK economic policies and practices. Agriculture, but specifically rice cultivation, was the CPK's comparative advantage in the promotion of its economic policy based on import substitution. Moreover, for the CPK, the overriding environmental obstacle associated with increased rice production—and, by extension, the economic development and defense of Democratic Kampuchea—was the problem of water.[13] As indicated in the CPK's Four-Year Plan, it was necessary to "increase the degree of mastery over the water problem from one year to another."[14] The plan further noted, "In order to gain mastery over water there must be a network of dikes and canals as the basis. There must also be canals, reservoirs, and irrigation pumps stationed in accordance with our strategy."[15] Moreover, as detailed earlier, the CPK calculated that rice production would need to be tripled, to a national average yield of three tons per hectare. Moreover, it was determined that a national grid system (i.e., chessboard pattern) of agricultural fields should be implemented. Over time, both of these preliminary objectives were discarded—although, as noted later, these elements became solidified through song.[16]

To convey their economic policies to the masses, as well as provide justification and legitimation for the hardships endured, the CPK promoted a collective and public form of education based on physical labor and communal sacrifice. Thus within songs both performed and broadcast over the radio, an equivalency was established whereby nurturing rice fields would equate with cultivating political consciousness. In their totality, however, these songs not only conveyed specific policies; they also narrated a story of collective transformation. Indeed, it was not uncommon for songs to begin with reference to the recent revolutionary victory: "We destroyed the American invaders from our land and won war in a great leap manner," and "On 17 April our great revolution perfectly defeated all the enemies, establishing a new Kampuchea."[17] Another song explains, "The Super Great 17 April is the new chapter of Cambodian history. It is the new era of our revolution, new Cambodia, and we move forward very fast."[18] This latter theme, of a new chapter, is repeated elsewhere: "They are determined to build new rice dikes, as a new chapter for our Cambodia, male and female soldiers, cadres, and men and women."[19]

If the previous chapter of Cambodia's history was marked by victory over the imperialists, songs explained that subsequent chapters were predicated on achieving victory over environmental problems. Thus while the CPK acknowledged, "We must estimate the water-power available. We must know where to construct dams and where to dig canals", so too did songs.[20] The necessity of constructing irrigation projects was a common refrain: "We push for new Kampuchea where there is rice, there is water. When we have rice, we have everything. We are no longer afraid of having no rain when we have rice dikes."[21]

Khmer Rouge songs were often quite specific in their translation of policy into verse. Apart from the construction of dikes, canals, and reservoirs, many songs described the conversion of rice fields into neatly arranged chessboard patterns or the need to produce three tons of rice per hectare. Thus songs instructed audiences: "We build big rice dikes, divide them into chessboard pattern, and make them look so beautiful. We merge small rice dikes with one another. We work together for the Cambodian revolution."[22] Another verse goes: "It is the rainy season. Therefore, Comrade, please work hard. We gather our workforces, work without wasting our time, and grow rice in a one hectare field three times a year."[23] Likewise, lyrics explain that "all big and small dams are filled with water because of the rain. The floodgates are closed and opened in order to stock and release water from the reservoir, distributing water to all fields."[24]

Lyrics represented the detailed tasks that were required for a successful and bright future. As one song reflected, "When there are rice dikes and canals, there are ways to irrigate water. We can transport our rice, sheaves of rice, husked rice, salt, pots, and jars, improving the people's living conditions."[25] Another song emphasized, "We have had more and new rice dikes and canals which distribute water to all fields. . . . All are the same in the chessboard patterns of rice fields. The canals are full of water, and they are connected from one to another, making the rural areas become prosperous."[26]

Heroic efforts to overcome environmental obstacles were to be communal. The mastery of water was thus a collective endeavor. Communes and agricultural collectives were to become the locus of daily life. Thus songs extolled the virtues of cooperation: "In handicraft warehouses, people do all types of work, and they work all the time. They are working actively the same as soldiers who fought and smashed the enemies during the war. In every village, commune, district, region, and zone, people do not stay still and do nothing. They work and keep active with self-mastery."[27] Other lyrics were equally straightforward: "Our peasants work in groups in the cooperative, storm attack, and collaboratively build rice dikes and finish them very quickly, enabling the village cooperative to move forward."[28]

If one wondered why cooperatives were considered the key to success, many songs identified how communal efforts had secured victory for the revolution: "Given that our cooperatives were the strong backbone of our great revolution, the soldiers and people were able to claim victory and defeat the imperialists."[29] Consequently, this same approach would achieve victory over nature and contribute to a new, utopian society: "Our cooperative produces products and contributes to building great Democratic Kampuchea with new rice dikes in chessboard patterns."[30] This theme is repeated often: "Like the Sun which rises so bright in the morning, our revolution shines with great and sharp light all over the country, mountainous areas and rural areas which went through such transformations on 17 April. / It rains in our new land, making our rice paddy turn green in chessboard pattern. Water flows along the canals and hits the floodgates, distributing water all over the fields."[31] Here we are readily asked to contemplate the fruition of labor, of major infrastructure projects. As with a new day, Democratic Kampuchea was envisioned as coming into light through communal efforts. The physical transformation of Cambodia, exemplified by orderly green rice fields and a network of life-giving water, was the reward for personal sacrifice and cooperation.

Nevertheless, clear separations of work by gender and age were identified. Consider, for example, the following lyrics. One song describes women's work: "Female peasants in our cooperative are working hard to transplant young rice seedlings. They are laughing happily and singing songs together. Their surrounding environment looks so peaceful and beautiful."[32] Likewise, another song offers a woman's narration: "We, the female youth, work fast and use our hands to put rice seeds in buckets and throw them into the fields. We throw both rice seeds and fertilizer into the fields. Then rice seedlings grow healthy and become green."[33] Similarly, for men, it was noted, "If we look further to the feet of the mountains, our male youth are plowing paddy fields. They have plowed hundreds of rice fields, and they are plowing more to finish their task."[34] Youth, both male and female, were also portrayed as having definable roles in the new society: "Boys and girls are working in line and carrying earth, and they are singing at the same time. They look busy. Some are tending cattle at the feet of the mountains."[35]

It is noteworthy that the many songs themselves extolled the importance of music to the ongoing revolution and the transformation of nature. One song, for example, depicts a scene of daily life following work in the fields: "Pots and plates have been collected and used in the collective dining hall. There are foods which have been cooked and smell good in the hall. They are served for our people who have done their work. They are eating together. After [the] meal, they take a break and listen to the radio with regard to beautiful music, voices of workers and peasants, literatures, and our prosperous cultures."[36]

Cooperation and hard work would, according to the lyrical narratives, transform Democratic Kampuchea into a bountiful landscape replete with fields laden with rice, vegetables, and other foodstuffs. Lyrics would announce: "Our rural area has changed its image. Each unit of the cooperative has moved forward and increased its economic, social, political, and other sectors. Everything has improved beautifully."[37] Such were the repeated refrains that must have sat uncomfortably next to the all-too-obvious shortages of food. Nevertheless, songs continue to proclaim, "Our rice fields are strong and tall, are in chessboard patterns, and stretch all over the fields and to the streams and lakes, making the rural areas look so lovely. They look so straight, transforming the new image of the rural areas."[38] According to another, "The image of the rural area turns to a completely new and beautiful. Rice dikes in chessboard pattern are everywhere and full of water."[39] Yet another song describes how the workers were "transforming rural areas to be beautiful and wealthy, and there is water during the dry and rainy season, and there are all types of fruits."[40]

Underlying the transformation of Democratic Kampuchea's agricultural landscape, however, was the lesson that society itself was being transformed. Hence, lyrics would teach that "under the great lines and leadership of the Revolutionary Kampuchea, we have changed the living condition of our people, and we are determined to work together and smash the enemies."[41] Another song concludes, "The collective stance of people is good. They agree upon one another to solve small and big problems together as well as to build and defend our country."[42] In other words, through collective efforts, discipline, and hard work, anything was possible: the perceived environmental problems—including starvation itself—could be overcome.[43]

The Materiality of Musical Performances

What remains of performances? This seemingly straightforward question has long troubled scholars of theater and poses a similar challenge to those who study the historiography of the Khmer Rouge. Simply put, many components of quotidian life within Democratic Kampuchea remain tantalizingly close yet frustratingly distant. The performance of music is one such element. To date, there has been little in-depth examination of Khmer Rouge performances. In part, this relates to the presumption that artistic performances, similar to poetry and musical lyrics, are simply propaganda materials and thus constitute modes of promoting party ideology. More problematic is the presumption that performances are ephemeral and hence nothing remains to be documented.

Within theatrical studies, it is widely held that live performances are immaterial, that nothing remains to be documented or archived. Peggy Phelan explains that "performance cannot be saved, recorded, documented, or otherwise participate in the circulation of representations of representations: once it does so it becomes something other than performance. . . . Performance . . . becomes itself through disappearance."[44] Marcia Siegel likewise argues that performances such as dance exist "at a perpetual vanishing point"; they are events that disappear in the very act of materializing.[45] More recent scholarship, however, has challenged the seeming impermanence of live performances.

Rebecca Schneider has taken up this challenge. She asks, "If we consider performance as of disappearance, of an ephemerality read as vanishment and loss, are we limiting ourselves to an understanding of performance predetermined by our cultural habituation to the logic of the archive?"[46] In other words, preexisting practices of archiving potentially circumscribe explanations before questions may even be posed. Yet Schneider counters that "the definition of performance as that which disappears, which is continually lost in time, is a definition well suited to the concerns of art history and the curatorial pressure to understand performance in the museal context where performance appeared to challenge object status and seemed to refuse the archive its privileged 'savable' original."[47] She elaborates: "In privileging an understanding of performance as a refusal to remain, do we ignore other ways of knowing, other modes of remembering, that might be situated precisely in the ways in which performance remains, but remains differently?"[48] In this penultimate section, I take up Schneider's challenge. In so doing, I make a double move, however. On the one hand, I consider what actually remains of Khmer Rouge musical performance and how material remnants may further support my overall thesis. On the other hand, I reconsider musical performances as a mode of public pedagogy and question what this says about the CPK's attempt to build socialism in Democratic Kampuchea.

To begin, we must confront head-on the *representation* of performances, for as Sarah Jones and her colleagues write, "Defining the nature of performances is at the root of all difficulties regarding their representation."[49] Noting that for many scholars transience is the principle characteristic of performance, they suggest that "it is worth reflecting for a moment on the meaning of this in terms of archiving," for if the "significant property of performance is its transience, are all attempts to archive performance futile?"[50] It is possible, for example, that photographs or other recordings of performances remain; likewise, *something* of the performance may be transmitted through oral testimony. There may also be material traces, such as ticket stubs or promotional posters. Yet do any of these remnants actually convey the essence of live performances? Jones and her coauthors acknowledge that "the representations that are usually created, such as the photographs and drawings, are often discounted as inadequate and unfaithful—they provide a window onto an event yet do not recreate the experience."[51]

Diana Taylor makes a distinction between the material representation of performances, such as photographs and promotional posters, and the immateriality, or remembrance, of performances.[52] Jones and her colleagues also expand on this concept, suggesting that "if we consider the development of performers' signature practices and embodied knowledge . . . each instantiation of a performance can itself be thought of as simply one part of an ongoing creative process that is constantly feeding back into itself. The identification of immaterial traces that are in a constant state of re-enactment counters the notion that performance disappears."[53] At stake is nothing less than the very ontology of performances.

Archives are generally thought of as repositories of material documents, as places that store physical objects of the past. Accordingly, attention often centers on specific artifacts or documents that may be collected, processed, recorded, and stored for future reference. More precisely, archives are understood as "sources of authoritative history."[54] This is revealed in the etymology of the term "archive," derived from the Greek *arkhe*, meaning government or rule, and *arkheion*, meaning government building. Thus following Francis Blouin and William Rosenberg, "archives endured as repositories of basic transactions, a symbol of historical continuity, order, and truth."[55] Is it appropriate, therefore, to consider performances as that which may be archived? On the one hand, "performances are constantly in a state of becoming and have no definable end. The archive consequently enforces a false sense of completeness on a performance event that is part of a much wider work. It is impractical to separate individual instantiations of a performance from the process of their creation and unrepresentative to force them to fit this model of archives."[56] From this perspective, there is no singular performance: to limit one's understanding, say, to a particular dance or show is to discount both the processes leading up to that moment and also the continuation of the performance. With respect to the former, one needs to consider the rehearsals, the development of choreography, the composing of musical scores, and so on. As to the latter, we could consider the memories of the performance and the emotive and visceral responses to the performance. On the other hand, the "immaterial traces and embodied knowledge" of performances find consonance with the purpose of archives.[57] As Blouin and Rosenberg explain, archives are also "places that permanently memorialize what societies and institutions regard as essential transactions." In short, "archives and their records somehow engage a society's 'memory' by preserving the authentic records of its past."[58]

It is this paradox of immateriality and the quality of being archived that frames my understanding of Khmer Rouge musical performances. To begin, very little empirical materials (e.g., films, photographs, or audio recordings) remain of actual performances. Nevertheless, these physical remnants, notably photographs, provide a first glance into the staging of performances by the CPK. However, these are also, quite literally, snapshots of singular performances. As Julia Hudson cautions, "in dance, as in most performing arts, there is no single 'authoritative' performance. Works are different each time they are performed; they may use different performers, or be one choreographer's variation on another's piece."[59] It is necessary, therefore, to evaluate Khmer Rouge performances beyond the material remnants and to consider the immateriality of performances—both from a historical standpoint and from the vantage of the Khmer Rouge.

The historiography of Democratic Kampuchea has been greatly expanded through the collection of oral testimonies by the Documentation Center of Cambodia, including interviews conducted with Khmer Rouge performing artists and those who witnessed such performances. In general, survivor accounts

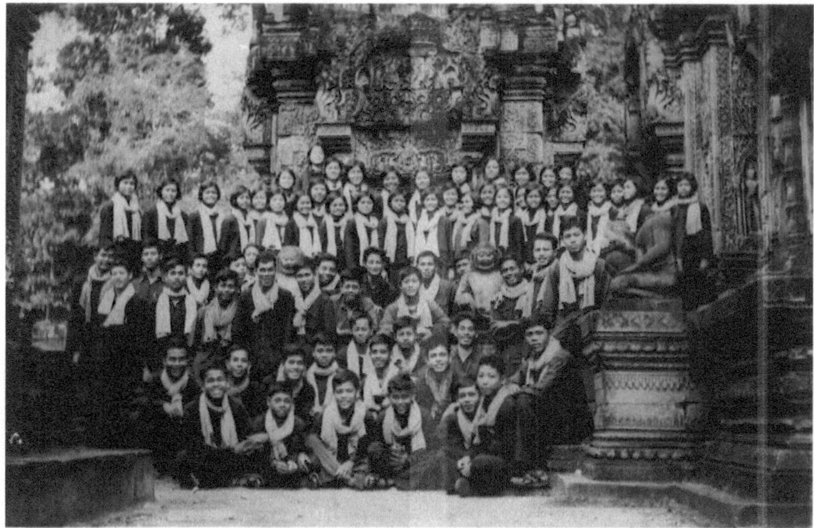

Figure 4.2. Male and female Khmer Rouge performers at the Banteay Srey Temple. Courtesy of the Documentation Center of Cambodia Archives.

indicate that live performances were fairly common and broadly understood as serving an ideological role. As detailed by Sok-Kheang Ly, throughout the civil war and following the revolution, Khmer Rouge officials would form *artistic groups*, composed of young women and men.[60] It was not uncommon, for example, that local dance troupes would be formed within cooperatives, and men and women would learn and rehearse artistic performances during breaks between work.[61] The Khmer Rouge made use also of mobile performing-arts troupes. These were normally composed of approximately thirty members each and included singers, musicians, and dancers. They would travel, replete with instruments, stage props, and portable generators, to particular performance sites. When not performing, the artists would engage in agricultural work or serve as soldiers in combat operations.

Often performances were held during special events, such as the inauguration of a newly constructed irrigation project (figure 4.5) or the reception of foreign dignitaries. When performed on-site or onstage, Khmer Rouge songs were sung as choruses, with both male and female performers singing particular refrains. As detailed above, songs included lyrics specific to men and

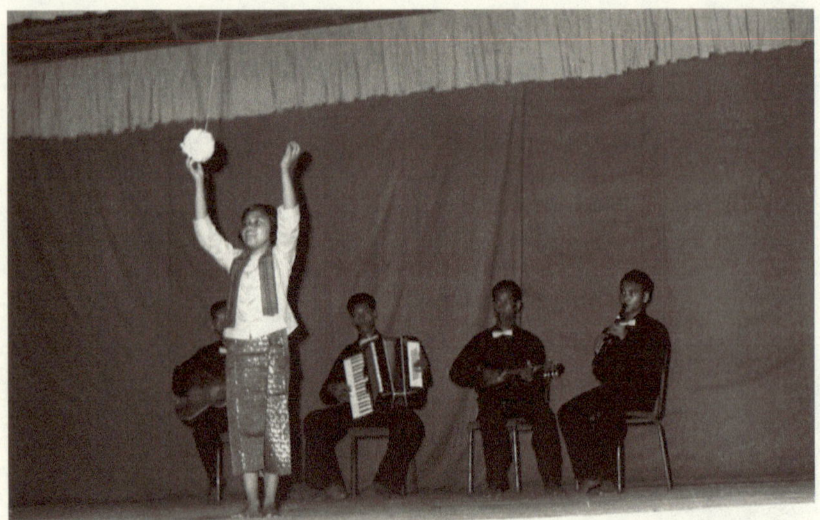

Figure 4.3. A Khmer Rouge dance performance. Courtesy of the Documentation Center of Cambodia Archives.

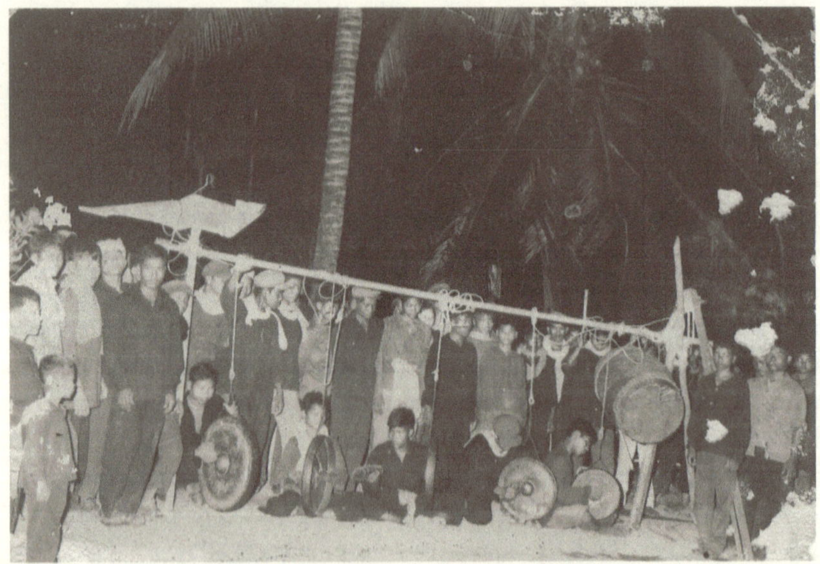

Figure 4.4. A performance in the Khmer Rouge liberated zone of Kratie Province. Courtesy of the Documentation Center of Cambodia Archives.

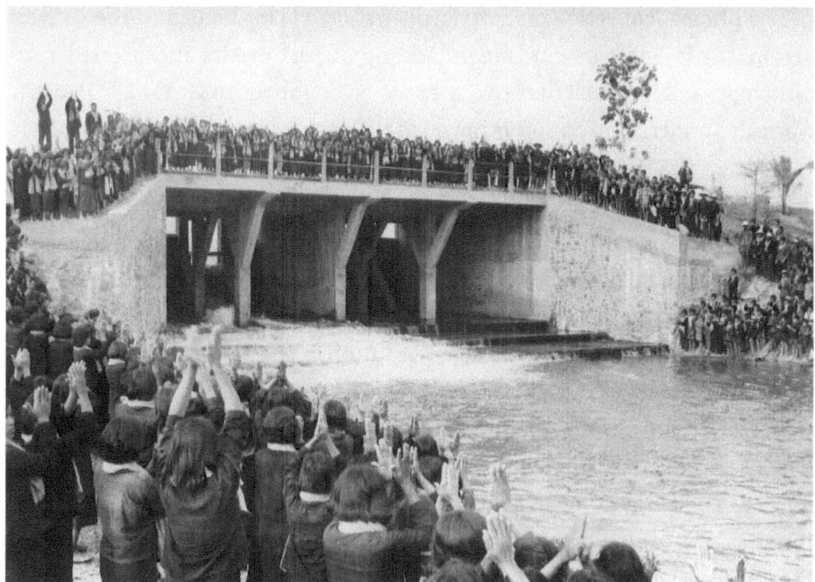

Figure 4.5. Celebration after the completion of an irrigation project. Courtesy of the Documentation Center of Cambodia Archives.

women, based mostly on sex-segregated occupational tasks, and props would emphasize these roles. When singing about agriculture, performers would carry hoes and baskets; when signing about work projects, they would dance with shovels or other tools. Public performances thus provided a visual image of ideal behavior. No individual performer was to be singled out; all was collective, both in verse and in action.

The actual performances—the *staging* of songs—contributed to the cultivation of a proper revolutionary attitude and political consciousness. However, the *totality* of performing—of the choreographing of dance routines, the composition of songs, and the repeated rehearsals—combined with the emotive remembrance, must be understood as an ongoing form of public pedagogy, a mode of instruction that worked through the collective memory of participating in or witnessing artistic performances. Simply put, the immateriality of performances—of that which cannot be archived—did in fact constitute a political process and legal ordering of society more pervasive than formal education could provide.

The phrase "collective memory" conceptually brings much to the conversation, for it "informs our understanding of past events and present relationships, and it contributes to our expectations about the future."[62] In other words, to understand the ways in which the past acts on the present, we have to address the broader frames of meaning that configure individual memories and in the process construct a particular sense of the past.[63] As Wulf Kansteiner explains, "Individual memories only assume collective relevance when they are structured, represented, and used in a social setting."[64] Collective memories, therefore, are not synonymous with historical reality but instead constitute a particular reconfiguration of the past. As James Wertsch and Henry Roediger explain, "In collective remembering, the past is tied interpretatively to the present, and if necessary part of an account of the past may be deleted or distorted in the service of present needs."[65] A critical element of the CPK's attempt to build socialism was to concurrently construct the past. For example, during a meeting held on March 3, 1976, members of the Central Committee of the CPK codified thirteen "Days of Recollection of Historical Events." These included April 17, 1975, as the "Independence Celebration"; August 15, 1973, as "The Day of the Great Defeat of the Imperialist American Air War"; April 12, 1975, as "The Fundamental Great Defeat of the War of Aggression of Imperialist America"; and July 10, 1961, as "The Birth of the Democratic Kampuchea Women's Organization."[66] This litany of decisive dates is significant in that it highlights the active construction of the past; and it was these dates of "historical significance" that were choreographed, rehearsed, performed, and remembered.

According to Aleida Assmann, "Once memories are verbalized in the form of a narrative or represented by a visual image, the individual's memories become part of an intersubjective symbolic system and are, strictly speaking, no longer a purely exclusive or unalienable property."[67] Here, we may follow Michael Shudson's lead that "memory is social. . . . [It] is located in institutions rather than in individual human minds in the form of rules, laws, standardized procedures, and records, a whole set of cultural practices through which people recognize a debt to the past."[68] Artistic performances, manifest in the material traces of photographs and song lyrics, were immaterial institutions that narrated the historiography of Democratic Kampuchea and the Communist Revolution as imagined by the CPK. In this way, the preeminent lessons of building socialism through the transformation of society through the transformation of nature were to become part of the Khmer Rouge's collective memory.

Conclusions

In Democratic Kampuchea, a particular imaginative geography was constructed through music, song, and performance. Ideological landscapes, enunciated in lyrics and represented through dance, were designed to mimic the paddy fields and irrigation systems being constructed under the watchful eyes of the Khmer Rouge. Songs and other artistic practices, consequently, must be viewed not as simple elements of propaganda or indoctrination but as authentic simulacra, for it was through these practices that the CPK envisioned future society and hence governed accordingly. Indeed, high-ranking members of the CPK readily understood the transformative power of music. In Democratic Kampuchea, music, radio, and performing arts were not only *not* dismantled but rather evidence reveals that cultural arts, such as music, were themselves *transformed* by the CPK in accordance with larger political and economic policies. In short, there was a greater degree of continuity between prerevolutionary and postrevolutionary performance practices than is commonly acknowledged. Such transformations were crucial in that they underscore the fundamental "humanist" concerns of the CPK, namely, the negation of individuality and the promotion of a collective political consciousness.

The use of music as a political form of public pedagogy by the CPK was of course not exceptional. As many studies document, songs and other performances are routinely used by political elites in an attempt to inculcate national loyalty and support.[69] What is significant is that Khmer Rouge artistic performances represent a dialectic of political economy, culture, and the environment. Hence, the transformation of *physical* nature under the Khmer Rouge was vitally important to the subsequent attempt to transform *human* nature; songs were used as a form of public pedagogy to identify specific environmental problems and how these were to be overcome. The primary contribution of this chapter, therefore, is not identifying the banal connection between music and landscape but rather emphasizing the *work* that music performs. Throughout Democratic Kampuchea, songs and performances were used as political instruments in an effort to radically transform the political consciousness of the men, women, and children who were subjected to CPK rule. Consequently, as the agrarian landscape was transformed through physical labor, including but not limited to the establishment of irrigation projects, so too was the citizenry of Democratic Kampuchea to be mentally and behaviorally transformed. The transformation of Democratic Kampuchea's natural environment would, according to the CPK, result in a transformation of consciousness; in turn, a proper political consciousness would lead to additional transformations of the country's natural resources. And it was through this dialectical unity, according to the Khmer Rouge, that any production quota could be achieved. This, in effect, was the nature of revolution.

5 Picturing the Revolution

On the surface, the photograph is a scene of everyday life. Two middle-aged women, seemingly deep in concentration, are weaving *smok* (baskets) made of bamboo. There is nothing particularly significant about the baskets; these are very common throughout Cambodia and are used to store a variety of goods, including rice grain, cooked rice, *prahok* (fish paste), and corn. One could easily imagine the photograph appearing in an issue of *National Geographic*. Little is known about the photograph. It was probably taken around 1975 or 1976, possibly earlier. The two women's names are not known; neither is the photographer identified. What is certain, however, is that a Khmer Rouge cadre took the photograph.

As detailed earlier, upon assuming power leading officials of the Communist Party of Kampuchea understood their tenuous hold on power and lack of popular support. Not only did the CPK leadership need to build socialism; it also needed to produce and disseminate an imagined geography of the country. This returns us to the photograph of two women weaving baskets, for this chapter will argue for the salience of photography in the attempt to build socialism in Democratic Kampuchea.

In his seminal work *Camera Lucida*, Roland Barthes introduces the concepts of *stadium* and *punctum*.[1] For Barthes, there is often a typical viewing, or *stadium*, of a photograph that refers to the banal, self-evident referential quality of a photograph. Thus, in figure 5.1, we see two women weaving baskets. However, there may also be something that interrupts, or disturbs, the photograph. Highly idiosyncratic, the *punctum* is neither a technical artifact nor a product of the photographer's intention; it is a quality derived from an active, engaged viewing of the photograph. Thus when we look more closely at figure 5.1, we notice the enlarged earlobe of the woman on the right. This

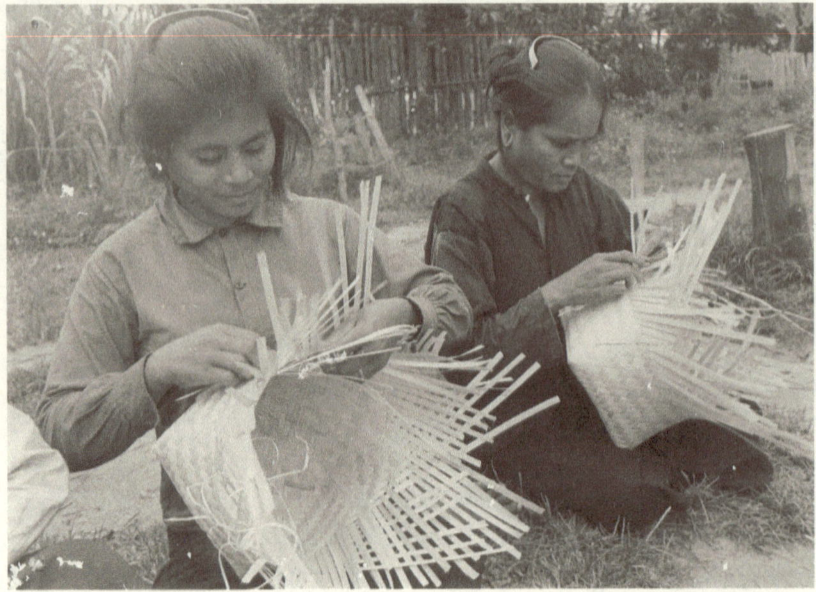

Figure 5.1. Women making *smok* (baskets) in Democratic Kampuchea. Courtesy of the Documentation Center of Cambodia Archives.

indicates that the women are perhaps affiliated with one of the indigenous groups of Cambodia. They are not Khmer, but perhaps Jarai, Bunong, or Tampeun. Also, the women are dressed not in indigenous clothing but in garb most commonly associated with the Khmer Rouge: black and what appears to be olive-green khaki.

There are sufficient contradictions apparent in figure 5.1 to lead us to question the presumed authenticity of the photograph. Given the context of the image—taken during the Khmer Rouge era—one begins to speculate that it forms part of an archive of photographic representations of *landscapes* that circulated throughout Democratic Kampuchea as a means of promoting a particular geographical imagination of a state in the making. In this chapter, landscape "is positioned . . . as a material signifier of identification with land, territory and environments which contribute towards formal and informal connectedness with national cultures and citizenship."[2]

As James Duncan explains, "by becoming part of the everyday, the taken-for-granted . . . the landscape masks the ideological nature of its form and content."[3] This holds for landscape photography and relates to my overall thesis. In this manner, landscape photography was a mode of public pedagogy that effectively captures the visuality of geographical knowledge.[4] Here visuality refers to the ways we see but also to how and what we are able, or allowed, to see.[5] As Gillian Rose writes, a key issue is "the ways in which particular visualities structure certain kinds of geographical knowledges, knowledges—and thus visualities—that are always saturated with power relations."[6] An engagement with visuality, in short, enables scholars to view cultural products, such as photographs, as "having meaning and value beyond their textual content."[7]

Landscape photography is not simply a mimetic representation of the landscape but an active participant in framing and constructing landscapes around certain political-geographic imaginaries.[8] This chapter explores Khmer Rouge–era photographs, many of which appeared in various issues of *Revolutionary Flag* or *Revolutionary Youth*, and argues that these images were circulated in an attempt to convey a particular geographical imagination of nation building. The concept of authentic simulacra is further developed as a means of moving beyond rote binaries of photographs—that is, as either truthful representations or propaganda. In short, photographs constitute a visual aspiration to the type of society to be built.

Landscape Photography as Political Instrument

Following Richard Schein, the representation of landscape is "central to ongoing cultural and social reproduction."[9] The representation of landscapes, in other words, is not simply a neutral activity; it is highly politicized—although the depth of this politicization may not be self-evident. As Don Mitchell writes, "Landscapes transform the facts of place into a controlled representation, an imposition of order in which . . . dominant ways of seeing are substituted for all ways of seeing and experiencing."[10]

Since its inception, photography has emerged as a widely employed media of landscape representation and, by extension, a politically important instrument of nation building. Indeed, the photograph "extended the authority of visual truth from the realm of actual experience to the verisimilitude of photographic realism."[11] Tim Hall, to this end, notes that "the idea of the photograph as a true record is almost universally accepted."[12] Steven Hoelscher likewise writes of the "thoroughly convincing illusion of factuality" of photographs.[13] The power of photography derives from its apparent mimetic quality—its ability to ostensibly represent the real world in an authentic, truthful, objective manner—thereby obfuscating its artificial basis. From this vantage point, one that judicial systems are often quick to uphold, photographs become key documentary and evidential sources. Photographs introduce a *legal ordering* to that which is depicted, a seemingly clear picture of reality. Herein lies the power and paradox of photographic representation. Photographs are powerful devices that purport to authentically represent reality, yet the images produced and reproduced are anything but authentic.[14] Viewed from this perspective, the photograph appears less "a record of reality" or "evidential document" than "something that is embedded within and part of a number of cultural contexts."[15] Photographs of everyday landscapes, for example, are selected and framed: What (or who) is included in the photography? From what angle is the photograph taken? Myriad decisions underlie the physical act of taking a photograph. Likewise, of the innumerable photographs taken, which will be reproduced? In what context will the images be shown?

Geographers especially have reconsidered the photographic representation of place. As Gillian Rose finds, "Instead of using [photographs] as descriptive illustrations that simply show what a location looked like when the shutter snapped, increasing numbers of geographers are thinking about the ways that photographs can be active players in the construction of a range of different kinds of geographical knowledge."[16] These methodologies, Mia Hunt explains, "see photographs as partial fragments and tend to use them as objects of analysis, embedded and meaningful in the cultural context of their production, capture, and site of viewing."[17] Consequently, geographers "have begun engaging directly with creative arts practice."[18] This engagement is important insofar as it calls attention to a greater sensitivity to the production of artistic productions and the inherent power dimensions of geographic representations. Photographs are thus not merely objects of interpretation; rather their appearance—both in terms of content and of coming into existence—signifies a complex and relational process. In short, photographic research methods of landscape interpretation "promote reflexive engagements" and "have the potential to open up questions around the politics of representation."[19]

This reflexive engagement is necessary when interpreting the Khmer Rouge photographic record and affords us the opportunity to see photographs not solely or exclusively as instruments of propaganda but rather as active participants in the CPK's attempt to build socialism.

A helpful analogy to understand Khmer Rouge photography as authentic simulacra is that of contemporary writings on the "subjunctive documentary." In recent years, considerable attention has been directed toward the production and viewing of fiction-driven science documentaries, especially those reliant on technological advances in computer-generated imaging.[20] To this end, Mark Wolf explains, "Whereas most documentaries are concerned with documenting events that have happened in the past, and attempt to make photographic records of them, computer imagining and simulation are concerned with what could be, would be or might have been: they form a subgenre of documentary we might call subjective documentary, following the use of the term subjunctive as a grammatical tense."[21] Clearly the Khmer Rouge did not have access to technologies anywhere approaching CGI; yet, in a rudimentary sense, their use of photographs in revolutionary magazines was founded on a comparable instrumentality of representation. Subjunctive documentaries, for example, "are profoundly aggressive in their insistence that the fictions they are 'documenting' not only could be real but truly are real."[22] Likewise, the photographs reproduced by the Khmer Rouge in various political outlets were fictional in that they were often staged—but they were real in the sense of authentically projecting an image of what a socialist society would look like. Through a photographic representation of everyday life, the future was made present and rendered actionable.[23]

The landscape photographs of the Khmer Rouge are authentic simulacra of an anticipatory future. They are truthful copies of a future landscape that existed virtually in the rhetoric of the CPK. They are material representations of an immaterial geography imagined but not realized: scenes of communal and harmonious everyday life that were never experienced but served as pedagogic devices informing citizens of how life *should* be lived; of how life *could* be lived, if society adhered to the policy prescriptions forwarded by the CPK. Poetry, song, and dance conveyed lessons of proper behavior and correct attitudes that were normative in scope. Landscape photographs reinforced these lessons and—critically important for a semiliterate society—provided visual "proof" of what society was to become. The artistic reproduction of communal life worked in unison with other creative expressions advanced by the CPK. That the landscape photographs of the Khmer Rouge appeared in public magazines and, especially, elementary school textbooks is therefore not inconsequential. The appearance of landscape photographs in Khmer Rouge publications served to reinforce ongoing efforts both to build socialism and to build Democratic Kampuchea itself.[24] Khmer Rouge photographs are thus understood as a form of public pedagogy, namely, a visual teaching instrument.[25] However, we must remain cognizant—as were the Khmer Rouge—that photographs are anything but neutral, apolitical material objects.[26] The CPK, I suggest, well understood the political power of photographic representation and that the effectiveness of photographs is found in the supposed truthfulness of photography's apparent mimetic quality.

The Authenticity of Geographical Imaginations

The CPK, we have seen, achieved victory but lacked widespread popular support. Moreover, the CPK realized that it was necessary to build socialism and to cultivate a proper political consciousness among its citizenry. This in turn required the nurturing of a collective vision of what Democratic Kampuchea was to become. Geographic education, therefore, would assume prominence in the nation-building practices of the Khmer Rouge. Having smashed most conventional modes of instruction, the CPK initiated several pedagogic practices that utilized artistic productions: poetry, song, and dance. Print materials, including textbooks and magazines, would disseminate lessons creatively, often focused on the everyday life of men, women, and children—that is, the imagined everyday life of a prosperous, communal society.

Both the textbooks and the magazines produced by the Khmer Rouge were especially visual, with numerous photographs reproduced in them. In part, the frequent use of photographs is tied to the dismal literacy of Democratic Kampuchea's citizens. Literacy prior to the Khmer Rouge victory was limited throughout the country, and the CPK made little concrete progress in promoting the ability to read or write. Consequently, photography was an important means of communicating to the citizenry the proper political consciousness required by the CPK in its effort to build socialism. Photographs were also important to portray Democratic Kampuchea as it might be. Geographical imaginations "make it possible to create a future that is different from the

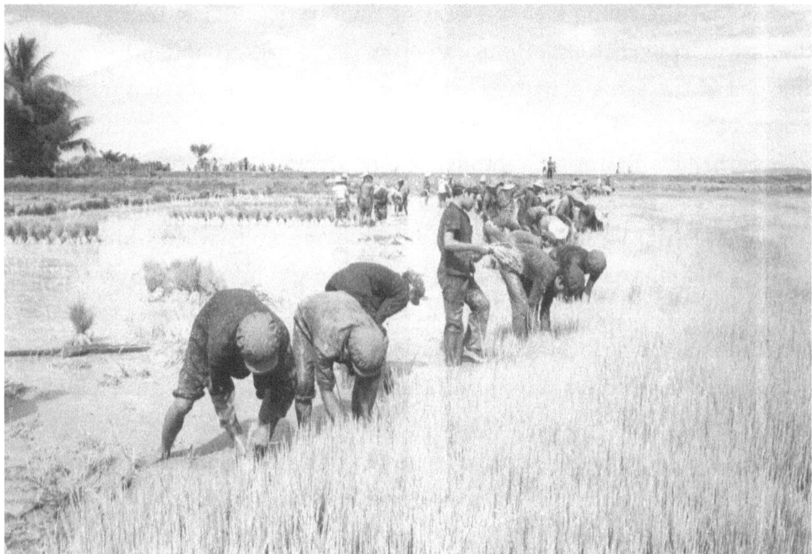

Figure 5.2. Khmer Rouge soldiers harvesting rice. Courtesy of the Documentation Center of Cambodia Archives.

present although its seeds are in the present."[27] Stated differently, the future geographies of Democratic Kampuchea were to be built on the present conditions of revolution; proper attitudes, ideas, and behaviors of present-day activities provided the path forward, and these were to be illustrated in myriad depictions of everyday landscapes.

Gillian Rose argues that "the production, circulation and consumption of photographs produce and reproduce the imagined geographies of the social group or institution for which they were made."[28] Just so, it would be too simplistic to dismiss Khmer Rouge–era photographs as propaganda (in the conventional usage of this term) or as inauthentic representations of a planned communal utopia. It is more appropriate to view these images as authentic simulacra of an imagined geography. Figure 5.2, for example, depicts a scene that would be, at a certain level, immediately recognizable to the majority of men, women, and children throughout Democratic Kampuchea. In the foreground, a group of young men are gathering *dak samnap* (rice seedlings) and tying these together into *kandap* (bundles) for transplanting. Closer inspection reveals that the young men are wearing military-issue caps, indicating that they are most likely Khmer Rouge soldiers. In the background, other men are engaged in the same activity. These men, however, are wearing traditional woven hats.

Superficially, figure 5.2 reproduces a moment not out of the ordinary; indeed, it is a scene that one finds every planting season in Cambodia today. What is significant is the apparent cooperation between Khmer Rouge soldiers and villagers. Stylistically, the photograph informs the viewer that there is no distinction between the Khmer Rouge and ordinary citizens. This is a common theme reflected in countless Khmer Rouge songs, slogans, and poems, in that soldiers were also farmers, and farmers were also soldiers. Collectively, all citizens of Democratic Kampuchea were to produce for their country. It should be noted that all people depicted in the photograph are young and healthy, and the seemingly endless rice paddies convey a sense of prosperity and abundance. Both nature and society exhibit a palpable vitality, a life full of promise and potential. The lesson is clear: through cooperation and hard work, Democratic Kampuchea would become a cornucopia.

A similar photograph (not reproduced here) appears in the October 1975 issue of *Revolutionary Youth*.[29] This photograph, however, depicts several young women transplanting rice; the caption indicates that the photograph was taken at the Trapeang Thom Subdistrict Cooperative in Takeo Province. Here the dialectics of photograph and text are readily apparent, in that the photograph is incorporated within an article titled "In the New Current Phase of the Revolution, Our Youth Must Constantly Strengthen Their Stance of Absolute and Seething Class Struggle." The article begins with the pronouncement "Peace has come to Kampuchean territory again." This statement is depicted visually, in that photographs illustrate agrarian activities as opposed to armed conflict. The article continues: "The new Kampuchean society is a society without exploiters, a society in which the worker-peasant people live in equality, in harmony, in an atmosphere of solidarity where everyone performs labor on offensives together to produce night and day in order to defend and built the country. This is a concrete fact that cannot be denied."[30] Both text and visual images reinforce the solidarity of communal labor, of the necessary sacrifices that are required of all youth. The article warns, however, that animosity and incorrect views have not been eliminated. "There are still ideologies of status, ranks, position, function, and personal achievements," the article continues, and "there is not yet to be seen any correct revolutionary worldview toward the matters of honor, dignity, glory, or superiority at all." Indeed, the article states, "In today's new Kampuchean society, whether in the production cooperatives or in the offices, ministries, or in the various work sites of the revolution or in each unit of the army of inside each of us individually, there is ongoing combat between personal feelings and communal feelings, between individual interests and collective interests." Therefore, readers are warned that "revolutionary youth must continue to strive and concentrate on strengthening a constantly seething stance of class struggle." This is to be accomplished, in part, through a constant "fight to build, indoctrinate, strengthen, and expand the Party's proletarian stance to reach one's self, to reach the ranks of our revolutionary youth" and to arm themselves with "the four essential proletarian qualities of the Party: the highest sacrifice, the sharpest combat, unconditional respect for organizational discipline, and unceasing innovation and building."[31] The photographs of young men and women tending to the harvest, accordingly, provide visual reinforcement to the text-based lessons of collective labor, discipline, hard work, and sacrifice. Thus even if readers were only semiliterate, the photographic depiction of everyday scenes served as pedagogic instruments that reinforced party policy. At this point, it matters little if the photographs were staged or not, for they functioned as authentic simulacra of what could be achieved in Democratic Kampuchea.

Landscape photographs of agrarian work teams provided another key lesson: these activities were (seemingly) ubiquitous throughout the country, as young men and women were working diligently, without complaint, in cooperatives organized by Angkar. When juxtaposed with one's immediate existence, the photographs functioned as subtle lessons to remain ever vigilant in one's efforts. The unstated message is clear: You may be enduring hardships, you may experience starvation and disease, but with the proper work ethic and the correct political consciousness, you too might elevate your cooperative to the scenes depicted in the magazine. A better life is possible, as illustrated by healthy young people working amid plentiful rice fields.

Both figures 5.3 and 5.4 convey analogous messages. Figure 5.3 depicts four young men working in a *rong masin a-chheu* (small-scale sawmill). At least two of the men are wearing *krama* (traditional checkered scarves), while a third is wearing a military-issue cap. As in the agricultural photograph, this image

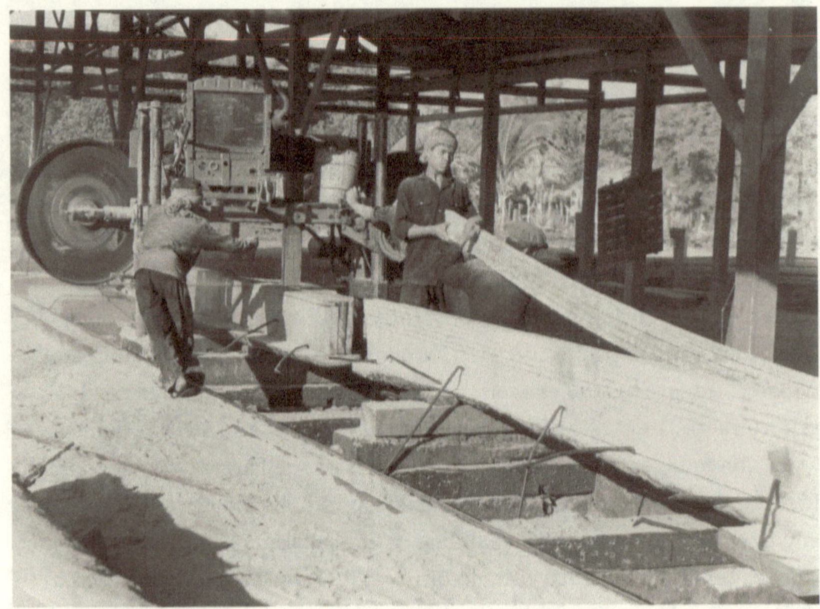

Figure 5.3. Khmer Rouge cadre working in a sawmill. Courtesy of the Documentation Center of Cambodia Archives.

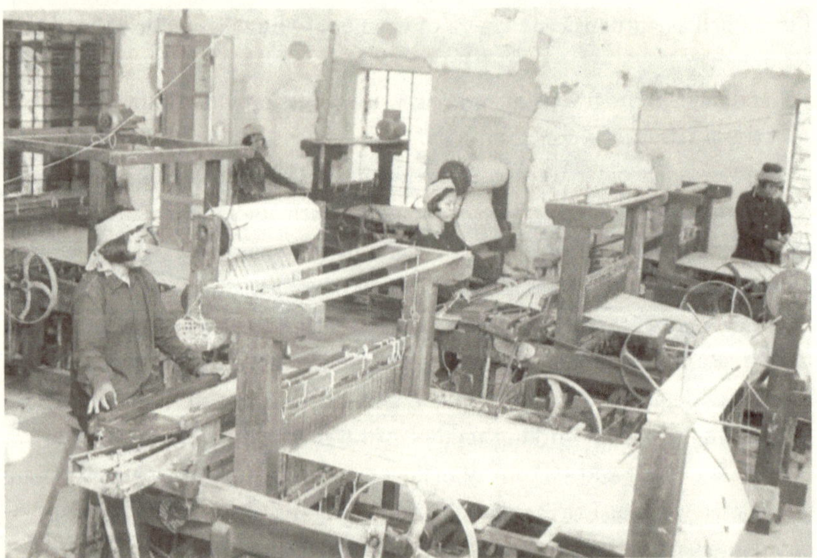

Figure 5.4. Female Khmer Rouge cadre working in a textile factory. Courtesy of the Documentation Center of Cambodia Archives.

expresses the close cooperation between soldier and citizen. Furthermore, the photograph highlights the industrial potential of Democratic Kampuchea through the use of modern technology. This is a theme developed as well in figure 5.4, in which three young women, all dressed in identical black pants and blouses, are making textiles—possibly *krama*—with semiautomatic machines (*kei dambanh peak kandal svay prawat*). The women are deep in concentration, focused solely on their activities. Moreover, the wide-angle view of the photograph emphasizes the abundance of machines producing textiles: a modern factory, similar to the rice fields, promising abundance and prosperity through communal—and dedicated—labor.

In terms of photographic style, figures 5.5 and 5.6 depict an aesthetic quality that viewers, then and now, might imagine on a postcard. Shot at an angle, and thus giving the illusion of extending into infinity, figure 5.5 illustrates a series of *phteah kumrou* (houses) being constructed. All houses are identical, with a single staircase leading to a single door, two windows, and pitched roofs. The style of house is common throughout rural Cambodia, as is the communal activity of house building. The landscape surrounding the houses has been recently cleared, and a dining hall is visible in the lower right background. Building materials include timber, cement, and iron. This photograph thus conveys a scene that is immediately familiar, yet it also highlights other economic strategies promoted by the CPK. Increases in agricultural production were required; these necessitated the expansion of agricultural lands and the large-scale use of irrigation. Forested lands were to be cleared, dams, canals, dikes, and reservoirs to be built. This often necessitated the forced relocation of people to the work sites and, in the process, the construction of new settlements. Figure 5.5 therefore naturalizes both the territorial expansion of Khmer Rouge economic activities and the continuity with pre–Khmer Rouge village life.

Crucially, the depiction of communal living in figure 5.5 normalizes the concentration of men, women, and children into communes. Various forms of communes and cooperatives were established as early as 1973, but following victory in 1975, the CPK intensified its effort to bring its citizenry together in camps. Within Democratic Kampuchea, communes and cooperatives were crucial nodes in the purported effort to improve the people's livelihoods and increase surplus value through the export of agricultural commodities. As detailed in 1975, following liberation of the country, the "co-operative movement [had] been mightily and ceaselessly strengthened and expanded."[32] Indeed,

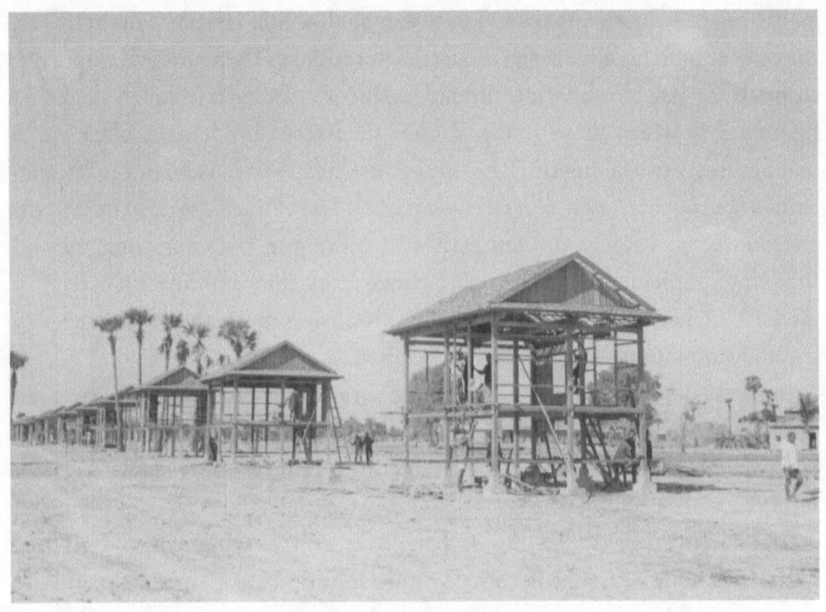

Figure 5.5. Model houses (*phteah kumrou*) constructed in Democratic Kampuchea. Courtesy of the Documentation Center of Cambodia Archives.

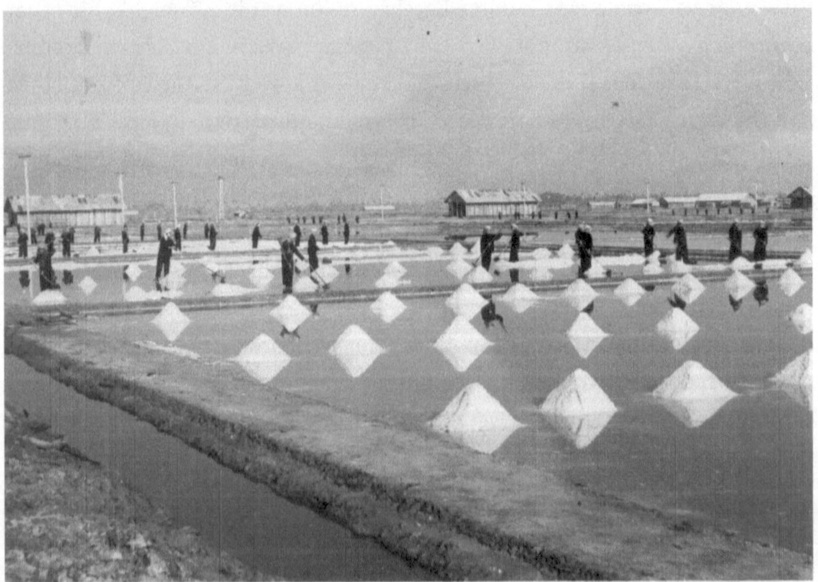

Figure 5.6. Salt production in Democratic Kampuchea. Courtesy of the Documentation Center of Cambodia Archives.

according to this account provided by the CPK, "Since liberation 99.9 percent of the Cambodian people [had] all been obliged to live in the country so as to be able to participate in the movement to increase production to sustain themselves and contribute to defending and building the country."[33]

As Virginia Blum and Anna Secor explain, material spaces, that is, the lived, day-to-day spaces, are not simply lived in recognizable, Euclidean terms; rather, these material spaces are also psychic spaces.[34] From this observation, we understand that the spaces of environmental transformation—the cleared forests, the canals and reservoirs, and the agricultural fields—are also spaces of psychological transformation. The establishment by the CPK of communes and cooperatives in Democratic Kampuchea demonstrates clearly how "material and psychic spaces are inseparable from one another."[35] According to the CPK leadership, "In the cooperatives there is correct and clear organization, firm and conscientious organizational discipline, lifestyle meetings, regularly held criticism/self-criticism meetings, constant political and cultural study meetings. . . . [The] cooperative movement is constantly and mightily agitating, rapidly progressing in terms of political stances and revolutionary ideology, organization, work capacity, culture, and daily living standards."[36] As concentrations of forced laborers, communes and cooperatives facilitated the transformation of Cambodia's physical environment and, subsequently, the production and distribution of agricultural commodities; however, as biopolitical technologies of control, these camps also served to transform political consciousness in conformity with the ongoing revolution. In turn, the photographic representation of communal living was a necessary condition to normalize such transformations and to imply continuity with traditional Khmer practice.

Figure 5.6 likewise illustrates the continuity of pre–Khmer Rouge practice with CPK policy. Also shot from an angle, figure 5.6 depicts *pumnouk* (salt production). In the heat and humidity of Cambodia, salt is extremely important for preserving fish and other foodstuffs. However, salt flats are not ubiquitous throughout the country; indeed, only a few sites are noted for salt production. Although the precise location is not indicated on this photograph, it was most likely taken at Sre Ampil, located in present-day Kampot Province. This region was, and remains, Cambodia's principle source of salt. Here, the photograph depicts scores of women—all dressed identically—tending to the production of salt. Closer inspection reveals that the women are posed; they are not actually working. The symmetry of the photograph belies also the reality of salt production as a backbreaking activity. Furthermore, many of the women in the photograph are simultaneously holding salt brooms *and* rifles. As a staged photograph, figure 5.6 highlights that the women likewise were to function as both soldiers and workers.

Taken as a whole, the photographs reveal key dominant narratives. It should be noted, for example, the very apparent sex and age segregation of the photographs. This dovetails with the overall divisions of labor forwarded by the CPK. In Democratic Kampuchea, the Khmer Rouge's Revolutionary Army served as a model for citizens to emulate. Laboring masses of people became "fighting forces," and work efforts were promoted in the language of offensive operations. Functionally, the citizenry of Democratic Kampuchea were divided into teams based on age and sex. As discussed in chapter 2, adults, people between fourteen and fifty years old, were assigned to groups known as *kang chalet*. Males served in *kang boroh* and females in *kang neary*. These two groups often performed the heaviest tasks, including plowing fields and constructing irrigation projects. Older members of Democratic Kampuchea—those fifty and above—were grouped into work teams known as *senah chun*. These teams were also segregated by sex, with males assigned to *senah chun boroh* and females to *senah chun neary*. Last, children (i.e., those under fourteen) were organized into *kang komar*, with boys and girls separated into *kang komara* and *kang khomarie*, respectively. These age- and sex-based divisions of labor are routinely naturalized throughout the photographs circulated by the CPK; indeed, rare is the photograph that depicts men and women in the same scene.[37]

Another narrative common to these photographs is the depiction of men and women actively performing labor. Simply put, in all photographs, people are *laboring*. There is no evidence of indolence or idleness; both citizens and soldiers are vigorously—but stoically—attacking and transforming nature. Consequently, landscape photographs circulated by the CPK illustrate an ongoing effort to transform nature into productive uses and, in the process, cultivate a proper political consciousness. These visual lessons are again reinforced in text. An undated issue of *Revolutionary Youth*, for example, includes an article titled "The New Revolutionary Worldview of Our Kampuchean Youth with Regard to Knowledge."[38] Here the CPK's geographical imagination is plainly intertwined with the attempt to build socialism. "After the liberation of the whole country," the article explains, "the Party educated our Kampuchean youth to love the nation, to love the territory, to love the people, and agitated for all of them to join in the great movement to increase production in order to defend and build the country rapidly." The article continues: "Our Kampuchean youth all joined the great movement to increase production because of the Party's education and propaganda and indoctrination in terms of worldview and political, ideological and organizational stances. Also, *when they joined intimately in the life of the worker-peasant people and became personally involved in doing productive labor, the worldview of our Kampuchean youth rapidly changed.*"[39] This last sentence effectively presents the CPK's understanding of the transformative potential of physical labor. Only when the youth began to actively transform nature productively did their worldview change. Consequently, not only is the promotion of artistic productions, such as poems, songs, and photographs, employed as a form of public pedagogy but also labor itself becomes a form of education, learning activities that dialectically suture policies between the base and the superstructure. The article concludes:

> Now, our Kampuchean youth see clearly that the major and the highest knowledge in the world is the knowledge and know-how of increasing production. Anyone who knows how to increase production can then live in honor and dignity. Therefore, our Kampuchean youth concentrate on going all-out to study rice farming, to study plowing and harrowing and transplanting, to study cattle tending, to join in the movement to put up dams, to put up paddy dikes in order to sort out the problems of water to increase production non-stop, day and night. . . . This is the worldview of Kampuchean youth toward the social knowledge and know-how that they must study.[40]

Last, what is distinctive about these photographs is precisely their indistinctiveness. There is a comfortable familiarity, a reassuring continuity between past, present, and future. No doubt viewers would immediately recognize these photographs as representations of their everyday world. Thus despite the revolution and the newly established government, life—as depicted in the photographs—was for the most part unchanged. Yet there are multiple absences in the photographs: familial attachments, for example, are not visible. There is no *personal* connection; individuals are present, but social relations are missing. Likewise, hardships and suffering are not made visible. At this point, the reception of these photographs by those who suffered and endured during the reign of the Khmer Rouge remains unclear. One can only speculate at this point on the contradictions that must have been experienced by those men, women, and children who lived and died in a reality far removed from the imaginative geographies depicted in these photographs. Further research is required to flesh out the disconnection between the landscapes inhabited by the viewers and the landscapes depicted.

Conclusions

The Communist Party of Kampuchea achieved military victory on April 17, 1975. However, despite having emerged triumphant on the battlefield, the CPK still needed to secure political consolidation of Cambodia. In 1975, the CPK was a relatively weak political organization; it did not have the widespread support of the majority of Cambodia's population. Consequently, it used both force and artwork in its effort to build socialism. Geographic education was thus crucial to the nationalist agenda set forth by the CPK; this included both the production of educational textbooks and magazines and, in the process, the widespread circulation of photographs.

Geographers and other social scientists have made important contributions to the important role of photography in bearing witness to the unimaginable horrors that consumed much of the twentieth century.[41] Photography, in this sense, provides a crucial evidentiary role. However, scholarship has also revealed the inauthenticity of photographs, that photographs are also used as instruments of aesthetic interventions or brute propaganda. Photographs are thus viewed as *inauthentic* from the standpoint of "truthful" representations. For scholars—but also activists in pursuit of social and legal justice—this paradox of photographic truth and nontruth poses a dilemma.

In recognition of the paradox of photography, this chapter reconsiders landscape photographs produced and reproduced during the Khmer Rouge era not as simple forms of propaganda but as modes of instruction. When viewing these photographs, we are witnessing the *photographic production of a nationalist landscape*. As a result, such photographs are *authentic simulacra* in their truthful or faithful representation of how the CPK envisioned both the revolution and the subsequent administration of Democratic Kampuchea. These photographs depict scenes that are immediately familiar yet convey a sense of the new. However, photographs often hide as much as they reveal.

Accordingly, it is necessary to consider not only what is *present* in the image but also what is *absent*. In recent years, geographers have given attention to absence in a variety of settings, including, for example, landscapes of industrial ruins and necro-geographies.[42] Here, the concept of "absent-presence" is especially salient in an examination of landscape photographs.

Following Avril Maddrell, an absent-presence "reflects the apparently contradictory binding together of things absent with the present."[43] In other words, conceptually, it is necessary to articulate both what is *represented* in the photograph and what is *not presented*. This poses, as Maddrell rightly notes, an apparent oxymoron: how is it possible to see what is not seen? For historical research, this poses less of a problem, in that we have the benefit of hindsight. In the case of Cambodia, for example, we know that upward of two million people died, yet in the landscape photographs distributed for public consumption, there are (understandably) no corpses visible. This is not to deny that the CPK did not photograph those who died or were killed. Indeed, numerous postmortem photographs exist from Democratic Kampuchea.[44] My concern at this point, however, is less that overt violence is absent in landscape photographs than that ideology is present in the landscape. As political instruments, landscape photography and geographic education were just as central to nation building in Democratic Kampuchea as were forms of political violence.

6 Conclusions

In a well-known passage appearing late in the third volume of *Capital*, Marx differentiates between the "realm of necessity" and the "true realm of freedom." His comments appear in the context of labor productivity, surplus value, and, broadly, the length of the working day. He begins: "The realm of freedom really begins only where labor determined by necessity and external expediency ends; it lies by its very nature beyond the sphere of material production proper."[1] Reflecting his materialist conception of history, Marx seems to imply that true freedom can only come about *after the basic conditions of life* have been satisfied, that is, food, water, and shelter. He explains, "Just as the savage must wrestle with nature to satisfy his needs, to maintain and reproduce his life, so must civilized man, and he must do so in all forms of society and under all possible modes of production."[2] In other words, humanity cannot escape its biological constraints; and any mode of production—presumably, therefore, even Communism—would be forever limited by the necessary conditions of social reproduction. Certainly, these conditions change with transformations in social organization and technology. Marx writes, "This realm of natural necessity expands with his development, because his needs do too; but the productive forces to satisfy these expand at the same time."[3] Implicitly Marx calls attention to the increased economic productivity under capitalism. However, he cautions that mere economic growth does not lead to "freedom" because the demands of individuals and society also change. This captures his fundamental observation and critique of capitalism, that under this mode of production wealth was accumulated at a greater rate, and to a larger extent, than at any other moment in human history, yet amid all this affluence countless men, women, and children still lived in poverty. Freedom in other words was not possible simply because of increased productivity. Something else was missing.

A partial answer is provided by Marx. He continues: "Freedom, in this sphere [i.e., the realm of necessity], can consist only in this, that socialized man, the associated producers, govern the human metabolism with nature in a rational way, bringing it under their collective control instead of being dominated by it as a blind power; accomplishing it with the least expenditure of energy and in conditions most worthy and appropriate for their human nature."[4] At this point, Marx postulates that within communal society, where society is organized collectively and human beings are no longer constrained by unseen forces, freedom can exist within the realm of necessity. However, this is not true freedom, for humanity is still compelled to work to reproduce life itself. In other words, the realm of necessity is forever a sphere of necessary production. True or authentic freedom for Marx appears only *beyond* this realm. He concludes: "The true realm of freedom, the development of human powers as an end in itself, begins beyond it, though it can only flourish with this realm of necessity as its basis."[5] What constitutes this utopian realm of freedom that lies beyond the sphere of necessary production and, more precisely, why does Communism alone seem to promise an escape from ceaseless toil and unfreedom? The answer, I maintain, provides insight not only into the creative expression of art under the Communist Party of Kampuchea but also clarifies a political praxis for contemporary society. Consequently, in this concluding chapter, I move beyond Democratic Kampuchea, to draw lessons from the dialectics of art and politics under the Khmer Rouge in an effort to recontextualize a Marxist-based progressive politics.

Freedom, Necessity, and the Khmer Rouge

Marx's writings on freedom and necessity, especially as they appear in the third volume of *Capital*, have attracted much interest and have generated substantial debate.[6] Notably, these debates pivot on the fundamental question of revolutionary transformations. As introduced earlier, for Marx, systemic contradictions within any given mode of production will necessarily lead to revolutionary transformations. Within capitalism, for example, the contradictions between the forces of production and the relations of production would grow to a point whereby the proletariat would become aware of their alienated existence and subsequently overthrow the exploitative ruling class. Once free of their oppressors, workers would live in a nonexploitative, harmonious, and unalienated communal society. Yet, does the passage in volume 3 indicate for Marx a "less hopeful and more realistic" view of Communism, a future where alienation remains albeit under a different guise?[7] Indeed, many commentators read into this passage a proposal that necessary labor—the labor required to satisfy basic human needs—is incompatible with genuine freedom.[8] Thus many scholars find in this passage proof that Marx, writing later in life, had changed his views on Communism. Specifically, his positing of humanity's inability to escape the realm of necessity is read as confirmation that alienation is an enduring feature of the human condition and not a defining feature of capitalism.[9] Herbert Marcuse, for example, notes that "the realm of necessity would remain a realm of alienation."[10]

To begin, it is first necessary to define more precisely our terms of operation. For Marx, the realm of necessity is relatively straightforward. This is the sphere of necessary production; it includes those activities required for individual and collective survivability. Consequently, regardless of the overall mode of production, humanity is always conditioned by the requirements of biological reproduction. Of course, as noted in the above passage, with advances in technology, coupled with more efficient and effective production methods, men and women theoretically should achieve more freedom from the exigencies of their natural condition.[11] In other words, with greater social organization, humanity moves beyond the limitations imposed by nature; rather than being subjected to the blind forces of the physical world, men and women begin to assume more direct control over their own reproduction. Under capitalism, however, something curious happens. On the one hand, "productive power reaches unprecedented levels of development" and thus "should provide the means to humanize labor," but in actuality "the rich development of the social production is in stark contrast to the stunted development of the individual."[12] Men and women are freed from the physical limits of nature but remain mired in a condition of unfreedom. Why? According to Marx, the answer is that seemingly blind market forces have replaced the physical forces of nature, leading to a condition of alienation. Consequently, as noted in chapter 1, men and women living within a capitalist society are precluded from developing an unestranged consciousness. A Communist transformation is therefore necessary, for it is through collective *self-determination* that men and women exercise full, conscious control over their economic activities.[13] It is no surprise, therefore, that in Democratic

Kampuchea the promise of collective self-determination was a common refrain. Public speeches, internal reports, but also poems and songs reference themes of freedom from both physical nature and oppressive social relations of production. Only through collective labor, the CPK promised, could society be truly free and people would live in harmony.

Returning to Marx, true freedom is only found *beyond* the realm of necessity. For Kandiyali, freedom in this sense "is essentially one of individual self-realization, which consists . . . in the deployment and development of one's distinctly human powers and capacities."[14] David James expands on this idea, noting that freedom here refers not simply to the absence of constraints—whether these are "natural" or market related—but to a condition of expressive freedom.[15] This expressive freedom remains unrealized within capitalism, given that alienation is a systemic feature of a system of production for exchange. Within Communism, however, men and women are both free from constraints *and* positioned to cultivate their human capacities. James writes that, under Communism, "an individual's conscious, purposive activity and the results of this activity produce an external confirmation of his or her human essence. At the same time, he or she is able to realize him- or herself in the sense of exercising and developing certain powers associated with this essence by means of conscious activity which is free in that it is performed in accordance with ends which the agent has formed and chooses to realize through its own activity."[16] In short, whereas the realm of necessity is a realm of collective determination, the realm of true freedom is a realm of individual self-realization.

This reading of Marx's famous passage, I believe, is more faithful both to his materialist understanding of history and to a dialectical positioning of the individual within society. On the one hand, men and women can never leave the inescapable condition of their own physical constitution; some level of economic productivity will always be required, for the simple fact that unless food, water, and shelter are obtained, life is not possible. On the other hand, while all modes of production offer certain practices to obtain these basic material needs, only through the self-determination of individuals working collectively can a conditional freedom be achieved. True freedom, however, is only found beyond this limited realm of freedom. In other words, the realm of necessity and the true realm of freedom are not oppositional spheres of life but instead constitute a dialectical relationship between self-determination and self-realization. The former facilitates the latter; the latter materializes from the former.

When Marx postulates that "the realm of freedom actually begins only where labor which is determined by necessity and mundane considerations ceases," he is calling attention to the potential of realizing one's true creative expression. Under Communism, therefore, *individual* self-realization is made possible through *collective* self-determination. For this reason, "the paradigm of 'truly' free activity is art: an activity that is undetermined by the pressures and considerations of physical necessity, an end in itself."[17] Trotsky recognized this capacity, noting that "true art is unable not to be revolutionary, not to aspire to a complete and radical reconstruction of society."[18]

Throughout his writings, Trotsky contextualizes creative expression and artistic production as existing beyond the realm of necessity. For example, he suggests that "in the realm of artistic creation, the imagination must escape from all constraints and must under no pretext allow itself to be placed under bonds."[19] Artists, in other words, must be free from the worry of their own social reproduction; the basic conditions of life must be assured. This is not to say that artists do not labor in society. Instead, it indicates that men and women must have the time necessary to express themselves creatively. This modality of individual self-realization can only happen under a condition of self-determination whereby all members of society interact communally under conditions free from oppression and exploitation. Trotsky elaborates:

> In a society which will have thrown off the pinching and stultifying worry about one's daily bread, in which community restaurants will prepare good, wholesome and tasteful food for all to choose, in which communal laundries will wash clean everyone's good linen, in which children, all the children, will be well-fed and strong and gay, and in which they will absorb the fundamental elements of science and art as they absorb albumen and air and the warmth of the sun, in a society in which electricity and the radio will not be the crafts they are today, but will come from inexhaustible sources of superpower at the call of a central button, in which there will be no "useless mouths," in which the liberated egotism of man . . . will be directed wholly towards the understanding, the transformation and the betterment of the universe—in such a society the dynamic development of culture will be incomparable with anything that went on in the past.[20]

In Democratic Kampuchea, communal forms of living were proposed and implemented: eating, cleaning, raising children were to be collective endeavors, reflecting the overall objective of the CPK to radically impose a society organized around collective self-determination, self-reliance, and self-mastery. Yet the crucial element of individuality was missing, for members of the CPK understood any semblance of personal identity as reactionary. The homogenization of all facets of life, from the style of dress to the type of haircut allowed, was in direct disagreement with the promise of freedom that, according to Marx and Trotsky, began beyond the realm of necessity. Artistic expression under the Khmer Rouge, consequently, reflected this misreading both in the manner in which poems, songs, and other art forms were produced and in the subject matter expressed in these productions. Artistic creations throughout Democratic Kampuchea were by and large not produced through individual free will; poems and songs were written not as ends in themselves but instead as objects produced as a means to an end. Art under the Khmer Rouge was produced by the party itself, designed to serve pragmatic ends, namely, pedagogic lessons of how socialism was to be built. Accordingly, artistic productions emphasized collective determination but remained silent on individual self-realization.

Trotsky warned that "the domain of art is not one in which the party is called upon to command."[21] Indeed, he was adamant that within the sphere of artistic production, "no one [was] going to prescribe themes to a poet or intend[ed] to prescribe them."[22] For Trotsky, "the actual development of art, and its struggle for new forms [were] not part of the Party's tasks, nor [was] it its concern."[23] He concludes: "The new forms must find for themselves, and independently, an access into the consciousness of the advanced elements of the working class as the latter develop culturally. Art cannot live and cannot develop without a flexible atmosphere of sympathy around it."[24]

Trotsky's pronouncements were written with an eye toward the heavy-handed and bureaucratic appropriation of art within the Soviet Union. His comments are equally applicable to Democratic Kampuchea, in that both societies exemplified a decidedly nondialectical understanding of collective self-determination and individual self-realization. Trotsky writes: "When the [futurists] propose to throw overboard the old literature of individualism, not only because it has become antiquated in form, but because it contradicts the collectivist nature of the proletariat, they reveal a very inadequate understanding of the dialectic nature of the contradiction between individualism and collectivism."[25] Likewise, the assertion among members of the CPK that individualism constituted a reactionary element that required being smashed revealed their misunderstanding of freedom itself. Indeed, an engagement with the production of art under the Khmer Rouge illustrates clearly how the concept of self-determination was misapplied with tragic consequences. Individual self-expression was anathema to the Khmer Rouge and thus marked a significant deviation from Marxist political philosophy. It does indicate, however, a greater degree of consonance with the bureaucratic functionality of Stalin's Soviet Union, whereby all segments of society—the arts, science, and so forth—were co-opted to serve not free individuals within a free collective society but instead the dictates of a vanguard party that ruled as a minority over the majority.

For Trotsky, the "very purpose of communism" was to "free finally and once and for all the creative forces of mankind from all pressure, limitation and humiliating dependence."[26] To this end, Trotsky averred that "personal relations, science and art will not know any externally imposed 'plan,' nor even any shadow of compulsion."[27] That such a society failed to materialize in Democratic Kampuchea following the Khmer Rouge's so-called Communist revolution is beyond question. What is necessary is to articulate more precisely how artistic productions were made to work in the CPK's attempt to build socialism.

Artistic Productions and Geographical Imaginations

Thus far I have argued that artistic productions under the Khmer Rouge reflect a misreading of Marx, that individual self-realization was brutally suppressed in a misguided attempt to reorganize society in a collective fashion. Simply put: the negation of individuality within a collective society marked a decidedly nondialectical understanding of both history and revolution. That being said, the Khmer Rouge did anticipate that art may provide a crucial means of building socialism. Given that the conditions for revolution were not present during the years of civil war, the CPK acted as a vanguard and brought about through military action the overthrow of the previous regime. The widely acknowledged need to build socialism was based on the plain fact that the people of Cambodia did not exhibit a proper political consciousness.

This posed a significant threat to the Khmer Rouge in that both economic productivity and national security were jeopardized. Poems, songs, dance, and photography were thus used as a form of public pedagogy, as political instruments engendered to instruct men, women, and children of the necessity and legitimacy of revolution but also of the society that would become. As Thomas Reed notes, "It is one thing to hear a political speech and remember an idea or two. It is quite another to sing a song and have its politically charged verses become emblazoned on your memory."[28]

Artistic productions appear as material records of the CPK's attempt to build socialism. Indicative of Marx and Engels's premise that "it is not consciousness that determines life, but life that determines consciousness," the CPK compelled by direct force hundreds of thousands of men, women, and children to labor incessantly for the party.[29] Through the transformation of nature—itself a stalwart of the operational objective of rapidly increasing economic productivity—individuals would also be transformed; a proper political consciousness of society writ large, one geared exclusively toward the dictates of Angkar, would in turn propel Democratic Kampuchea forward. Consequently, the dialectic of nature-society interactions figured prominently in poems, songs, dance, and photography.

The party-controlled production of art by the Khmer Rouge illustrates, to a certain extent, Trotsky's premise that "the revolution lays out the ground for a new society. But it does so with the methods of the old society, with the class struggle, with violence, destruction and annihilation."[30] Poems, songs, dance, and photography produced by the Khmer Rouge capture both the past and the future. On the one hand, artistic productions reflect the violent struggle of liberation, of the necessity of armed intervention in the overthrow of the former government and its civil and military apparatuses. On the other hand, these productions—but notably poems, song, and dance—marked a continuity with previous forms of creative expression. New lyrics were set to old musical scores, as were revolutionary ideas and ideals written in traditional forms of poetry. Where the Khmer Rouge departed was in its pragmatic and utilitarian repurposing of art.

The production of art under the Khmer Rouge was normative. These objects represented a particular geographical imagination of what Democratic Kampuchea was to become. Although outwardly illustrative of reality, artistic productions were in fact authentic simulacra, in that these materials expressed a faithful and genuine portrayal of how the CPK saw the future. Stripping aside their penchant for using the fiery rhetoric of waging war on agriculture or industry, the geographical imagination of the CPK was, at one level, that of a harmonious existence whereby all members of society benefited from collective self-determination amid a bountiful nature. Yet, at another level, this geographical imagination revealed a dark underbelly, where external and internal enemies threatened to destroy and negate past sacrifices. Vigilance was therefore required, and justice would be swift in an attempt to smash all who stood in opposition. Ironically, it was the systemic contradiction between an imagined and creatively expressed society resplendent with abundance and the brutal realities of hardship and suffering that engendered a pervasive sense of alienation among the people of Democratic Kampuchea. Few could fail to notice the disparities between the poetically expressed landscape bursting with melons and pumpkins and the harsh conditions of starvation food rations or of the discrepancy between healthy men and women happily dancing while working in rice fields with the stark presence of emaciated and diseased figures who labored under threat of execution. For the men, women, and children of Democratic Kampuchea, the freedoms promised through artistic expression were but a grim reminder of their decidedly unfree and alienated existence.

The Power of Artistic Productions

Recent years have witnessed a flourishing of scholarly studies on the progressive potential of art. The discipline of geography especially has experienced what some have described as a creative (re)turn—and for good reason.[31] Whereas geographers have long recognized the "relationship between geographical knowledge-making and creative practices," this recent turn has raised new "questions concerning politics and power."[32] Indeed, "engagement with the artful," Harriet Hawkins explains, "proffers the means to grasp the messy, unfinished and contingent—in everything from spatial imaginaries to knowledge-making practices—that a more scientifically inclined geography might orient us away from."[33] Yet we should remain mindful of Alan Ingram's injunction that any assessment of art and politics should begin with a critical and evaluative approach to the supposed emancipatory possibilities that have preoccupied much of the literature to date.[34]

To this end, an interpretation of the Khmer Rouge through *its artistic productions* offers an alternative reading of how violence transpired throughout Democratic Kampuchea. Rather than dismissing poems and songs as propaganda, one can reflect critically on the normative geographies imagined by the Khmer Rouge and how these creative expressions materialized in social, political, and economic policies and practices. However, an examination of artistic practice conducted under the Khmer Rouge provides a cautionary tale, a reminder that "creative interventions are best viewed as a form of power, an educational practice subject to wider social, political and economic contestations."[35] Creative geographies, Hawkins writes, "are often celebrated for challenging the spaces, strictures and structures of geographical knowledge making."[36] Poems and song, for example, may constitute political interventions that challenge hegemonic structures such as class, race/ethnicity, gender, and sexuality. The Khmer Rouge did not understand artistic productions as creative expressions of individuality, but poems, songs, dance, and photography were produced as political interventions necessary for a revolutionary transformation of society. High-ranking cadres of the CPK were anti-imperialist in orientation; they were anti-capitalist in orientation; they decried formal schools and other governmental institutions as apparatuses of the ruling class. Similar pronouncements are made repeatedly and routinely among progressive scholars today. Think, for example, of the myriad calls to challenge if not radically oppose the neoliberal university.[37]

A critical geographical understanding of art, Janet Banfield writes, "recognizes the power of art to shape as well as to reflect socio-spatial environments."[38] Such an approach calls into question the interplay of people, place, and nature but also of justice, freedom, and democracy. The political finds material expression in artistic production. Accordingly, as Hawkins concludes, "as creative practices increasingly become a part of the making of geographical knowledge, it is important that we remain alert not only to the potentials but also to the responsibilities of these practices."[39] Indeed, following Eric Magrane, "a poem can be a collaborator or an act of resistance."[40]

Over the past forty years, the Khmer Rouge has become the face of unmitigated evil. However, this portrayal—while not without justification—has been and continues to be politically charged. More precisely, the "actually existing socialism" of Democratic Kampuchea hangs as an albatross around the neck of progressive politics and potentially stymies efforts by geographers and other scholars to promote a leftist or progressive agenda.[41]

The Khmer Rouge is variously described as the embodiment of a "pure" socialism or Communism or Marxism or Stalinism or Maoism, or some combination thereof. Consider the statements of Benjamin Valentino on the Cambodian genocide specifically but Communist society in general. He writes that the "communist utopias" of the Soviet Union, China, and Cambodia represent "history's greatest slaughterhouses" and that it is "the revolutionary desire to bring about the rapid and radical transformation of society that distinguishes radical communist regimes from all other forms of government."[42] And existing scholarship has, in my opinion, largely failed in challenging these assertions. So what? Is not the Khmer Rouge a relic of the past? Beyond historical curiosity, why should we—and here I'm speaking primarily of scholars oriented to the political Left—pay any attention to the revolution and mass violence that defined Cambodia forty years ago?

A primary reason, I suggest, is because the Khmer Rouge is routinely held up by conservative scholars, commentators, and public pundits as exemplary of all things Marxist and thereby serve to counter the promotion of progressive agendas and critiques of neoliberalism. To the saying "there is no alternative to capitalism," conservatives can readily and happily call attention to the Khmer Rouge: *there is an alternative, and this is it*. If you don't like the free market, if you don't like private property, if you don't like deregulation, here is what you get. And leftist academics in particular are hamstrung in their response. Efforts to promote a critical pedagogy, for example, risk uncritical associations with the critical pedagogy advanced by the Khmer Rouge.

The Khmer Rouge and Marxist geographers drank from the same well; both studied Marx's *Capital* and Lenin's *Thesis on Imperialism*. It is no surprise, therefore, that rhetoric and hyperbole are disturbingly similar. The anti-imperialist and anticolonialist sentiments exhibited by the Khmer Rouge are echoed by contemporary calls for the decolonialization of education and critiques of the neoliberal university. Lurking beneath these proclamations of progressive and radical change, however, for conservative scholars and pundits, the bogeyman of the Khmer Rouge as an exemplar of "pure" Communism (or socialism or Marxism, or Maoism, or Stalinism, or whatever) remains a potent rejoinder. How is it possible, therefore, for leftist scholars to advocate progressive change when confronted with the menace of the Khmer Rouge?

We need, as Peter McLaren writes in *Antipode*, "to remain mindful of the Marxist humanist concern of revolutions turning into their opposite."[43] This is crucial, for the specter of the Khmer Rouge continues to haunt—and inform—American geopolitics.

The CPK advocated in theory a form of public pedagogy; it understood also the emancipatory potential of artistic practices. It erred, however, by imposing a stultifying—and ultimately oppressive and violent—system of mass conformity and discipline. It failed in that a truly communal society is conditioned on individual self-realization and liberation from systemic structures of oppression. If this factor is ignored, as Paula Allman and John Wallis explain, we end up with the kind of dogmatic, undemocratic, totalitarian practices that became the norm in states such as Democratic Kampuchea that claimed to be socialist or Communist.[44]

Caught in the crosshairs of neoliberal performativity, Gregory Martin and Tony Brown write, "The challenge for academics is to make 'defiant choices' in their teaching roles that are committed, political, and risky."[45] To this end, they explain, critical pedagogy is focused on creating and supporting contexts and forms of praxis capable of imagining alternative futures and enacting alternative ways of understanding the present.[46] Necessary, therefore, is an opportunity for thoughtful critique of all forms of inequality—class inequality, sexism, racism, ableism, discrimination against gay, lesbian, and transgendered persons—and of how these forms of inequality are structured within society.[47]

A critical pedagogy must be premised on the possibilities of transcending systemic forms of oppression; it must be able to present students with alternative geographical imaginations of the kinds of social relations on which a just society might be based. In other words, it is necessary, following Jane Wellens and her colleagues, both to teach about social transformation and to teach for social transformation. Thus "teaching about social transformation can lead to teaching for social transformations as the students' views are affected through a wider understanding of society."[48] Accordingly, artistic interventions, along with the study of such interventions, may provide an emancipatory challenge to the neoliberal university.[49] The Khmer Rouge forwarded a vulgar form of aesthetic politics that was counter to the emancipatory possibilities of artistic practices. Educators must not follow this same misguided path. For artistic practices to be truly liberating, such interventions must be engaged with open eyes. A critical engagement with artworks may effectively challenge structures of oppression but must be approached reflexively. The promotion of such practices must be situated within a context of individual self-realization and collective self-determination; students and activists must be afforded the space for full creative expression. To this end, artistic practices are understood as pedagogic interventions that employ "creative means to question and explore social problems and conflicts without necessarily prescribing solutions . . . and encourage more democratic alternatives."[50] To promote a progressive politics is to imagine geography differently, and a progressive politics is realized when we are able to freely express ourselves, creatively, unfettered by the violence of intolerance and injustice.

NOTES

Introduction

1. Etcheson, *Rise and Demise*; Kiernan, *How Pol Pot Came*; Chandler, *Tragedy of Cambodian History*; Kiernan, *Pol Pot Regime*; Becker, *When the War Was Over*; Heder, *Cambodian Communism*; Hinton, *Why Did They Kill?*; and Nhem, *Khmer Rouge*.

2. See, for example, LeVine, *Love and Dread in Cambodia*; and Mertha, *Brothers in Arms*.

3. On the nexus of art and politics, see, for example, Barron, *"Degenerate Art"*; Adam, *Art of the Third Reich*; and Petropoulos, *Art as Politics*. On the spatiality of aesthetic politics, see, for example, Gracyk, "Searching for the 'Popular'"; Dixon, "Creating the Semi-Living"; Ingram, "Making Geopolitics Otherwise"; Dikeç, "Beginners and Equals"; Hawkins, "Geography and Art"; Marston and De Leeuw, "Creativity and Geography"; V. Vickery, "Beyond Painting, beyond Landscape"; and Ingram, "Rethinking Art and Geopolitics."

4. Lukács, *History and Class Consciousness*; Lunn, "Marxism and Art"; Kadarkay, "Georg Lukács's Road"; Benjamin, "Work of Art"; Rancière, *Politics of Aesthetics*; Lewis, "Art or Propaganda?"; Rancière, "From Politics to Aesthetics?"; Rancière, "Thinking between Disciplines"; Rancière, *Dissensus*; and M. Jackson, "Aesthetics, Politics, and Attunement."

5. Pol Pot, *Long Live the 17th Anniversary*.

6. Au, *Reclaiming Communist Philosophy*, 1.

7. Eagleton, *Why Marx Was Right*, 184.

8. Ibid., 184.

9. Ibid., 17.

10. Au, *Reclaiming Communist Philosophy*, xxi.

11. Tyner, *From Rice Fields*. See also Tyner, "Violence"; Tyner, "Radical Geography and the Legacy"; and Tyner and Rice, "Cambodia's Political Economy of Violence."

12. Chandler, *Tragedy of Cambodian History*, 108.

13. Kiernan, "Conflict in Cambodia," 484.

14. Ibid.

15. The Communist movement in Cambodia, never a unified party to begin with, was further divided in accordance with Vietnamese needs. In an effort to protect the embattled KPRP, approximately one thousand Khmer Communists traveled to the DRV to receive military and political training; these men and women would not return until the early 1970s. A second group of Khmer revolutionaries would remain in Cambodia, with some participating overtly in political opposition to Sihanouk, while others worked covertly in an attempt to recruit party members.

16. Heder, *Cambodian Communism*. For alternative readings, see Kiernan, "Origins of Khmer Communism"; Thion, "Cambodian Idea of Revolution"; Etcheson, *Rise and Demise of Democratic Kampuchea*; Kiernan, *How Pol Pot Came*; and K. Jackson, "Ideology of Total Revolution."

17. Heder, *Cambodian Communism*, 32.

18. Pol Pot, *Long Live the 17th Anniversary*.

19. Etcheson, *After the Killing Fields*, 5.

20. Seekins, "Historical Setting," 43–44.

21. Etcheson, *After the Killing Fields*, 7.

22. Bombing raids would continue until the U.S. Congress called a halt to all American military operations in Cambodia in 1973.

23. Short, *Pol Pot*, 218.

24. Harvey, *Spaces of Capital*, 213.

25. Said, *Orientalism*.

26. Ashcroft and Ahluwalia, *Edward Said*, 61.

27. Gregory, "Lightning of Possible Storms."

28. Daniels, "Geographical Imagination," 182.

29. DeLeyser, "Authenticity on the Ground," 612.

30. Aitken and Zonn, "Re-Presenting the Place Pastiche," 16.

31. Hopkins, "Mapping of Cinematic Places," 60.

32. Baudrillard, *Simulacra and Simulation*.

33. Rancière, "Thinking between Disciplines," 1.

34. Dixon, "Creating the Semi-Living," 412.

35. Ibid.

36. Compare Ingram, "Making Geopolitics Otherwise," 218.

37. Ross, "Understanding Propaganda," 16.

38. Bartlett, *Aims of Political Propaganda*, 6. See also Lee, *How to Understand Propaganda*. For more recent historiographies of propaganda and politics, see Roberts, *Forward Soviet!*, and R. Taylor, *Film Propaganda*.

39. Compare Shaw and Sharp, "Playing with the Future," 342.

40. Ingram, "Making Geopolitics Otherwise," 218.

41. Beech, *Art and Value*, 211.

42. Ibid., 211.

43. Ibid., 213. See also Merleau-Ponty, *Adventures of the Dialectic*.

44. Beech, *Art and Value*, 213.

45. Jacoby, "Western Marxism," 581. See also P. Anderson, *Considerations on Western Marxism*; Gouldner, *Two Marxisms*; Long, "Marx and Western Marxism."

46. Jacoby, "Western Marxism," 582.

47. Ibid.

48. Beech, *Art and Value*, 213.

49. Ibid., 214.

50. Compare Castree, "Teaching History, Philosophy and Theory."

51. Beech, *Art and Value*, 215.

52. Harvey, *Spaces of Hope*, 5.

53. Henning, *Philosophy after Marx*, 13–14.

54. Ingram, "Rethinking Art and Geopolitics," 12.

55. Sharp, "Towards a Critical Analysis," 333.

56. Sherry and Schouten, "Role for Poetry," 218.

57. Sandlin and Milam, "Mixing Pop (Culture) and Politics"; Von Blum, "Paul Robeson"; Allsup and Shieh, "Social Justice and Music Education"; Loopmans, Cowell, and Oosterlynck, "Photography"; and Waldner and Dobratz, "Graffiti as a Form."

58. Giroux, "Public Pedagogy," 11.

59. Schuermans, Loopmans, and Vandenabeele, "Public Space," 676.

60. Schuermans, Loopmans, and Vandenabeele, "Public Space," 680.

61. Marston, "Khmer Rouge Songs."

62. Hall, "Camera Never Lies?," 455.

63. Hoelscher, "Photographic Construction of Tourist Space," 549.

64. Herb, "Double Vision," 143.

65. Harvey, *Spaces of Hope*.

66. N. Smith, "Neo-Critical Geography," 14.

Chapter 1. The Materiality of Art and Politics

1. Document No. E3/130 (00184022), "Communist Party of Kampuchea—Statute," archived by the Extraordinary Chambers in the Court of Cambodia (ECCC), http://www.eccc.gov.kh/en.

2. Cherne, "Cambodia—Auschwitz of Asia," 22. Admittedly in a previous publication I made a similar statement. See Tyner, *Genocide and the Geographical Imagination*, 15.

3. Marx and Engels, *German Ideology*, 36–37.

4. Ibid., 37.
5. Peet, *Global Capitalism*, 59.
6. D'Amato, *Meaning of Marxism*, 34.
7. Banaji, *Theory as History*, 51–52.
8. Marx, *Contribution to the Critique*, 20–21, emphasis added.
9. D'Amato, *Meaning of Marxism*, 35.
10. Ollman, *Dance of the Dialectic*, 12.
11. Ingersoll, Matthew, and Davison, *Philosophic Roots of Modern Ideology*, 119.
12. Marx and Engels, *German Ideology*, 42, emphasis added.
13. Marx, *Capital*, 1:103.
14. Marx and Engels, *German Ideology*, 42.
15. Marx, *Contribution to the Critique of Political Economy*, 11.
16. Paolucci, *Marx's Scientific Dialectics*, 194.
17. D'Amato, *Meaning of Marxism*, 35.
18. Marx, *Contribution to the Critique*, 21.
19. Ibid.
20. D'Amato, *Meaning of Marxism*, 36.
21. Ibid., 37.
22. Banaji, *Theory as History*, 47.
23. D'Amato, *Meaning of Marxism*, 37.
24. Banaji, *Theory as History*, 47–48.
25. Ibid., 48.
26. Ibid.
27. Quoted in D'Amato, *Meaning of Marxism*, 37.
28. Ibid., 38.
29. Marx and Engels, *Communist Manifesto*, 34–35.
30. D'Amato, *Meaning of Marxism*, 97.
31. Ibid., 113.
32. Hallas, "Toward a Revolutionary Socialist Party," 52.
33. Marx and Engels, *German Ideology*, 67.
34. Ibid.
35. Holt, *Social Thought of Karl Marx*, 52.
36. Eyerman, "False Consciousness and Ideology," 43.
37. Marx and Engels, *Communist Manifesto*.
38. D'Amato, *Meaning of Marxism*, 114.
39. Ibid.
40. Lenin, *Essential Works*, 153.
41. Ibid.
42. R. N. Hunt, *Political Ideas*, 322.

43. R. N. Hunt, *Political Ideas of Marx*, 323.

44. Quoted in R. N. Hunt, *Political Ideas*, 319.

45. Chan, *Chinese Marxism*, 8.

46. Johnstone, "Marx and Engels"; Johnstone, "Paris Commune and Marx's Conception"; Laibman, "Modes of Production"; Gottlieb, "Historical Materialism"; V. Chibber, "What Is Living."

47. Chan, *Chinese Marxism*, 15.

48. Ollman, *Alienation*, 12.

49. Castree, *Nature*, 35.

50. Marx, *Capital*, 1:283.

51. N. Smith, *Uneven Development*, 54.

52. N. Smith, *Uneven Development*, 55.

53. Marx, *Economic and Philosophic Manuscripts*, 76.

54. It should not go unnoticed that a similar Marxist position would hold that "humans" and "animals" are not distinct but instead must be dialectically related as well.

55. Marx, *Capital*, 1:283–84.

56. N. Smith, *Uneven Development*, 55–56.

57. Marx and Engels, *German Ideology*, 49–50.

58. N. Smith, *Uneven Development*, 63.

59. Marx, *Economic and Philosophic Manuscripts*; see also Ollman, *Alienation*, 136.

60. Petrović, "Alienation," 14.

61. Ollman, *Alienation*, 151.

62. Ibid., 134.

63. Klagge, "Marx's Realms," 769.

64. Petrović, "Marx's Theory of Alienation"; Sayers, "Creative Activity and Alienation"; Kandiyali, "Freedom and Necessity."

65. Kandiyali, "Freedom and Necessity," 107.

66. Ibid.

67. Ibid., 108.

68. Ibid., 109.

69. Ollman, *Alienation*, 81.

70. Kandiyali, "Freedom and Necessity," 109.

71. Contemporary scientists, from anthropologists to zoologists, may take issue with Marx's distinction of "humans" and "animals," and this is not the place to engage in a lengthy philosophical reflection on the veracity of Marx's claims, most notably his premise that humans are unique in their creative potential. The salience of Marx's assertion concerns how these ideas were—or were not—incorporated into the corpus of "Marxist" political philosophy and how these translated into the policies and programs of "actually existing" Communist societies.

72. Kandiyali, "Freedom and Necessity," 109.

73. Ollman, *Alienation*, 116.

74. Kandiyali, "Freedom and Necessity," 110.

75. Marx's understanding of artistic expression is heavily indebted to that of Hegel. See, for example, Sean Sayers.

76. Sayers, "Creative Activity and Alienation," 114.

77. This statement provides an opening to consider the commodification of art under capitalism, of the production of paintings, sculptures, music, and so forth not for aesthetic purposes or self-fulfillment but as commodities for exchange.

78. Marx, *Economic and Philosophic Manuscripts*, 77.

79. Marx, *Contribution to the Critique*, 21.

80. Trotsky, *Literature and Revolution*, 29.

81. Ibid., emphasis added.

82. Ibid., 31–33.

83. Ibid., 33.

84. Ibid.

85. Ibid.

86. Ibid., 62.

87. Ibid., 61.

88. Ibid., 62.

89. Ibid., 121.

90. Ibid., 136.

91. Ibid., 122.

92. Ibid., 143–44.

Chapter 2. Transformations

1. Marx, "Eighteenth Brumaire of Louis Bonaparte," 346.

2. Lenin, *Essential Works*, 290.

3. Ibid., 288.

4. Pol Pot, *Long Live the 17th Anniversary*.

5. Ibid., 15.

6. Ibid., 17.

7. Ibid.

8. Lenin, *Essential Works*, 292.

9. Quoted in Slocomb, *People's Republic of Kampuchea*, 21.

10. Communist Party of Kampuchea (CPK), "Party's Four-Year Plan," 45.

11. Tyner, *Killing of Cambodia*, 11.

12. Said, *Orientalism*. See also Ashcroft and Ahlwalia, *Edward Said*, 61.

13. Hinton, *Why Did They Kill?*, 48.

14. Document No. E3/130 (00184022), "Communist Party of Kampuchea—Statute," archived by the Extraordinary Chambers in the Court of Cambodia (ECCC), http://www.eccc.gov.kh/en.

15. Ibid.

16. Ben Kiernan, "Khmer Rouge Biographical Questionnaire," available online at Yale University Genocide Studies Program, http://gsp.yale.edu/khmer-rouge-biographical-questionnaire.

17. Johnstone, "Democratic Centralism," 135.

18. Angle, "Decent Democratic Centralism," 525. See also Lin and Lee, "Constitutive Rhetoric of Democratic Centralism," 151.

19. Pol Pot, *Long Live the 17th Anniversary*.

20. Ibid.

21. It remains unclear if the senior leadership of the CPK even intended for the workers to assume decision-making capabilities, as theorized in democratic centralism, or if this was a ruse from the outset.

22. Document No. D55874, archived at the Documentation Center of Cambodia, Phnom Penh.

23. M. Vickery, *Cambodia*, 71–73.

24. Office of the Co-Prosecutors, *Co-Prosecutors' Rule 66 Final Submission* (public redacted version), Case No. 002/19/09/20007–ECCC/OCIJ, 53.

25. "Mobile" here refers to the development of mobile work detail committees that would oversee the mobilization of work groups that would be deployed to various work sites.

26. Membership fluctuated and normally consisted of upward of thirty men and women. Apart from the Standing Committee members (who served on both committees), the Central Committee included Khieu Samphan, Koy Thuon, Ney Saran, and Ke Pok. The Central Committee also included the Specialist Military Committee, which included Pol Pot, Nuon Chea, Son Sen, So Phim, and Ta Mok; Vorn Vet and Ke Pauk would later be added. See also Office of the Co-Investigating Judges (OCIJ), *Closing Order*, Case File No. 002/19-09-2007–ECCC/OCIJ, page 18.

27. Ibid., 17.

28. Documentary evidence indicates that the CPK Standing Committee decided as early as October 9, 1975, on these positions. See Office of the Co-Prosecutors, *Co-Prosecutors' Rule 66 Final*, 51. For a thorough overview of these ministries, see Mertha, *Brothers in Arms*, 35–53.

29. Details of the establishment of these ministries are found in Document No. D21227, archived in the Documentation Center of Cambodia (DC-CAM), Phnom Penh, Cambodia.

30. The respective ministers of these committees are Chey Soun, Cheng An, Koy Thuon, Ek Sophon, Mei Brang, and Ta Che. It is unclear how active any of these committees truly were; preliminary archival evidence suggests that the agriculture and commerce committees were most active. See Document No. D21227.

31. Nhem, *Khmer Rouge*, 46–47.

32. This section is heavily indebted to the work of Andrew Mertha.

33. Mertha, *Brother in Arms*, 44; George Chigas and Dmitri Mosyakov, "Literacy and Education under the Khmer Rouge," available at Yale University Genocide Studies Program, http://gsp.yale.edu/literarcy-and-education-under-khmer-rouge.

34. The following narrative is based on Kim Vun's testimony provided at the Extraordinary Chambers in the Court of Cambodia (ECCC), cf. Document No. E1/111.1 (00839615), "Transcript of Trial Proceedings, Case File No. 002/19-09-2007-ECCC/TC, 21 August 2012, Trial Day 99," archived by the Extraordinary Chambers in the Court of Cambodia (ECCC), http://www.eccc.gov.kh/en; Document No. E1/112.1 (00841140), "Transcript of Trial Proceedings, Case File No. 002/19-09-2007-ECCC/TC, 22 August 2012, Trial Day 100," archived by the Extraordinary Chambers in the Court of Cambodia (ECCC), http://www.eccc.gov.kh/en; and Office of the Co-Investigating Judges, "Criminal Case File No. 002/14-08-2006," archived by the Extraordinary Chambers in the Court of Cambodia (ECCC), http://www.eccc.gov.kh/en.

35. Document No. E1/111.1 (00839615), "Transcript of Trial Proceedings, . . . 21 August 2012, Trial Day 99."

36. Document No. E1/112.1 (00841140), "Transcript of Trial Proceedings, . . . 22 August 2012, Trial Day 100."

37. Ibid.

38. Ibid.

39. Ibid.

40. The CPK oversaw the publication of at least three textbooks, a beginning-level math book, and first-grade and second-grade geography texts.

41. Mertha, *Brothers in Arms*, 45.

42. Ibid., 47.

43. CPK, "Party's Four-Year Plan," 51.

44. Tyner, "Violence"; Tyner and Rice, "Cambodia's Political Economy of Violence"; Tyner and Rice, "To Live and Let Die"; and Tyner, *From Rice Fields*.

45. T. Smith, "Underdevelopment of Development Literature."

46. Todaro, *Economic Development*, 428.

47. Document No. D00698, "Cooperation with the Ministry of Commerce," archived at the Documentation Center of Cambodia, Phnom Penh.

48. Ibid.

49. CPK, "Report of Activities," 200.

50. Ibid.

51. CPK, "Party's Four-Year Plan," 46.

52. CPK, "Preliminary Explanation," 131.

53. CPK, "Party's Four-Year Plan," 51.

54. Ibid., 132.

55. Ibid., 89.

56. Ibid.

57. For an in-depth discussion of CPK water-management policies, see Tyner and Will, "Nature and Post-Conflict Violence."

58. CPK, "Preliminary Explanation," 131.

59. Ibid.

60. Ibid., 133.

61. See, for example, the following: interview with Bou Mao by Sok Vannak (June 16, 2011); interview with Mun Mut by Dany Long (June 16, 2011); interview with Lot Suoy by Dany Long (no date); interview with Pann Chhuong by Dany Long (June 18, 2011); interview with Mean Sambath by Dany Long (December 12, 2010); and interview with Chhit Yoeuk by Dany Long (June 16, 2011). Transcripts of these interviews are on record at the Documentation Center of Cambodia.

62. CPK, "Preliminary Explanation," 134.

63. Ibid., 137.

64. Ibid., 133.

65. CPK, "Excerpted Report," 34.

66. Ibid. The CPK did have a "cartography division." At this point, it is not known under which ministry or committee this division was placed.

67. Ibid.

68. Fraser, Mabee, and Slaymaker, "Mutual Vulnerability, Mutual Dependence."

69. Marx, *Critique of the Gotha Program*, 10. The simplicity of Marx's statement belies a complexity not readily apparent. Indeed, Marx explains that this form of distributive justice is infeasible. See, for example, Sen, "Merit and Justice."

70. Mam, "Endurance of the Cambodian Family," 134–35.

71. CPK, "Party's Four-Year Plan," 45–46.

72. Ibid., 46.

73. Ibid., 49.

74. CPK, "Excerpted Report," 16–17.

75. Ibid., 18.

76. Ibid.

77. Ibid., 19.

78. Ibid.

79. Ibid., 30.

80. Ibid., 33.

81. Document No. E3/724 (00089735), "July 1975," archived by the Extraordinary Chambers in the Courts of Cambodia (ECCC), http://www.eccc.gov.kh/en.

82. Ibid.

83. Ibid.

84. Ibid.

85. Document No. E3/729 (00184230), "July 1975," archived by the Extraordinary Chambers in the Courts of Cambodia (ECCC), http://www.eccc.gov.kh/en.

86. Ibid.

87. Ibid.

88. Marx and Engels, *German Ideology*, 42.

89. Marx, "Theses on Feuerbach," 173.

90. CPK, "Report of Activities," 202.

Chapter 3. Poetic Geographies

1. Sheers, "Poetry and Place," 173.

2. Lorimer, "Poetry and Place," 181.

3. Communist Party of Kampuchea (CPK), "Preliminary Explanation," 131, 147.

4. Ibid., 147.

5. Ibid.

6. Wright, "Geography in Literature," 659.

7. Wright, "Terrae Incognitae," 12.

8. Pocock, "Geography and Literature"; Noble and Dhussa, "Image and Substance"; Brosseau, "Geography's Literature"; and Lando, "Fact and Fiction."

9. Lando, "Fact and Fiction," 6.

10. Salter and Lloyd, *Landscape in Literature*, 28.

11. Ibid.

12. See, for example, Hones, "Text as It Happens"; and Saunders, "Literary Geography."

13. Saunders, "Literary Geography," 437.

14. Pred, *Past Is Not Dead*; Lorimer, "Poetry and Place"; Rawling, "Poetry and Place"; Eshun and Madge, "Now Let Me Share This"; Cresswell, "Displacements"; Cresswell, "Geographies of Poetry"; Madge, "On the Creative (Re)turn"; Magrane, "Situating Geopoetics"; and Eshun and Madge, "Poetic World-Writing."

15. Lorimer, "Poetry and Place," 182.

16. Madge, "On the Creative (Re)turn," 178.

17. Ward, "Art of Writing Place," 764.

18. Uline, Tschannen-Moran, and Wolsley, "Walls Still Speak."

19. Giroux, "Cultural Studies," 60.

20. Sandlin, O'Malley, and Burdick, "Mapping the Complexity," 338. See also Hickey-Moody, Savage, and Windle, "Pedagogy Writ Large."

21. Biesta, "Becoming Public."

22. Loopmans, Cowell, and Oosterlynck, "Photography."

23. Biesta, "Becoming Public," 693.

24. Ibid.

25. Sandlin, O'Malley, and Burdick, "Mapping the Complexity."

26. Sharp, "Publishing American Identity"; and Dittmer, "Captain America's Empire."

27. Biesta, "Becoming Public."

28. Document No. E3/749 (00182614), "Minutes—Meeting of the Standing Committee 9 January 1976," archived by the Extraordinary Chambers in the Court of Cambodia (ECCC), http://www.eccc.gov.kh/en.

29. Document No. E3/226 (00183363), "Minutes of Meeting on Health and Social Affairs 10-06-76," archived by the Extraordinary Chambers in the Court of Cambodia (ECCC), http://www.eccc.gov.kh/en.

30. Clayton, "Building the New Cambodia"; Ayers, "Khmer Rouge and Education"; Clayton, "Re-orientations in Moral Education."

31. George Chigas and Dmitry Mosyakov, "Literacy and Education under the Khmer Rouge," Yale University Genocide Project, available at http:www.yale.edu/cgp/literacyandeducation.html.

32. Sharp, "Towards a Critical Analysis," 333.

33. Lefebvre, *Production of Space*, 54.

34. Marx and Engels, *German Ideology*, 67.

35. See, for example, Clegg, Pina e Cunha, and Rego, "Theory and Practice of Utopia."

36. Of course, the Khmer Rouge also targeted those without education. Such "purges" were not so clear cut but hinged on the interaction of other variables, including, for example, one's perceived loyalty.

37. Mertha, *Brothers in Arms*.

38. This explains also the supposed paradox of many CPK officials having achieved high levels of education, including doctorates, yet forwarding an anti-intellectual society.

39. Chigas and Mosyakov, "Literacy and Education."

40. Ibid.

41. CPK, "Party's Four-Year Plan," 114.

42. Document No. E3/231 (00528385), "Minutes of the 8 March 1976 Meeting on Propaganda," archived by the Extraordinary Chambers in the Court of Cambodia (ECCC), http://www.eccc.gov.kh/en.

43. Schuermans, Loopmans, and Vandenabeele, "Public Space."

44. Chandler, "Normative Poems"; Thompson, "Oh Cambodia!"; and McCullough, "Tuning in to the Poetry."

45. Chandler, "Normative Poems," 271.

46. Ibid., 274.

47. CPK, "Party's Four-Year Plan," 113.

48. Ibid., 114.

49. Ibid.

50. Document No. L0001434, "Report of Region 1," archived at the Documentation Center of Cambodia, Phnom Penh.

51. Document No. E3/231 (00528385).

52. See, for example, Fanon, *Wretched of the Earth*. At this point, scholars have only speculated on the influence of Fanon on the Khmer Rouge. It is common, for example, to string together a list of influences, including Marx, Lenin, Stalin, Mao, Amin, and even Fanon. I am not aware of any concrete documentation that would directly connect Fanon's writings with CPK policy.

53. Shapiro-Phim, "Dance."

54. CPK, "Party's Four-Year Plan," 113.

55. Dy, "Khmer Literature since 1975"; Ledgerwood, Ebihara, and Mortland, introduction; and Sam, "Khmer Traditional Music Today."

56. Dy, "Khmer Literature since 1975," 29. Documentary evidence does show that some Khmer, perhaps as a form of resistance, composed their own private poetry and art. This is found, for example, in various Khmer Rouge notebooks, now archived at the Documentation Center of Cambodia. I am unaware of any systematic analysis of these materials.

57. Poems referenced in this chapter have been translated by staff members of, and are archived at, the Documentation Center of Cambodia, Phnom Penh.

58. Reproduced in *Searching for the Truth*, no. 19 (2001), back cover.

59. Originally published in *Revolutionary Youth*, no date; reprinted in *Searching for the Truth*, no. 11 (2000), back cover.

60. "Male and Female Revolutionary Youths Determine to Fight, Defend, and Rebuild the Country in Great Leaps," published in *Revolutionary Youth*, no. 12 (December 1976); reprinted in *Searching for the Truth*, no. 23 (2001), back cover.

61. For a more extensive discussion of Khmer Rouge security practices, including surveillance strategies, see Tyner, *Politics of Lists*.

62. For supporting slogans to this effect, see Locard, *Pol Pot's Little Red Book*.

63. Springer, "Earth Writing."

64. Ibid.

Chapter 4. The Lyrics of Revolution

1. Chandler, *Voices from S-21*; Hinton, *Why Did They Kill?*; Kasumi, *Gender-Based Violence*; DeFalco, "Accounting for Famine"; Cunha et al., "Organization (Angkar) as a State"; DeFalco, "Justice and Starvation in Cambodia"; Tyner and Rice, "To Live and Let Die"; and Tyner and Rice, "Cambodia's Political Economy of Violence."

2. Siebers, "Hitler and the Tyranny," 105. See also Mandel, "Rethinking 'After Auschwitz'"; Potter, "Arts in Nazi Germany"; and Potter, "What Is 'Nazi Music'?"

3. Mamula, "Starting from Nowhere?," 30.

4. Kong, "Music and Cultural Politics"; Kong, "Popular Music in Geographical Analysis"; Valentine, "Creative Transgressive Space"; S. J. Smith, "Beyond Geography's Visible Worlds"; Connell and Gibson, *Sound Tracks*; Revill, "Performing French Folk Music"; Morton, "Performing Ethnography"; Wood, Duffy, and Smith, "Art of Doing"; Moss, "Still Searching"; Wood, "Playing with 'Scottishness'"; and Knights, *Music*.

5. Leyshon, Matless, and Revill, "Place of Music," 426.

6. Sayana Ser, "Khmer Rouge Songs and Poems," unpublished report, on file at the Documentation Center of Cambodia, Phnom Penh.

7. Marston, "Khmer Rouge Songs."

8. Wood, "Playing with 'Scottishness,'" 199.

9. Marston, "Khmer Rouge Songs."

10. No sustained research has questioned the reception of songs by men or women while living under Khmer Rouge rule. Published accounts and memories indicate a range of attitudes, including anger or indifference. Vannak Som, for example, states, "At the worksite [the Khmer Rouge] played revolutionary songs that described and complemented the . . . work. . . . However, such songs never interested me at all. Frankly, I never paid attention to them." See Som, "Crime Deserves Judgement," 56. Pal Vannareak likewise notes that although "there was always sound played over a loudspeaker . . . [these] song[s] did nothing to help people." Indeed, according to Vannareak, "everyone was annoyed by the sound coming from that loudspeaker." See Vannareak, "Wait for Tomorrow," 60.

11. Marston, "Khmer Rouge Songs," 103.

12. From the song "Best Wishes for the Great Cambodian People," archived at the Documentation Center of Cambodia, Phnom Penh.

13. For an extended discussion, see Tyner and Will, "Nature and Post-Conflict Violence."

14. Communist Party of Kampuchea (CPK), "Party's Four-Year Plan," 89.

15. Ibid.

16. Oral testimonies of survivors speak often of the chessboard patterns of rice fields and the necessity of obtaining three tons per hectare. Consequently, these

accounts have been widely incorporated into scholarly and popular histories of the Khmer Rouge. Detailed empirical work, however, casts doubts on the ubiquity of these policies. Moreover, documentary evidence indicates that subsequent policy pronouncements of the CPK modified these initial quotas. It is possible that survivors are narrating particular understandings based on the repeated performance of songs as opposed to accurate policies forwarded by the CPK.

17. From the song "Our Cooperative Is Determined to Increase Production to Build Democratic Kampuchea," archived at the Documentation Center of Cambodia, Phnom Penh.

18. From the song "We Are Working Aggressively to Build Rice Dikes," archived at the Documentation Center of Cambodia, Phnom Penh.

19. From the song "We Are Determined to Build New Rice Dikes 'Chessboard Pattern,'" archived at the Documentation Center of Cambodia, Phnom Penh.

20. CPK, "Preliminary Explanation," 134.

21. From the song "We Are Working Aggressively to Build Rice Dikes."

22. Ibid.

23. From the song "During the Rainy Season, We Gather Our Workforce to Do Farm Work," archived at the Documentation Center of Cambodia, Phnom Penh.

24. From the song "New Image of Rural Cambodia during the Rainy Season," archived at the Documentation Center of Cambodia, Phnom Penh.

25. From the song "We Are Working Aggressively to Build Rice Dikes."

26. From the song "We Are Determined to Build New Rice Dikes 'Chessboard Pattern.'"

27. From the song "New Image of Rural Cambodia during the Rainy Season."

28. From the song "Our Cooperative Is Determined to Increase Production to Build Democratic Kampuchea."

29. Ibid.

30. Ibid.

31. From the song "Our Rural Area Has Transformed Completely," archived at the Documentation Center of Cambodia, Phnom Penh.

32. Ibid.

33. From the song "During the Rainy Season, We Gather Our Workforce to Do Farm Work."

34. From the song "Our Rural Area Has Transformed Completely."

35. Ibid.

36. Ibid.

37. Ibid.

38. From the song "We Are Working Aggressively to Build Rice Dikes."

39. From the song "New Image of Rural Cambodia during the Rainy Season."

40. From the song "Our Cooperative Is Determined to Increase Production to Build Democratic Kampuchea."

41. From the song "People along the Riverbank Are Determined to Increase the Agricultural Product," archived at the Documentation Center of Cambodia, Phnom Penh.

42. From the song "Our Rural Area Has Transformed Completely."

43. It should be noted that many songs predating the Khmer Rouge celebrated agricultural work and often included political agendas. However, according to Marston ("Khmer Rouge Songs," 106), while farming activities were romanticized—similar to the Khmer Rouge—a key difference is that earlier songs emphasized familial activities, whereas Khmer Rouge songs promoted the collective.

44. Phelan, *Unmarked*, 146.

45. Siegel, *At the Vanishing Point*, 1.

46. Schneider, "Performance Remains," 139.

47. Ibid.

48. Ibid.

49. Jones, Abbott, and Ross, "Redefining the Performing Arts Archive," 166.

50. Ibid.

51. Ibid., 167.

52. D. Taylor, *Archive and the Repertoire*.

53. Jones, Abbott, and Ross, "Redefining the Performing Arts Archive," 167.

54. Blouin and Rosenberg, *Processing the Past*, 16.

55. Ibid., 17.

56. Jones, Abbott, and Ross, "Redefining the Performing Arts Archive," 169.

57. Ibid.

58. Blouin and Rosenberg, *Processing the Past*, 17.

59. Hudson, "Access and Collective Memory," 288.

60. Ly, "Artistic Roles," 13.

61. Ibid., 14.

62. Edy, "Journalistic Uses of Collective Memory," 71.

63. Confino, "Collective Memory and Cultural History," 1386.

64. Kansteiner, "Finding Meaning in Memory," 190.

65. Wertsch and Roediger, "Collective Memory," 320.

66. Document No. E3/12 (00182809), "Decision of the Central Committee Regarding a Number of Matters," archived by the Extraordinary Chambers in the Courts of Cambodia (ECCC), http://www.eccc.gov.kh/en.

67. Assmann, "Transformations between History and Memory," 50.

68. Schudson, "Dynamics of Distortion," 347.

69. See, for example, Meyer, *Politics of Music*; and Ho, "Social Change and Nationalism"; Sonevytsky and Ivakhiv, "Late Soviet Discourses."

Chapter 5. Picturing the Revolution

1. Barthes, *Camera Lucida*.

2. Tolia-Kelly, "Materializing Post-Colonial Geographies," 675.

3. Duncan, *City as Text*, 19.

4. Crang, "Hair in the Gate."

5. Foster, *Vision and Visuality*.

6. Rose, "On the Need to Ask," 213.

7. Tolia-Kelly, "Materializing Post-Colonial Geographies," 675.

8. See, for example, Schwartz, "*Geography Lesson*."

9. Schein, "Methodological Framework," 382.

10. Mitchell, *Lie of the Land*, 27.

11. Schwartz, "Records of Simple Truth," 11.

12. Hall, "Camera Never Lies?," 455.

13. Hoelscher, "Photographic Construction of Tourist Space," 549.

14. Rose, "Practising Photography"; Sidaway, "Photography as Geographical Fieldwork"; and Rose, "Using Photographs as Illustrations."

15. Hall, "Camera Never Lies?," 456.

16. Rose, "Using Photographs as Illustrations," 151.

17. M. A. Hunt, "Urban Photography/Cultural Geography," 154.

18. Ibid., 154–55.

19. Hall, "Reframing Photographic Research Methods," 329.

20. Metz, "Fantasy Made Real."

21. Wolf, "Subjunctive Documentary," 274.

22. Metz, "Fantasy Made Real," 334.

23. Salazar, "Anticipatory Modes," 56. See also B. Anderson, "Preemption, Precaution, Preparedness."

24. Herb, "Double Vision," 143.

25. Sanders, "Developing Geographers through Photography."

26. Compare Rose, "Practising Photography"; Sidaway, "Photography as Geographical Fieldwork"; and Hall, "Camera Never Lies?"

27. Masini, "Rethinking Futures Studies," 1163.

28. Rose, "Practising Photography," 555.

29. Document No. E3/729 (00357900), "Revolutionary Youth Issue No. 10, October 1975," archived by the Extraordinary Chambers in the Court of Cambodia (ECCC), http://www.eccc.gov.kh/en.

30. Ibid.

31. Ibid.

32. Document No. E3/729, "Kampuchean Youth Must Forge and Re-Fashion Themselves in the Movement to Strengthen and Expand Production Cooperatives," archived by the Extraordinary Chambers in the Courts of Cambodia (ECCC), http://www.eccc.gov.kh/en.

33. Ibid.

34. Blum and Secor, "Psychotopologies."

35. Ibid., 1031.

36. Document No. E3/729, "Kampuchean Youth Must Forge."

37. A notable example of photographs showing men and women are those depicting communal wedding ceremonies.

38. Document No. E3/729 (00357923), "Revolutionary Youth," archived by the Extraordinary Chambers in the Court of Cambodia (ECCC) at http://www.eccc.gov.kh/en.

39. Ibid., emphasis added.

40. Ibid.

41. Hoelscher, "Angels of Memory," 196.

42. Edensor, "Ghosts of Industrial Ruins"; Edensor, "Waste Matter"; Ginn, "Death, Absence and Afterlife"; and Maddrell, "Living with the Deceased."

43. Maddrell, "Living with the Deceased," 504.

44. Compare Caswell, *Archiving the Unspeakable*; Tyner and Devadoss, "Administrative Violence"; and Tyner, *Politics of Lists*.

Chapter 6. Conclusions

1. Marx, *Capital*, 3:958–59.

2. Ibid., 3:959.

3. Ibid.

4. Ibid.

5. Ibid.

6. Marcuse, "Realm of Freedom"; Gray, "Marxian Freedom"; Klagge, "Marx's Realms"; Maidan, "Alienated Labour and Free Activity"; Musto, "Revisiting Marx's Concept of Alienation"; Kandiyali, "Freedom and Necessity"; and James, "Compatibility of Freedom and Necessity."

7. Plamenatz, *Karl Marx's Philosophy of Man*, 171.

8. For a helpful overview, see James, "Compatibility of Freedom and Necessity."

9. See Kandiyali for an informative discussion on the various readings of this passage.

10. Marcuse, "Realm of Freedom," 22.

11. Kandiyali, "Freedom and Necessity," 109.

12. Ibid.

13. Ibid., 110.

14. Ibid.

15. James, "Compatibility of Freedom and Necessity."

16. Ibid.

17. Kandiyali, "Freedom and Necessity," 113.

18. Trotsky, *Art and Revolution*, 133.

19. Ibid., 134.

20. Ibid., 50.

21. Ibid., 63.

22. Ibid., 36.

23. Trotsky, *Literature and Revolution*, 122.

24. Ibid., 136.

25. Ibid., 65.

26. Ibid., 108.

27. Ibid.

28. Reed, *Art of Protest*, 28.

29. Marx and Engels, *German Ideology*, 42.

30. Trotsky, *Art and Revolution*, 51.

31. Hawkins, "Dialogues and Doings"; Hawkins, "Geography and Art"; Marston and De Leeuw, "Creativity and Geography"; Madge, "On the Creative (Re)turn"; Hawkins, "Creative Geographic Methods"; Magrane, "Situating Geopoetics"; and Philo, "Squeezing, Bleaching, and the Victims' Fate."

32. Marston and De Leeuw, "Creativity and Geography," iii and xi.

33. Hawkins, "Creative Geographic Methods," 248.

34. Ingram, "Rethinking Art and Geopolitics," 12.

35. Eshun and Madge, "Poetic World-Writing," 784.

36. Hawkins, "Geography and Art," 66.

37. Castree and Sparke, "Introduction"; Heyman, "Research, Pedagogy, and Instrumental Geography"; Chatterton, Hodkinson, and Pickerill, "Beyond Scholar Activism."

38. Banfield, *Geography Meets Gendlin*, 26.

39. Hawkins, "Creative Geographic Methods," 264.

40. Magrane, "Situating Geopoetics," 97.

41. For an expanded discussion specific to geography, see Tyner, "Radical Geography and the Legacy"; see also Amin and Thrift, "What's Left? Just the Future"; and N. Smith, "Neo-Critical Geography."

42. Valentino, *Final Solutions*, 93.

43. McLaren, "This Fist Called My Heart," 474.

44. Allman and Wallis, "Praxis."

45. Martin and Brown, "Out of the Box," 387.

46. Ibid.

47. Rikowski, "Marx and the Education," 567.

48. Wellens et al., "Teaching Geography for Social Transformation," 120.

49. Pinder, "Urban Interventions"; Diprose, "Negotiating Contradiction"; C. Smith, "Art as a Diagnostic"; and Desai and Darts, "Interrupting Everyday Life."

50. Pinder, "Urban Interventions," 731.

BIBLIOGRAPHY

Adam, Peter. *Art of the Third Reich*. New York: Abrams, 1992.

Aitken, Stuart C., and Leo E. Zonn. "Re-Presenting the Place Pastiche." In *Place, Power, Situation, and Spectacle: A Geography of Film*, edited by Stuart C. Aitken and Leo E. Zonn, 3–25. Lanham, Md.: Rowman & Littlefield, 1994.

Allman, Paula, and John Wallis. "Praxis: Implications for 'Really' Radical Education." *Studies in the Education of Adults* 22, no. 1 (1990): 14–30.

Allsup, Randall Everett, and Eric Shieh. "Social Justice and Music Education: The Call for a Public Pedagogy." *Music Educators Journal* 98, no. 4 (2012): 47–51.

Amin, Ash, and Nigel Thrift. "What's Left? Just the Future." *Antipode* 37, no. 2 (2005): 220–38.

Anderson, Ben. "Preemption, Precaution, Preparedness: Anticipatory Action and Future Geographies." *Progress in Human Geography* 34, no. 6 (2010): 777–98.

Anderson, Perry. *Considerations on Western Marxism*. New York: New Left Books, 1976.

Angle, Stephen C. "Decent Democratic Centralism." *Political Theory* 33, no. 4 (2005): 518–46.

Ashcroft, Bill, and Pal Ahluwalia. *Edward Said*. New York: Routledge, 1999.

Assmann, Aleida. "Transformations between History and Memory." *Social Research* 75 (2008): 49–72.

Au, Wilson W. S. *Reclaiming Communist Philosophy: Marx, Lenin, Mao and the Dialectics of Nature*. Charlotte, N.C.: Information Age, 2017.

Ayers, David. "The Khmer Rouge and Education: Beyond the Discourse of Destruction." *History of Education* 28, no. 2 (1999): 205–18.

Banaji, Jairus. *Theory as History: Essays on Modes of Production and Exploitation*. Chicago: Haymarket Books, 2011.

Banfield, Janet. *Geography Meets Gendlin: An Exploration of Disciplinary Potential through Artistic Practice*. New York: Palgrave Macmillan, 2016.

Barron, Stephani, ed. *"Degenerate Art": The Fate of the Avant-Garde in Nazi Germany* (New York: Abrams, 1991).

Barthes, Roland. *Camera Lucida: Reflections on Photography*. New York: Hill & Wang, 1981.

Bartlett, Frederic C. *The Aims of Political Propaganda*. New York: Octagon, 1940.

Baudrillard, Jean. *Simulacra and Simulation*. Translated by Sheila Faria Glaser. Ann Arbor: University of Michigan Press, 1994.

Becker, Elizabeth. *When the War Was Over: Cambodia and the Khmer Rouge Revolution*. New York: Public Affairs, 1998.

Beech, Dave. *Art and Value: Art's Economic Exceptionalism in Classical, Neoclassical and Marxist Economics*. Chicago: Haymarket Books, 2016.

Benjamin, Walter. "The Work of Art in the Age of Its Technological Reproducibility." In *Walter Benjamin: Selected Writings*, vol. 3, *1935–1938*, edited by H. Eiland and M. W. Jennings, 101–33. Cambridge, Mass.: Harvard University Press, 2002.

Biesta, Gert J. J. "Becoming Public: Public Pedagogy, Citizenship and the Public Sphere." *Social & Cultural Geography* 13, no. 7 (2012): 683–97.

Blouin, Francis X., Jr., and William G. Rosenberg. *Processing the Past: Contesting Authority in History and the Archives*. Oxford: Oxford University Press, 2011.

Blum, Virginia, and Anna Secor. "Psychotopologies: Closing the Circuit between Psychic and Material Space." *Environment and Planning D: Society and Space* 29, no. 6 (2011): 1030–47.

Brosseau, Marc. "Geography's Literature." *Progress in Human Geography* 19, no. 3 (1994): 333–53.

Castree, Noel. *Nature*. New York: Routledge, 2005.

———. "Teaching History, Philosophy and Theory: Notes on Representing Marxism and 'Marxist Geography.'" *Journal of Geography in Higher Education*, 18, no. 1 (1994): 33–42.

Castree, Noel, and Matthew Sparke. "Introduction: Professional Geography and the Corporatization of the University; Experiences, Evaluations, and Engagements." *Antipode* 32, no. 3 (2000): 222–29.

Caswell, Michelle. *Archiving the Unspeakable: Silence, Memory, and the Photographic Record in Cambodia*. Madison: University of Wisconsin Press, 2014.

Chan, Adrian. *Chinese Marxism*. New York: Continuum, 2003.

Chandler, David P. "Normative Poems (Chbap) and Pre-Colonial Cambodian Society." *Journal of Southeast Asian Studies* 15, no. 2 (1984): 271–79.

———. *The Tragedy of Cambodian History: Politics, War, and Revolution since 1945*. New Haven, Conn.: Yale University Press, 1991.

———. *Voices from S-21: Terror and History in Pol Pot's Secret Prison*. Berkeley: University of California Press, 1999.

Chatterton, Paul, Stuart Hodkinson, and Jenny Pickerill. "Beyond Scholar Activism: Making Strategic Interventions inside and outside the Neoliberal University." *ACME: An International E-Journal for Critical Geographies* 9, no. 2 (2010): 245–75.

Cherne, Leo. "Cambodia—Auschwitz of Asia." *Worldview* 21, no. 7–8 (1978): 21–25.

Chibber, Vivek. "What Is Living and What Is Dead in the Marxist Theory of History." *Historical Materialism* 19, no. 2 (2011): 60–91.

Clayton, Thomas. "Building the New Cambodia: Educational Destruction and Construction under the Khmer Rouge." *History of Education Quarterly* 38, no. 1 (1998): 1–16.

———. "Re-orientations in Moral Education in Cambodia since 1975." *Journal of Moral Education* 34, no. 4 (2005): 505–17.

Clegg, Stewart, Miguel Pina e Cunha, and Arménio Rego. "The Theory and Practice of Utopia in a Total Institution: The Pineapple Panopticon." *Organization Studies* 33, no. 12 (2012): 1735–57.

Communist Party of Kampuchea. "Decisions of the Central Committee on a Variety of Questions." In *Pol Pot Plans the Future: Confidential Leadership Documents from Democratic Kampuchea, 1976–1977*, edited by David Chandler, Ben Kiernan, and Chanta Boua, Yale University Southeast Asia Studies 33, 3–8. New Haven, Conn.: Yale Center for International and Area Studies, 1988.

———. "Excerpted Report on the Leading Views of the Comrade representing the Party Organization at a Zone Assembly." In *Pol Pot Plans the Future: Confidential Leadership Documents from Democratic Kampuchea, 1976–1977*, edited by David Chandler, Ben Kiernan, and Chanta Boua, Yale University Southeast Asia Studies 33, 13–35. New Haven, Conn.: Yale Center for International and Area Studies, 1988.

———. "The Party's Four-Year Plan to Build Socialism in All Fields, 1977–1980." In *Pol Pot Plans the Future: Confidential Leadership Documents from Democratic Kampuchea, 1976–1977*, edited by David Chandler, Ben Kiernan, and Chanta Boua, Yale University Southeast Asia Studies 33, 45–119. New Haven, Conn.: Yale Center for International and Area Studies, 1988.

———. "Preliminary Explanation before Reading the Plan, by the Party Secretary." In *Pol Pot Plans the Future: Confidential Leadership Documents from Democratic Kampuchea, 1976–1977*, edited by David Chandler, Ben Kiernan, and Chanta Boua, Yale University Southeast Asia Studies 33, 124–63. New Haven, Conn.: Yale Center for International and Area Studies, 1988.

———. "Report of Activities of the Party Center according to the General Political Tasks of 1976." In *Pol Pot Plans the Future: Confidential Leadership Documents from Democratic Kampuchea, 1976–1977*, edited by David Chandler, Ben Kiernan, and Chanta Boua, Yale University Southeast Asia Studies 33, 182–212. New Haven, Conn.: Yale Center for International and Area Studies, 1988.

Confino, Alon. "Collective Memory and Cultural History: Problems of Method." *American Historical Review* 102, no. 5 (1997): 1386–403.

Connell, John, and Chris Gibson. *Sound Tracks: Popular Music Identity and Place*. London: Routledge, 2003.

Crang, Mike. "The Hair in the Gate: Visuality and Geographical Knowledge." *Antipode* 35, no. 2 (2003): 238–43.

Cresswell, Tim. "Displacements: Three Poems." *Geographical Review* 103, no.2 (2013): 285–87.

———. "Geographies of Poetry/Poetries of Geography." *Cultural Geographies* 21, no. 1 (2014): 141–46.

Cunha, Miguel Pina, Stewart Clegg, Arménio Reg, and Michele Lancione. "The Organization (Angkar) as a State of Exception: The Case of the S-21 Extermination Camp, Phnom Penh." *Journal of Political Power* 5, no. 2 (2012): 279–99.

D'Amato, Paul. *The Meaning of Marxism*. Chicago: Haymarket Books, 2006.

Daniels, Stephen. "Geographical Imagination." *Transactions of the Institute of British Geographers* 36 (2011): 182–87.

DeFalco, Randle C. "Accounting for Famine at the Extraordinary Chambers in the Courts of Cambodia: The Crimes against Humanity of Extermination, Inhumane Acts and Persecution." *International Journal of Transitional Justice* 5, no. 1 (2011): 142–58.

———. "Justice and Starvation in Cambodia: The Khmer Rouge Famine." *Cambodia Law and Policy Journal* 2 (2014): 45–84.

DeLeyser, Dydia. "Authenticity on the Ground: Engaging the Past in a California Ghost Town." *Annals of the Association of American Geographers* 89, no. 4 (1999): 602–32.

Desai, Dipti, and David Darts. "Interrupting Everyday Life: Public Interventionist Art as Critical Public Pedagogy." *International Journal of Art & Design Education* 35, no. 2 (2016): 183–96.

"Determine to Turn Our Great Cambodian Homeland to Bright Green Rice and Crop Fields." *Revolutionary Youth* 8 (August 1976). Repr., *Searching for the Truth*, no. 20 (August 2001).

Dikeç, Mustafa. "Beginners and Equals: Political Subjectivity in Arendt and Rancière." *Transactions of the Institute of British Geographers* 38 (2012): 78–90.

Diprose, Gradon. "Negotiating Contradiction: Work, Redundancy and Participatory Art." *Area* 47, no. 3 (2015): 246–53.

Dittmer, Jason. "Captain America's Empire: Reflections on Identity, Popular Culture, and Post-9/11 Geopolitics." *Annals of the Association of American Geographers* 95, no. 3 (2005): 626–43.

Dixon, Deborah. "Creating the Semi-Living: On Politics, Aesthetics and the More-Than-Human." *Transactions of the Institute of British Geographers* 34 (2009): 411–25.

Duncan, James A. *The City as Text: The Politics of Landscape Interpretation in the Kandyan Kingdom*. Cambridge: Cambridge University Press, 1990.

Dy, Khamboly. "Khmer Literature since 1975." In *Cambodian Culture since 1975: Homeland and Exile*, edited by May M. Ebihara, Carol Anne Mortland, and Judy Ledgerwood, 27–38. Ithaca, N.Y.: Cornell University Press, 1994.

Eagleton, Terry. *Why Marx Was Right*. New Haven, Conn.: Yale University Press, 2011.

Edensor, Tim. "The Ghosts of Industrial Ruins: Ordering and Disordering Memory in Excessive Space." *Environment and Planning D: Society and Space* 23, no. 6 (2005): 829–49.

———. "Waste Matter—The Debris of Industrial Ruins and the Disordering of the Material World." *Journal of Material Culture* 10, no. 3 (2005): 311–32.

Edy, Jill A. "Journalist Uses of Collective Memory." *Journal of Communication* 49, no. 2 (1999): 71–85.

Eshun, Gabriel, and Clare Madge. "'Now Let Me Share This With You': Exploring Poetry as a Method for Postcolonial Geography Research." *Antipode* 44, no. 4 (2012): 1395–428.

———. "Poetic World-Writing in a Pluriversal World: A Provocation to the Creative (Re)turn in Geography." *Social & Cultural Geography* 17, no. 6 (2016): 778–85.

Etcheson, Craig. *After the Killing Fields: Lessons from the Cambodian Genocide*. Lubbock: Texas Tech University Press, 2005.

———. *The Rise and Demise of Democratic Kampuchea*. Boulder, Colo.: Westview Press, 1984.

Eyerman, Ron. "False Consciousness and Ideology in Marxist Theory." *Acta Sociologica* 24, no. 1–2 (1981): 43–56.

Fanon, Frantz. *The Wretched of the Earth*. New York: Grove, 1963.

Foster, Hal, ed. *Vision and Visuality*. Seattle: Bay Press, 1988.

Fraser, Evan, Warren Mabee, and Olav Slaymaker. "Mutual Vulnerability, Mutual Dependence: The Reflexive Relation between Human Society and the Environment." *Global Environmental Change* 13, no. 2 (2003): 137–44.

Ginn, Franklin. "Death, Absence and Afterlife in the Garden." *Cultural Geographies* 21, no. 2 (2014): 229–45.

Giroux, Henry A. "Cultural Studies, Public Pedagogy and the Responsibility of Intellectuals." *Communication and Critical/Cultural Studies* 1, no. 1 (2004): 59–79.

———. "Public Pedagogy and the Politics of Resistance: Notes on a Critical Theory of Educational Theory." *Educational Philosophy and Theory* 35, no. 1 (2003): 5–16.

Gottlieb, Roger S. "Historical Materialism, Historical Laws and Social Primacy: Further Discussion of the Transition Debate." *Science & Society* 51, no. 2 (1987): 188–99.

Gouldner, Alvin. *The Two Marxisms*. London: Macmillan, 1980.

Gracyk, Theodore. "Searching for the 'Popular' and the 'Art' of Popular Art." *Philosophy Compass* 2, no. 3 (2007): 380–95.

Gray, John. "Marxian Fom, Individual Liberty, and the End of Alienation." *Social Philosophy & Policy* 3, no. 2 (1986): 160–87.

Gregory, Derek. "The Lightening of Possible Storms." *Antipode* 36 (2004): 798–808.

Hall, Tim. "The Camera Never Lies? Photographic Research Methods in Human Geography." *Journal of Geography in Higher Education* 33, no. 3 (2009): 453–62.

———. "Reframing Photographic Research Methods in Human Geography: A Long-Term Reflection." *Journal of Geography in Higher Education* 39, no. 3 (2015): 328–42.

Hallas, Duncan. "Toward a Revolutionary Socialist Party." *Party and Class* (1971): 38–55.

Harvey, David. *Spaces of Capital: Towards a Critical Geography*. New York: Routledge, 2001.

———. *Spaces of Hope*. Berkeley: University of California Press, 2000.

Hawkins, Harriet. "Creative Geographic Methods: Knowing, Representing, Intervening; On Composing Place and Page." *Cultural Geographies* 22, no. 2 (2015): 247–68.

———. "Dialogues and Doings: Sketching the Relationship between Geography and Art." *Geography Compass* 5, no. 7 (2011): 464–78.

———. "Geography and Art: An Expanding Field; Site, the Body and Practice." *Progress in Human Geography* 37, no. 1 (2012): 52–71.

Heder, Steve. *Cambodian Communism and the Vietnamese Model: Imitation and Independence, 1930–1975*. Bangkok: White Lotus Press, 2004.

Henning, Christoph. *Philosophy after Marx: 100 Years of Misreadings and the Normative Turn in Political Philosophy*. Translated by Max Henninger. Chicago: Haymarket Books, 2015.

Herb, Guntram. "Double Vision: Territorial Strategies in the Construction of National Identities in Germany, 1949–1979." *Annals of the Association of American Geographers* 94, no. 1 (2004): 140–64.

Heyman, Rich. "Research, Pedagogy, and Instrumental Geography." *Antipode* 32, no. 3 (2000): 292–307.

Hickey-Moody, Anna, Glen C. Savage, and Joel Windle. "Pedagogy Writ Large: Public, Popular and Cultural Pedagogies in Motion." *Critical Studies in Education* 51, no. 3 (2010): 227–37.

Hinton, Alexander, L. *Why Did They Kill? Cambodia in the Shadow of Genocide*. Berkeley: University of California Press, 2005.

Ho, Wai-Chung. "Social Change and Nationalism in China's Popular Songs." *Social History* 31, no. 4 (2006): 435–53.

Hodkinson, Stuart. "Teaching What We (Preach and) Practice: The MA in Activism and Social Change." *ACME* 8, no. 3 (2009): 462–73.

Hoelscher, Steven. "Angels of Memory: Photography and Haunting in Guatemala City." *GeoJournal* 73, no. 3 (2008): 195–217.

———. "The Photographic Construction of Tourist Space in Victorian America." *Geographical Review* 88, no. 4 (1998): 548–70.

Holt, Justin. *The Social Thought of Karl Marx*. Los Angeles: Sage, 2015.

Hones, Sheila. "Text as It Happens: Literary Geography." *Geography Compass* 2, no. 5 (2008): 1301–17.

Hopkins, Jeffrey. "A Mapping of Cinematic Places: Icons, Ideology, and the Power of (Mis)Representation." In *Place, Power, Situation, and Spectacle: A Geography of Film*, edited by Stuart C. Aitken and Leo E. Zonn, 47–65. Lanham, Md.: Rowman & Littlefield, 1994.

Hudson, Julia. "Access and Collective Memory in Online Dance Archives." *Journal of Media Practice* 13, no. 3 (2012): 285–301.

Hunt, Mia A. "Urban Photography/Cultural Geography: Spaces, Objects, Events." *Geography Compass* 8, no. 3 (2014): 151–68.

Hunt, Richard N. The *Political Ideas of Marx and Engels*. Vol. 1, *Marxism and Totalitarian Democracy, 1818–1850*. Pittsburgh: University of Pittsburgh Press, 1974.

Ingersoll, David E., Richard K. Matthew, and Andrew Davison. *The Philosophic Roots of Modern Ideology: Liberalism, Communism, Fascism, Islamism*. 3rd ed. Upper Saddle River, N.J.: Prentice Hall, 2001.

Ingram, Alan. "Making Geopolitics Otherwise: Artistic Interventions in Global Political Space." *Geographical Journal* 177, no. 3 (2011): 218–22.

———. "Rethinking Art and Geopolitics through Aesthetics: Artist Reponses to the Iraq War." *Transactions of the Institute of British Geographers* 41 (2016): 1–13.

Jackson, Karl D. "The Ideology of Total Revolution." In *Cambodia 1975–1978: Rendezvous with Death*, edited by Karl D. Jackson, 37–78. Princeton, N.J.: Princeton University Press, 1989.

Jackson, Mark. "Aesthetics, Politics, and Attunement: On Some Questions Brought by Alterity and Ontology." *GeoHumanities* 2, no. 1 (2016): 8–23.

Jacoby, Russell. "Western Marxism." In *A Dictionary of Marxist Thought*, 2nd ed., edited by Tom Bottomore, 581–84. Malden, Mass.: Blackwell, 1991.

James, David. "The Compatibility of Freedom and Necessity in Marx's Idea of Communist Society." *European Journal of Philosophy*. https://doi.org/10.1111/ejop.12209.

Johnstone, Monty. "Democratic Centralism." In *A Dictionary of Marxist Throught*, 2nd ed., edited by Tom Bottomore, 134–37. Malden, Mass.: Blackwell, 1991.

———. "Marx and Engels and the Concept of the Party." *Socialist Register* (1967): 121–58.

———. "The Paris Commune and Marx's Conception of the Dictatorship of the Proletariat." *Massachusetts Review* 12, no. 3 (1971): 447–62.

Jones, Sarah, Daisy Abbott, and Seamus Ross. "Redefining the Performing Arts Archive." *Archival Science* 9 (2009): 165–71.

Kadarkay, Arpad. "Georg Lukács's Road to Art & Marx." *Polity* 13, no. 2 (1980): 230–60.

Kandiyali, Jan. "Freedom and Necessity in Marx's Account of Communism." *British Journal for the History of Philosophy* 22, no. 1 (2014): 104–23.

Kansteiner, Wulf. "Finding Meaning in Memory: A Methodological Critique of Collective Memory." *History and Theory* 41, no. 2 (2002): 179–97.

Kasumi, Nakagawa. *Gender-Based Violence during the Khmer Rouge Regime: Stories of Survivors from the Democratic Kampuchea (1975–1979)*. Phnom Penh: n.p., 2007.

Kiernan, Ben. "Conflict in Cambodia, 1945–2002." *Critical Asian Studies* 34, no. 4 (2002): 483–95.

———. *How Pol Pot Came to Power: A History of Communism in Kampuchea, 1930–1975.* London: Verso, 1985.

———. "Origins of Khmer Communism." *Southeast Asian Affairs* (1981): 161–80.

———. *The Pol Pot Regime: Race, Power, and Genocide in Cambodia under the Khmer Rouge.* New Haven, Conn.: Yale University Press, 1996.

Klagge, James C. "Marx's Realms of 'Freedom' and 'Necessity.'" *Canadian Journal of Philosophy* 16, no. 4 (1986): 769–78.

Knights, Vanessa. *Music, National Identity and the Politics of Location: Between the Global and the Local.* London: Routledge, 2016.

Kong, Lily. "Music and Cultural Politics: Ideology and Resistance in Singapore." *Transactions of the Institute of British Geographers* 20, no. 4 (1995): 447–59.

———. "Popular Music in Geographical Analysis." *Progress in Human Geography* 19, no. 2 (1995): 183–98.

Laibman, David. "Modes of Production and Theories of Transition." *Science & Society* 48, no. 3 (1984): 257–94.

Lando, Fabio. "Fact and Fiction: Geography and Literature." *GeoJournal* 38, no. 1 (1996): 3–18.

Ledgerwood, Judy, May M. Ebihara, and Carol Anne Mortland. Introduction to *Cambodian Culture since 1975: Homeland and Exile*, edited by May M. Ebihara, Carol Anne Mortland, and Judy Ledgerwood, 1–26. Ithaca, N.Y.: Cornell University Press, 1994.

Lee, Alfred. *How to Understand Propaganda.* New York: Rinehart, 1953.

Lefebvre, Henri. *The Production of Space.* London: Blackwell, 1991.

Lenin, Vladimir I. *Essential Works of Lenin: "What Is to Be Done?" and Other Writings.* Edited by Henry M. Christman. New York: Dover, 1987.

LeVine, Peg. *Love and Dread in Cambodia: Weddings, Births, and Ritual Harm under the Khmer Rouge.* Singapore: National University of Singapore Press, 2010.

Lewis, William S. "Art or Propaganda? Dewey and Adorno on the Relationship between Politics and Art." *Journal of Speculative Philosophy* 19, no. 1 (2005): 42–54.

Leyshon, Andrew, David Matless, and George Revill. "The Place of Music: Introduction." *Transactions of the Institute of British Geographers* 20, no. 4 (1995): 423–33.

Lin, Canchu, and Yueh-Ting Lee. "The Constitutive Rhetoric of Democratic Centralism: A Thematic Analysis of Mao's Discourse on Democracy." *Journal of Contemporary China* 22, no. 7 (2013): 148–65.

Locard, Henri. *Pol Pot's Little Red Book: The Sayings of Angkar.* Chiang Mai, Thailand: Silkworm Books, 2004.

Long, Tom. "Marx and Western Marxism in the 1970s." *Berkeley Journal of Sociology* 24 (1980): 13–66.

Loopmans, Maarten, Gillian Cowell, and Stijn Oosterlynck. "Photography, Public Pedagogy and the Politics of Place-Making in Post-Industrial Areas." *Social & Cultural Geography* 13, no. 7 (2012): 699–718.

Lorimer, Hayden. "Poetry and Place: The Shape of Words." *Geography* 93, no. 3 (2008): 181–82.

Lukács, Georg. *History and Class Consciousness*. Translated by Rodney Livingstone. Cambridge, Mass.: MIT Press, 1971.

Lunn, Eugene. "Marxism and Art in the Era of Stalin and Hitler: A Comparison of Brecht and Lukács." *New German Critique* 3 (1974): 12–44.

Ly, Sok-Kheang. "Artistic Roles in Khmer Rouge Revolution." *Searching for the Truth*, 2nd quarter (2008): 13–15.

Maddrell, Avril. "Living with the Deceased: Absence, Presence and Absence-Presence." *Cultural Geographies* 20, no. 4 (2013): 501–22.

Madge, Clare. "On the Creative (Re)turn to Geography: Poetry, Politics and Passion." *Area* 46, no. 2 (2014): 178–85.

Magrane, Eric. "Situating Geopoetics." *GeoHumanities* 1, no. 1 (2015): 86–102.

Maidan, Michael. "Alienated Labour and Free Activity in Marx's Thought." *Political Science* 41, no. 1 (1989): 59–73.

Mam, Kalyanee. "The Endurance of the Cambodian Family under the Khmer Rouge Regime: An Oral History." In *Genocide and Rwanda: New Perspectives*, edited by Susan E. Cook, 127–71. New Haven, Conn.: Yale Center for International and Area Studies, 2004.

Mamula, Stephen. "Starting from Nowhere? Popular Music in Cambodia after the Khmer Rouge." *Asian Music* 39, no. 1 (2008): 26–41.

Mandel, Naomi. "Rethinking 'After Auschwitz': Against a Rhetoric of the Unspeakable in Holocaust Writing." *Boundary* 228, no. 2 (2001): 203–28.

Marcuse, Herbert. "The Realm of Freedom and the Realm of Necessity: A Reconsideration." *Praxis* 5 (1969): 20–25.

Marston, John. "Khmer Rouge Songs." *Crossroads: An Interdisciplinary Journal of Southeast Asian Studies* 16, no. 1 (2002): 100–127.

Marston, Sallie, and Sarah de Leeuw. "Creativity and Geography: Toward a Politicized Intervention." *Geographical Review* 103, no. 2 (2013): iii–xxvi.

Martin, Gregory, and Tony Brown. "Out of the Box: Making Space for Everyday Critical Pedagogies." *Canadian Geographer* 57, no. 3 (2013): 381–88.

Marx, Karl. *Capital: A Critique of Political Economy*. Vol. 1. Translated by Ben Fowkes. New York: Penguin, 1990.

———. *Capital: A Critique of Political Economy*. Vol. 3. Translated by David Fernbach. New York: Penguin, 1991.

———. *A Contribution to the Critique of Political Economy*. Translated by S. W. Ryazanskaya. New York: International, 1970.

———. *Critique of the Gotha Program*. New York: International, 2009.

———. *Economic and Philosophic Manuscripts of 1844*. Translated by Martin Milligan. Amherst, N.Y.: Prometheus Books, 1988.

———. "The Eighteenth Brumaire of Louis Bonaparte." In *Karl Marx: Selected Writings*, 2nd ed., edited by David McLellan, 329–55. Oxford: Oxford University Press, 2000.

———. "Theses on Feuerbach." In *Karl Marx: Selected Writings*, 2nd ed., edited by David McLellan, 171–74. Oxford: Oxford University Press, 2000.

Marx, Karl, and Friedrich Engels. *The Communist Manifesto*. Translated by Samuel Moore. Chicago: Charles H. Kerr, 1945.

———. *The German Ideology: Including Theses on Feurbach and Introduction to the Critique of Political Economy*. Amherst, N.Y.: Prometheus Books, 1988.

Masini, Eleonora. "Rethinking Future Studies." *Futures* 38 (2006): 1158–68.

McCullough, Ken. "Tuning in to the Poetry of U Sam Oeur." *Manoa* 12, no. 1 (2000): 113–20.

McLaren, Peter. "This Fist Called My Heart: Public Pedagogy in the Belly of the Beast." *Antipode* 40, no. 3 (2008): 472–81.

Merleau-Ponty, Maurice. *Adventures of the Dialectic*. Translated by Joseph Bien. Evanston, Ill.: Northwestern University Press, 1973.

Mertha, Andrew. *Brothers in Arms: Chinese Aid to the Khmer Rouge, 1975–1979*. Ithaca, N.Y.: Cornell University Press, 2014.

Metz, Anneke M. "A Fantasy Made Real: The Evolution of the Subjunctive Documentary on U.S. Cable Science Channels." *Television & New Media* 9, no. 4 (2008): 333–48.

Meyer, Michael. *The Politics of Music in the Third Reich*. New York: Peter Lang, 1991.

Mitchell, Don. *The Lie of the Land: Migrant Workers and the California Landscape*. Minneapolis: University of Minnesota Press, 1996.

Morton, Frances. "Performing Ethnography: Irish Traditional Music Sessions and New Methodological Spaces." *Social & Cultural Geography* 6, no. 5 (2005): 661–76.

Moss, Pamela. "Still Searching for the Promised Land: Placing Women in Bruce Springsteen's Lyrical Landscapes." *Cultural Geographies* 18, no. 3 (2011): 343–62.

Musto, Marcello. "Revisiting Marx's Concept of Alienation." *Socialism and Democracy* 24, no. 3 (2010): 79–101.

Nhem, Boraden. *The Khmer Rouge: Ideology, Militarism, and the Revolution that Consumed a Generation*. Santa Barbara, Calif.: Praeger, 2013.

Noble, Allen G., and Ramesh Dhussa. "Image and Substance: A Review of Literary Geography." *Journal of Cultural Geography* 10, no. 2 (1990): 49–65.

Ollman, Bertell. *Alienation: Marx's Conception of Man in Capitalist Society*, 2nd ed. New York: Cambridge University Press, 1976.

———. *Dance of the Dialectic: Steps in Marx's Method*. Urbana: University of Illinois Press, 2003.

Paolucci, Paul. *Marx's Scientific Dialectics: A Methodological Treatise for a New Century.* Chicago: Haymarket Books, 2007.

Peet, Richard. *Global Capitalism: Theories of Societal Development.* New York: Routledge, 1991.

Petropoulos, Jonathan. *Art as Politics in the Third Reich.* Chapel Hill, N.C.: University of North Carolina Press, 1996.

Petrović, Gajo. "Alienation." In *A Dictionary of Marxist Thought*, 2nd ed., edited by Tom Bottomore, 11–16. Malden, Mass.: Blackwell, 1991.

———. "Marx's Theory of Alienation." *Philosophy and Phenomenological Research* 23, no. 3 (1963): 419–526.

Phelan, Peggy. *Unmarked: The Politics of Performance.* New York: Routledge, 1993.

Philo, Chris. "Squeezing, Bleaching, and the Victims' Fate: Wounds, Geography, Poetry, Micrology." *GeoHumanities* (2017): https://doi.org/10.1080/2373566x.2017.1291311.

Pinder, David. "Urban Interventions: Art, Politics and Pedagogy." *International Journal of Urban and Regional Research* 32, no. 3 (2008): 730–36.

Plamenatz, John P. *Karl Marx's Philosophy of Man.* Oxford: Clarendon Press, 1975.

Pocock, Douglas C. D. "Geography and Literature." *Progress in Human Geography* 12, no. 1 (1988): 87–102.

Pol Pot. *Long Live the 17th Anniversary of the Communist Party of Kampuchea.* Phnom Penh: Ministry of Foreign Affairs, 1977. Document no. D30882, archived at the Documentation Center of Cambodia, Phnom Penh.

Potter, Pamela M. "The Arts in Nazi Germany: A Silent Debate." *Contemporary European History* 15, no. 4 (2006): 585–99.

———. "What Is 'Nazi Music'?" *Musical Quarterly* 88, no. 3 (2006):428–55.

Pred, Allan R. *The Past Is Not Dead: Facts, Fictions, and Enduring Racial Stereotypes.* Minneapolis: University of Minnesota Press, 2004.

Rancière, Jacques. *Dissensus: On Politics and Aesthetics.* New York: Bloomsbury, 2015.

———. "From Politics to Aesthetics?" *Paragraph* 28, no. 1 (2005): 13–25.

———. *The Politics of Aesthetics.* London: Continuum, 2004.

———. "Thinking between Disciplines: An Aesthetics of Knowledge." *Parrhesia* 1 (2006): 1–12.

Rawling, Eleanor M. "Poetry and Place: Introduction." *Geography* 93, no. 3 (2008): 171.

Reed, Thomas V. *The Art of Protest: Culture and Activism from the Civil Rights Movement to the Streets of Seattle.* Minneapolis: University of Minnesota Press, 2005.

Revill, George. "Performing French Folk Music: Dance, Authenticity and Nonrepresentational Theory." *Cultural Geographies* 11, no. 2 (2004): 199–209.

Rikowski, Glenn. "Marx and the Education of the Future." *Policy Futures in Education* 2, no. 3 and 4 (2004): 565–77.

Roberts, Graham. *Forward Soviet! History and Non-Fiction Film in the USSR*. London: I. B. Tauris, 1999.

Rose, Gillian. "On the Need to Ask How, Exactly, Is Geography 'Visual'?" *Antipode* 35, no. 2 (2003): 212–21.

———. "Practising Photography: An Archive, A Study, Some Photographs and a Researcher." *Journal of Historical Geography* 26, no. 4 (2000): 555–71.

———. "Using Photographs as Illustrations in Human Geography." *Journal of Geography in Higher Education* 32, no. 1 (2008): 151–60.

Ross, Sheryl T. "Understanding Propaganda: The Epistemic Merit Model and Its Application to Art." *Journal of Aesthetic Education* 36, no. 1 (2002): 16–30.

Rouhani, Farhang. "Practice What You Teach: Facilitating Anarchism in and out of the Classroom." *Antipode* 44, no. 5 (2012): 1726–41.

Said, Edward. *Orientalism*. New York: Vintage Books, 1979.

Salazar, Juan F. "Anticipatory Modes of Futuring Planetary Change in Documentary Film." In *A Companion to Contemporary Documentary Film*, edited by Alexandra Juhasz and Alisa Lebow, 43–60. New York: John Wiley & Sons, 2015.

Salter, Christopher L., and William J. Lloyd. *Landscape in Literature*. Washington, D.C.: Association of American Geographers, 1977.

Sam, Sam-Ang. "Khmer Traditional Music Today." In *Cambodian Culture since 1975: Homeland and Exile*, edited by May M. Ebihara, Carol Anne Mortland, and Judy Ledgerwood, 39–47. Ithaca, N.Y.: Cornell University Press, 1994.

Sanders, Rickie. "Developing Geographers through Photography: Enlarging Concepts." *Journal of Geography in Higher Education* 31, no. 1 (2007): 181–95.

Sandlin, Jennifer A., and Jennifer L. Milam. "'Mixing Pop (Culture) and Politics': Cultural Resistance, Culture Jamming, and Anti-Consumption Activism as Critical Public Pedagogy." *Curriculum Inquiry* 38, no. 3 (2008): 323–50.

Sandlin, Jennifer A., Michael P. O'Malley, and Jake Burdick. "Mapping the Complexity of Public Pedagogy Scholarship: 1894–2010." *Review of Educational Research* 81, no. 3 (2011): 338–75.

Saunders, Anghard. "Literary Geography: Reforging the Connections." *Progress in Human Geography* 34, no. 4 (2010): 436–52.

Sayers, Sean. "Creative Activity and Alienation in Hegel and Marx." *Historical Materialism* 11, no. 1 (2003): 107–28.

Schein, Richard. "A Methodological Framework for Interpreting Ordinary Landscapes: Lexington, Kentucky's Courthouse Square." *Geographical Review* 99, no. 3 (2009): 377–402.

Schneider, Rebecca. "Performance Remains." In *Perform, Repeat, Record: Live Art in History*, edited by Amelia Jones and Adrian Heathfield, 137–50. Bristol, UK: Intellect Books, 2012.

Schudson, Michael. "Dynamics of Distortion in Collective Memory." In *Memory Distortion: How Minds, Brains, and Societies Reconstruct the Past*, edited by Daniel Schacter, 346–64. Cambridge, Mass.: Harvard University Press.

Schuermans, Nick, Maarten P. J. Loopmans, and Joke Vandenabeele. "Public Space, Public Art and Public Pedagogy." *Social & Cultural Geography* 13, no. 7 (2012): 675–82.

Schwartz, Joan M. "*The Geography Lesson*: Photographs and the Construction of Imaginative Geographies." *Journal of Historical Geography* 22, no. 1 (1996): 16–45.

———. "'Records of Simple Truth and Precision': Photography, Archives, and the Illusion of Control." *Archivaria* 50 (2000): 1–40.

Seekins, Donald. "Historical Setting." In *Cambodia: A Country Study*, edited by R. R. Ross, 3–71. Washington D.C.: U.S. Government Printing Office, 1990.

Sen, Amartya. "Merit and Justice." In *Meritocracy and Economic Inequality*, edited by Kenneth Arrow, Samuel Bowles, and Steven Durlauf, 5–16. Princeton, N.J.: Princeton University Press, 2000.

Shapiro-Phim, Toni. "Dance, Music, and the Nature of Terror in Democratic Kampuchea." In *Annihilating Difference: The Anthropology of Genocide*, edited by Alexander Hinton, 179–93. Berkeley: University of California Press, 2002.

Sharp, Jo P. "Publishing American Identity: Popular Geopolitics, Myth and the *Reader's Digest*." *Political Geography* 12, no. 6 (1993): 491–503.

———. "Towards a Critical Analysis of Fictive Geographies." *Area* 32, no. 3 (2000): 327–34.

Shaw, Ian G. R., and Joanne P. Sharp. "Playing with the Future: Social Irrealism and the Politics of Aesthetics." *Social & Cultural Geography* 14, no. 3 (2013): 341–59.

Sheers, Owen. "Poetry and Place: Some Personal Reflections." *Geography* 93, no. 3 (2008): 172–75.

Sherry, John F., Jr., and John W. Schouten. "A Role for Poetry in Consumer Research." *Journal of Consumer Research* 29, no. 2 (2002): 218–34.

Short, Philip. *Pol Pot: Anatomy of a Nightmare*. New York: Henry Holt, 2004.

Sidaway, James D. "Photography as Geographical Fieldwork." *Journal of Geography in Higher Education* 26, no. 1 (2002): 95–103.

Siebers, Tobin. "Hitler and the Tyranny of the Aesthetic." *Philosophy and Literature* 24, no. 1 (2000): 96–110.

Siegel, Marcia B. *At the Vanishing Point: A Critic Looks at Dance*. New York: Saturday Review Press, 1968.

Slocomb, Margaret. *The People's Republic of Kampuchea, 1979–1989: The Revolution after Pol Pot*. Chiang Mai, Thailand: Silkworm Books, 2003.

Smith, Christine. "Art as a Diagnostic: Assessing Social and Political Transformation through Public Art in Cairo, Egypt." *Social & Cultural Geography* 16, no. 1 (2015): 22–42.

Smith, Neil. "Neo-Critical Geography, or, the Flat Pluralist World of Business Class." *Antipode* 37, no. 5 (2005): 887–99

———. *Uneven Development: Nature, Capital, and the Production of Space*. 3rd ed. Athens: University of Georgia Press, 2008.

Smith, Susan J. "Beyond Geography's Visible Worlds: A Cultural Politics of Music." *Progress in Human Geography* 21, no. 4 (1997): 502–29.

Smith, Tony. "The Underdevelopment of Development Literature: The Case of Dependency Theory." *World Politics* 31, no. 2 (1979): 247–88.

Som, Vannak. "Crime Deserves Judgement." *Searching for the Truth*, 3rd quarter (2006): 55–58.

Sonevytsky, Maria, and Adrian Ivakhiv. "Late Soviet Discourses of Nature and the Natural: Musical *Avtentyka*, Native Faith, and 'Cultural Ecology' after Chernobyl." In *Current Directions in Ecomusicology: Music, Nature, Environment*, edited by Aaron Allen and Kevin Dawe, 135–46. New York: Routledge, 2015.

Springer, Simon. "Earth Writing." *GeoHumanities*. https://doi.org/10.1080/2373566x.2016.1272431.

Taylor, Diana. *The Archive and the Repertoire: Performing Cultural Memory in the Americas*. Durham, N.C.: Duke University Press, 2005.

Taylor, Richard. *Film Propaganda: Soviet Russia and Nazi Germany*. London: I. B. Tauris, 1998.

Thion, Serge. "The Cambodian Idea of Revolution." In *Revolution and Its Aftermath: Eight Essays*, edited by David P. Chandler and Ben Kiernan, 10–33. New Haven, Conn.: Yale University Southeast Asia Studies, 1983.

Thompson, Ashley. "Oh Cambodia! Poems from the Border." *New Literary History* 24, no. 3 (1993): 519–44.

Todaro, Michael P. *Economic Development in the Third World*. 4th ed. New York: Longman, 1989.

Tolia-Kelly, Divya. "Materializing Post-Colonial Geographies: Examining the Textural Landscapes of Migration in the South Asian Home." *Geoforum* 35, no. 6 (2004): 675–88.

Trotsky, Leon. *Art and Revolution: Writings on Literature, Politics, and Culture*. New York: Pathfinder Press, 1992.

———. *Literature and Revolution*. Chicago: Haymarket Books, 2005.

Tyner, James A. *From Rice Fields to Killing Fields: Nature, Life, and Labor under the Khmer Rouge*. Syracuse, N.Y.: Syracuse University Press, 2017.

———. *Genocide and the Geographical Imagination: Life and Death in Germany, China, and Cambodia*. Lanham, Md.: Rowman & Littlefield, 2012.

———. *The Killing of Cambodia: Geography, Genocide and the Unmaking of Space*. Aldershot, UK: Ashgate, 2008.

———. *The Politics of Lists: Bureaucracy and Genocide under the Khmer Rouge*. Morgantown: West Virginia University Press, 2018.

———. "Radical Geography and the Legacy of the Khmer Rouge." *Geopolitics* 20, no. 4 (2015): 741–44.

———. "Violence, Surplus Production, and the Transformation of Nature during the Cambodian Genocide." *Rethinking Marxism* 26 (2014): 490–506.

Tyner, James A., and Christabel Devadoss. "Administrative Violence: Prison Geographies and the Photographs of Tuol Sleng Security Center, Cambodia." *Area* 46, no. 4 (2014): 361–68.

Tyner, James A., and Stian Rice. "Cambodia's Political Economy of Violence: Space, Time, and Genocide under the Khmer Rouge, 1975–79." *Genocide Studies International* 10, no. 1 (2016): 84–94.

———. "To Live and Let Die: Food, Famine, and Administrative Violence in Democratic Kampuchea, 1975–1979." *Political Geography* 52 (2016): 47–56.

Tyner, James A., and Rachel Will. "Nature and Post-Conflict Violence: Water Management under the Communist Party of Kampuchea, 1975–1979." *Transactions of the Institute of British Geographers* 40, no. 3 (2015): 362–374.

Uline, Cynthia, Megan Tschanen-Moran, and Thomas D. Wolsley. "The Walls Still Speak: The Stories Occupants Tell." *Journal of Educational Administration* 47, no. 3 (2009): 400–426.

Valentine, Gil. "Creative Transgressive Space: The Music of kd lang." *Transactions of the Institute of British Geographers* 20, no. 4 (1995): 474–85.

Valentino, Benjamin A. *Final Solutions: Mass Killing and Genocide in the Twentieth Century*. Ithaca, N.Y.: Cornell University Press 2004.

Vannareak, Pal. "Wait for Tomorrow." *Searching for the Truth*, 3rd quarter (2009): 52–61.

Vickery, Michael. *Cambodia 1975–1982*. Chiang Mai, Thailand: Silkworm Books, 1984.

Vickery, Veronica. "Beyond Painting, beyond Landscape: Working beyond the Frame to Unsettle Representations of Landscape." *GeoHumanities* 1, no. 2 (2015): 321–44

Von Blum, Paul. "Paul Robeson: The Quintessential Public Intellectual." *Journal of Pan African Studies* 2 (2008): 70–81.

Waldner, Lisa K., and Betty A. Dobratz. "Graffiti as a Form of Contentious Political Participation." *Sociology Compass* 7, no. 5 (2013): 377–89.

Ward, Miranda. "The Art of Writing Place." *Geography Compass* 8, no. 10 (2014): 755–66.

Wellens, Jane, Andrea Berardi, Brian Chalkley, Bill Chambers, Ruth Healey, Janice Monk, and Jodi Vender. "Teaching Geography for Social Transformation." *Journal of Geography in Higher Education* 30, no. 1 (2006): 117–31.

Wertsch, James V., and Henry L. Roediger. "Collective Memory: Conceptual Foundations and Theoretical Approaches." *Memory* 16, no. 3 (2008): 318–26.

Wolf, Mark J. P. "Subjunctive Documentary: Computer Imaging and Simulation." In *Collecting Visible Evidence*, edited by J. M. Gaines and M. Renov, 274–91. Minneapolis: University of Minnesota Press, 1999.

Wood, Nichola. "Playing with 'Scottishness': Musical Performance, Non-Representational Thinking and the 'Doings' of National Identity." *Cultural Geographies* 19, no. 2 (2012): 195–215.

Wood, Nichola, Michelle Duffy, and Susan J. Smith. "The Art of Doing (Geographies of) Music." *Environment and Planning D: Society and Space* 25, no. 5 (2007): 867–89.

Wright, John K. "Geography in Literature." *Geographical Review* 14, no. 4 (1024): 659–60.

———. "Terrae Incognitae: The Place of Imagination in Geography." *Annals of the Association of American Geographers* 37, no. 1 (1947): 1–15.

INDEX

www.ingramcontent.com/pod-product-compliance
Lightning Source LLC
LaVergne TN
LVHW091148080826
845145LV00008B/2302